SO-AAA-398

THE SENATOR

MY TEN YEARS WITH TED KENNEDY

RICHARD E. BURKE

with WILLIAM and MARILYN HOFFER

SMP

ST. MARTIN'S PAPERBACKS

THE SENATOR: MY TEN YEARS WITH TED KENNEDY

Copyright © 1992 by A. L. P., Inc.

Cover photographs courtesy of F. P. G. International.

ISBN: 0-312-95133-7

Printed in the United States of America

St. Martin's Press hardcover edition/September 1992
St. Martin's Paperbacks edition/April 1993

10 9 8 7 6 5 4 3 2 1

*To my family, whose love and support
during this time of my life
gave me the strength to persevere.*

AUTHOR'S NOTE

This is a true story. Quotations have been re-cre-
ated from memory, to the best of my ability and, where
possible, I have checked the substance with other
sources. Much of the information contained herein is
based upon steno books outlining my daily activities,
maintained during most of the period from 1977 through
February 1981. Additional information was drawn from
volumes of personal and professional correspondence,
office memos, campaign notes, photographs, speech
manuscripts, and internal reports.

To ensure the privacy of certain individuals I have
changed the names, altered the identities and often the
professions and job descriptions of the following characters:

Cindy Marks, Mandi Carver, Sally Ryan, Jeannie,
Barbara Logan, Lori Dawson, Richard, Paula, Margo
Frye, Kitty Brewer, Pam Farmer, Betty McKay, Mi-
chelle, Josh, Peter, and Natasha. Cindy Marks, Lori
Dawson, and Betty McKay are composites.

The names of these individuals are fictitious, but their
stories are fact.

THE SENATOR

1 I was sitting in the choir loft of Holy Trinity Church in the nation's capital, waiting for the ten o'clock Mass on a Sunday morning in October 1971. Our Georgetown University Glee Club often sang here. Holy Trinity was founded in 1776, and it's the venerable Roman Catholic parish in Washington; many dignitaries are members of the congregation.

Shortly before Mass was to begin, I heard a murmur run through the gathering. Heads turned, my own included, to witness the entrance of Senator Edward Moore Kennedy. He stood a striking six feet two inches tall, a broad-shouldered man with a mop of brown hair, stylishly long. The jaw that jutted out like a granite ledge pointed unmistakably toward the future.

Here, before my eyes, was the unquestioned heir to the Kennedy throne. His stunning blond wife, Joan, was on his arm and his children followed them up the aisle. This was the storybook image of the idealized American family, sophisticated and involved. The Senator's deep-blue eyes made contact with an acquaintance, and he offered a half-wave and a wide, toothy grin. He exuded charisma, just as his brothers had, and the air in the church seemed to crackle with his presence.

Because my own political philosophies favored my mother's—who was a liberal Democrat, as opposed to my father's, who was a conservative Republican Connecticut businessman—I, being a scrub-faced, eighteen-year-old college freshman, was awed to see in person the most prominent liberal Democrat of all. He was, after all, the one responsible for my now being old enough to vote! That day I sang my bass part with gusto.

After the service the Senator attended our glee club reception. Like my father, he was a man who commanded the attention of everyone around him. When Dad entered a room, heads turned and conversation ceased; Senator Kennedy produced the same response. I introduced myself to him and said, "I used to live in Massachusetts. I have a sister in Wilbraham and another in Westfield."

He smiled and said, "I'm there all the time."

As I shook his hand I sensed power and authority.

I was completely overwhelmed. Kennedys had that effect on people and I knew then that I was no different.

I was only a youngster when President Kennedy, in a 1962 speech at Yale University, defined his political philosophy. He declared, "The central domestic problems of our time do not relate to basic clashes of philosophy and ideology, but to ways and means." He went on to make his point clear: We need to work within the system to bring about necessary change. But he never had the opportunity to fully test the philosophy.

Following the President's assassination, the torch passed to Robert Kennedy, who emphasized the importance of personal involvement in the political process.

Then, five years later, Robert Kennedy was assassinated, leaving Edward Moore Kennedy as the final "ripple of hope" for those who looked to the family to solve "the complex and obstinate problems" of the world.

In recorded history there has rarely been such a clearly inherited mandate. Edward Kennedy, by general acclamation, was now the torch bearer, carrying the dreams of a generation of idealists who longed for the resurrection of Camelot, who were quite willing to ask what they could do for their country.

Could he pull the sword from the stone?

One answer came during the height of the demonstrations against the Vietnam War. Senator Kennedy was scheduled to give a speech at Yale, the very location where his brother Jack had proclaimed the importance of working within the system. Arriving at the university, he found his path to the auditorium blocked by an angry, near-violent mob of antiwar student protesters. He grabbed a bullhorn, leaped atop a parked Volkswagen, and spoke to the hostile crowd:

> I am an authority on violence—all it brings is pain and suffering and there is no place for that in our society. I think that protest is becoming far too comfortable, like everything else in America. . . .We can protest anything now, using the same old procedures, writing the old slogans on the same old cardboards with detachable handles.
>
> If you want to bring an end to war—then work to elect men who agree with you and mount that political campaign this fall that we know was successful before. If you are still insistent on racial equality, then go where you are needed—to register blacks, to assist with their arguments in court, to offer your services to their cause. If you care about poverty, go live it.
>
> Teach the children, work with the addict, help them in their community programs. In short, act in a way meaningful to others than yourself.

Those words inspired me with a measure of the Senator's own vision, just the way Bobby's and Jack's had. As a freshman at Georgetown, majoring in accounting and finance, I had already volunteered to work in the student government, but now simple campus politics didn't seem enough. I wanted an opportunity to act upon my idealism.

So, a month after that Sunday in church, in November 1971, I walked into room 431 of the Russell Building where the office of the senior senator from Massachusetts was then located. Judy Epstein, a specialist on Massachusetts legislative issues, was at the front desk, filling in for longtime receptionist Melody Miller, who was on a break. She glanced at my shoulder-length curls—the collegiate badge of the early seventies—and asked, "Can I help you?"

"Yes, I'd like to volunteer."

"Great!" she replied. "We have a mailroom down the hall. Room four three seven. Go down there and ask for Lillian."

Lillian was a woman of frail appearance who was surprisingly full of life. Her confident presence made it clear that the mailroom was her domain. Within minutes of my arrival, I was seated at a large table covered with letters. Lillian explained that most senators received about one hundred letters each week; Kennedy received more than one thousand. Since the early 1960s, the volume of incoming mail and miscellaneous printed material that passed through this office had tripled. Despite the fact that earlier this year the Senator had been ousted from the key post of majority whip, he was still one of the most visible, popular, and/or controversial figures on the political scene. After the assassination of his brother Bobby, the Senate Rules Committee allowed him additional office space to accommodate the increased volume of mail, but they did not pay for additional staff members, so the Senator found it necessary to spend up to $100,000 of his personal funds annually to meet the office budget; thus, volunteers were highly valued.

Quickly, efficiently, Lillian set me to my task, which

was to open each letter and staple the pages to the envelope in order to preserve the address. Stacks of opened mail were returned to Lillian for sorting. Any mail relating to legislative matters was routed to Susan Riley, a paid staffer. Susan was an astute researcher and charged with the responsibility of writing letters to constituents on all legislative issues. She perused each letter quickly, before coding it and slipping it into the appropriate compartment, labeled SOCIAL SECURITY, HOUSING, WELFARE, EDUCATION, WOMEN'S RIGHTS, or some other important topic.

I volunteered in the mailroom one or two days a week and, before long, counted both Lillian and Susan among my friends. I was quiet and eager to learn, and they seemed to appreciate that.

Gradually, Lillian entrusted me with greater responsibilities. I was allowed to code and sort some of the mail myself, routing the letters to the appropriate staffer. For instance, Paul Kirk, a longtime Kennedy adviser and the Senator's chief political assistant, handled any correspondence regarding campaigns and other Democratic party business. Anything involving the turmoil in Ireland went straight to chief legislative assistant Carey Parker.

My work was of the drudge variety, but Lillian had the ability to make it enjoyable. The routine was occasionally broken by a letter from someone on the lunatic fringe who had managed to get a message past the security personnel in the main post office, located downstairs. Once I opened an envelope to find a mouse leg inside. Another correspondent sent the Senator a used condom. All of this aberrational material went into the box labeled HATE MAIL. If there seemed to be a truly alarming threat in the mail, the letter and envelope were turned over to the FBI and the Secret Service for the appropriate investigation. Given the history of the Kennedy family, nothing was ever taken for granted.

There was another category of mail that troubled me. An occasional "Kennedy-you're-no-good" letter came in accompanied by a tabloid clipping that hinted at improprieties in the Senator's personal life. There had been numerous rumors in the press about the Senator's free-wheeling life-style, as well as stories that his marriage was deteriorating—and of course there was the tragic Chappaquiddick incident of 1969—but I discounted the hate mail as the sort of nonsense that plagues the famous. The press at times was relentless. Invariably someone in the mailroom would glance at one of the scandalous clippings and comment, "Listen to this . . . it says the Senator was with—"

"—Trash," Lillian would interrupt, making it clear she didn't want to hear it. "That trash!"

Who could blame her? After all, here in the mailroom, we were die-hard Kennedy supporters. Our loyalty was reinforced by the Senator himself, who about once a week would thrust his head into the mailroom just to say hello and thank everyone for the work. I learned very quickly that no one here ever referred to the boss as "Kennedy" or "Ted." It was as if he had been christened "the Senator," and that was all the reference needed.

There were times, though, when the references were not always positive. Occasionally word would filter back to the mailroom that the Senator was "a little buzzed" after a particularly long lunch, usually on days when he had a light schedule. Work, we heard, would essentially cease while the Senator cut up with his staff or on the phone or with his friends, feeling no pain, and, being gregarious with all, even making his way back to the mailroom to say thanks, with a sloppy grin.

After a time, Lillian decided that I was ready to be entrusted with greater responsibility. She called Melody Miller in the Senator's main office and announced that she was sending "the new kid" up with the mail. She handed me a hefty stack of correspondence and told me to deliver it directly "to Angelique."

Melody smiled at me as I entered, and said, "Hi. How are you doing?"

She was a very attractive young woman with long blond hair; at first glance she reminded me of the Senator's wife, Joan.

The Senator's office, with thirty-five employees, was one of the busiest on the Hill, attracting callers and visitors from all over the world. Melody managed twin banks of constantly ringing phones, routing calls with skill. In addition, she dealt with scores of visitors every day, well aware that the impression she presented reflected upon the Senator. Beyond this, Melody was the first line of security. If a visitor aroused her suspicions, she was under standing orders to hit an alarm button that would alert staffers to bolt the inner doors.

Melody allowed me to pass into the suite, pointing the way to another, more inner office.

That office was very cramped. Off to one side, appointment secretary Chris Capito sat at her desk, phone in hand, busy ordering airline tickets, scheduling and rescheduling hotel reservations, coordinating details with advance men in various cities and, in general, plotting every moment of the Senator's life.

In the center rear was the paper-strewn desk of administrative assistant Eddy Martin, a veteran journalist who had been with the Senator since 1962. He stood only about five feet five inches tall, but displayed the stocky build of an ex-Marine. As the Senator's administrative assistant, Eddy and his secretary, Anne Strauss, coordinated every phase of the Senator's professional and political life.

Anne was in constant motion, chattering at Eddy, "Do this now. Sign this paper. You've got to call California."

The Senator's private life was the domain of personal

secretary Angelique Voutselas. She was an attractive Greek-American in her mid-forties, stylish, chic, and very professional. She glanced at me sternly for a moment, and then smiled warmly. "You're the new kid?" she asked, almost amused.

"Yes," I responded. "I brought the mail."

She accepted the stack of correspondence and whispered an aside to her secretary, "He's kind of cute."

I'm sure I must have blushed beet red, but without skipping a beat, Angelique turned her head and snapped, "Hurry up, Eddy, get that memo over here or the bag is going without it." Eddy Martin reacted with a sharp glance over the rim of his glasses, but said nothing directly.

After that I was heading into the inner office several times a day, bringing the mail. One could judge the time of day by the degree of deterioration in Eddy Martin's appearance. First thing in the morning, Eddy was neat and dapper. By the end of the day his shirttail hung out, his tie was loosened, his rolled-up cuffs were soiled with ink, and his normally pink complexion was several shades darker. His survival mechanism was a biting sense of humor.

Angelique was a warm, endearing person, but she was also a perfectionist, and her cool business style was calculated to shield the Senator. She had been with him since the mid-1960s and was fiercely protective of him. Her desk was situated adjacent to the door of the Senator's office; the route to him clearly led through her.

What fascinated me most were the dynamics of Angelique's relationship with Eddy. There was obvious tension between the two. Each was responsible for a major portion of the Senator's activities and each jockeyed for a preferred position.

Throughout the day various staffers deposited stacks of papers in the in box on Angelique's desk. She sorted these into categories and placed them in a huge open briefcase in the Senator's office. Whenever he had a spare moment, on the floor of the Senate, in the backseat of his car, on an airplane, or even as he ate lunch, the Senator maximized his time by digging through the paperwork, reading, amending, approving, and signing. A portion of Angelique's power lay in the fact that she was one of the few people who could decipher his chicken-scratch handwriting. By necessity, she translated most of his instructions to the rest of the staff.

Unless the Senator was in a meeting, his office door was usually open and, as often as not, he was calling out for Angelique or Chris to get him a particular file or requesting a briefing paper from Eddy. Sometimes, if Angelique was busy in the Senator's office, she beckoned for me to bring the mail inside.

The private office was truly an inner sanctum. On one side was a large desk that had once belonged to the Senator's father and had been used, in turn, by President Kennedy and Bobby. A replica of the President's famed White House rocking chair and both his personal American flag and presidential flag adorned the office. A fireplace, though never used, added a cozy feeling. A sofa and two comfortable chairs were provided for visitors.

On the wall near the Senator's desk was a small framed note, handwritten in 1932 on Milton Academy stationery. It was from fifteen-year-old John F. Kennedy, asking his mother Rose, "Can I be godfather for the baby?" The baby was the Senator, known to his family not as Ted, but as Eddie. The Senator often drew a visitor's attention to this.

Other framed mementos lined the walls: a letter to Ted from his mother, complaining about his spelling; his own report card from Milton Academy; a letter from President Kennedy congratulating his youngest brother on taking his oath to the U.S. Senate; the President's dog

tags from PT-109; photographs of the Senator in the
company of the world's most powerful men and women;
works of fine art; school papers from the Senator's children; a mobile that the Senator's son, Teddy, Jr., had
fashioned from Popsicle sticks. It was like a museum
presided over by an eclectic curator.

Also in this room was a framed quote from President
John Adams, which was a sort of family manifesto: "I
must study politics and war that my sons may have the
liberty to study mathematics and philosophy . . . in order
to give their children the right to study painting, poetry
and music."

On the far end of the suite, beyond the Senator's office
and private bathroom, was the legislative room, the domain of Carey Parker, a quiet, unassertive fellow in his
late thirties who worked fourteen-hour days as chief legislative assistant; he doubled as a speechwriter. The Senator valued his opinion immensely and did *nothing* to
promote any piece of legislation unless Parker was behind it.

The suite contained one other, smaller room for the
caseworkers who handled specific requests from constituents. Dick Drayne, the Senator's press secretary, had a
desk in the rear.

One floor below us, chief political assistant Paul Kirk
worked at a desk amid the staff of the Refugee Subcommittee, which the Senator chaired. The more I saw of
Kirk, the more I realized that he could have been a
politician himself. The thirty-three-year-old Harvard-
educated lawyer, son of a Boston-Irish judge, was a strikingly handsome six-footer, blessed with a low-key
personality that allowed him to stand as a pillar amid any
tempest.

I was inspired by the sense of moderately controlled
chaos in the office, and it didn't take me long to set a
goal. Yes, I would hustle in the mailroom, for as long as

necessary, but my aim was to move onto the Senator's working team, closer to where Angelique and Eddy handled the vital tasks. I did not know how high I could go, but I was determined to do the best possible job and see where it led me.

Lillian and Susan were very helpful and supportive. Once, I overheard Lillian talking to Eddy Martin about giving me more responsibilities. "He's awfully young," Eddy cautioned.

"What are you talking about?" Lillian retorted. "Who cares how young he is as long as he does his work well?"

My lucky break came around lunchtime on a warm day in the spring of 1972.

"Rick, do you drive?"

"Yes, of course," I replied.

"Would you like to drive the Senator?"

"Sure," I answered quickly.

Angelique explained that the regular driver, John Carlin, was off this day, and she needed a replacement. She asked me to come to the office for a briefing. When I arrived she handed me a set of car keys and said, "It's a blue Pontiac convertible, downstairs. Just drive over to The Monocle, park in front, go in, and tell him you are there. You are going over to St. Alban's, to Teddy's sports day."

I knew The Monocle. It was a favorite lunchtime spot for the legislators, just a few blocks away, near Union Station. But I did not know the location of the private school where Teddy, Jr., was enrolled. "I don't know where St. Alban's is," I protested.

"It's at the National Cathedral," Angelique said.

"I'm not sure where the National Cathedral is," I said, suddenly worried about what I'd gotten into and not wanting to let anyone down.

"Don't worry. He'll show you how to get there." Angelique handed me a briefcase to give to the Senator so that he could work during the short ride through north-west Washington.

It was an exhilarating feeling to pull the Senator's late-model convertible away from its curbside space in the reserved, guarded section adjacent to the Capitol. The top was down and the weather was perfect.

At the appointed hour of 2:00 P.M. I located the Senator in The Monocle. He was involved in a laughter-laden conversation with his good friend and former University of Virginia law school roommate, Senator John Tunney of California. "Senator," I interrupted politely, "I'm here to drive you."

"Great. I'll be out in fifteen minutes," he responded, still chuckling about something Tunney had said.

About half an hour later, running behind schedule, the Senator raced out of The Monocle, jumped into the "shotgun" seat at my side, and said, "Hi, we're going to St. Alban's." Without further comment, he opened the briefcase and set to his work.

"Senator," I said with embarrassment, "I don't know where St. Alban's is."

He glanced up sharply, his concentration broken. "Do you know where Constitution Avenue is?" he asked.

"Yes." It was the main thoroughfare that flanked the Capitol on the north side.

"Go on Constitution toward Massachusetts Avenue."

"Okay, fine." I was very nervous as I shifted the car into drive. *I know he wants to get there fast,* I thought. *I hope he's going to pay attention.* I prayed I could remain calm and appear in control.

I made my way along Constitution and negotiated the proper half-right turn onto Massachusetts. The midday traffic presented a mild congestion problem, but I managed to weave between the two lanes of traffic with a measure of dispatch. The Senator glanced up occasionally, particularly when we stopped at traffic lights. Invariably someone tooted a car horn to catch his attention and then waved. He was always ready with a genial smile and a casual return wave, happy to be recognized.

We sped up Massachusetts Avenue past Embassy Row and its blocks and blocks of old buildings, some of them stately, some of them overly ornate. Without looking up from his paperwork, the Senator mumbled, "Uh, when you get, uh, past the embassy area, tell me."

"Okay," I replied, stopping at a light. "We're there now."

He glanced about and said, "Oh, er, uh, take a right here."

One of the characteristics the Senator has been criticized for is his seeming inability to talk in direct sentences, peppering them instead with *ers, uhs, umms, uh-huhs,* and *ahs.* The Senator had always joked with reporters that this was because he was the youngest of the Kennedy children and had never had a chance to complete a sentence. Whatever the reason, one had to listen carefully to get the full sentence, especially while driving.

By now I was in the left lane. I glanced to my right and saw that the driver beside me had noticed us. I held up my palm and indicated that I wanted to pull in front. As the light changed, I eased the car across the lane of traffic, in front of the accommodating driver. The Senator slumped in his seat, somewhat chagrined by the exploitation of privilege. Clearly there were times to use it—and not use it.

St. Alban's was just ahead. The Senator directed me into the parking lot, jumped out, and said, "Oh, uh, park the car and come in." He strode off at a brisk pace.

I followed him to the athletic area, where we stood amid a small group of parents and other spectators. "Hi, Senator," someone said. He smiled and nodded in response. St. Alban's was an exclusive school and, therefore, this was an exclusive set of parents. The spectators included a smattering of legislators, bureaucrats, and even an ambassador.

It was Boys' Field Day and ten-year-old Teddy was with a group of student-athletes, preparing for the long jump and a relay race.

Suddenly the Senator said, "Oh! I want my camera." He turned to me and commanded, "Rick, go to my house and get my camera. It's in the front hall closet. If Rosalie is there—she's, er, Joan's secretary—just tell her you are doing it for me. I think Theresa is there, too, with Patrick. They'll know where to get the camera." He was referring to Theresa Fitzpatrick, the longtime governess, and his youngest child, four-year-old Patrick.

"There's one big problem," I said, somewhat embarrassed.

"What?"

"I don't know how to get to your house. I've never been to your house."

He was incredulous. "Oh, uh, well . . . You've never been to my house? Okay, you know how to get to Chain Bridge Road?" I nodded. Chain Bridge, the major route from the District to the fashionable Virginia suburb of McLean, was close to the university. "Go out here," the Senator continued, "take a right—"

"Yeah. . . ."

"Okay, go over the bridge. When you get to the light on Chain Bridge Road, it's exactly six-tenths of a mile past that. Take a right. The house is number six thirty-six." He glanced up at the field of boys in front of us and frowned. "This is going to be over in half an hour," he warned. "You've got ten minutes to get there and back."

Ten minutes? Was he joking? I was terrified as I sprinted through the parking lot. I sped the Senator's car across the Potomac River on Chain Bridge Road and worried, *What if it's not* exactly *six-tenths of a mile past the light? What if I get lost?*

To my relief, the directions were perfect. I located 636 Chain Bridge Road with ease and pulled into the long, curving driveway. I was surprised at the rather unassuming appearance of what looked like an average, gray-shingled ranch house. There wasn't even a gate. *What about security?* I wondered. I walked through a manicured courtyard, tried the front door, and found it unlocked. I was surprised that no one was around to challenge my unexpected appearance. I found the camera in the closet and raced back to the car.

I arrived at St. Alban's with a few minutes to spare.

"You made it!" the Senator said, beaming, immediately turning his attention to the athletics. With this man, I realized, every single second in his day counted. He snapped photos of Teddy running in the relay. One shot after another, click, click, click.

Eleven-year-old Kara, the Senator's oldest child, was now at his side. She was a student at the adjacent National Cathedral School. "Kara," the Senator asked suddenly, "do you know Rick?"

She smiled and said hello. She seemed to be a sweet young girl with bright green eyes and the chubby cheeks of preadolescence.

Teddy, finished with his relay race, came over to join us. He squirmed with boyish embarrassment as his father hugged him. "This is Rick," the Senator said, slapping him on the back.

"Hello," Teddy mumbled. He seemed very shy.

The Senator commanded his son and daughter to pose for a snapshot, which brought mild protests but dutiful obedience.

"Okay, Rick, uh, time to get back to the Hill. Let's go." And off we went.

That evening I called my parents to tell them all about my afternoon, still not believing how smoothly everything had gone, and how I'd been entrusted with what seemed like momentous responsibility. My mother was naturally thrilled, but when I told my father, he seemed totally unimpressed. At that moment I wondered if there was something deeper to my father's lack of enthusiasm. I knew it had nothing to do with me, but everything to do with the Senator. Though he never said it, I knew my father was wary of him.

2 **Very often the Senator flew to Boston for the** weekend. On Fridays, the Senate adjourned at 4:00 P.M. or shortly thereafter, so Chris usually booked him on a five o'clock flight from National Airport.

I quickly realized, while listening to John Carlin, for whom I often filled in on Fridays, that getting the Senator there on time was a real challenge. Just as the Senator was not known for his superb driving, he was also notorious for running late.

"Okay, Rick, the drill is this: Call the Delta Airlines office at National and ask for our contact, a man named Joe, who works in special services. Tell him that you are leaving the Hill at four-fifteen and you are going to try to make the five o'clock flight," John instructed. "Ask the airline man to meet you at the curb and get you through," John said. "You don't want to miss the flight, because the next one isn't until eight P.M., and you don't want to sit around for three hours with an angry boss. When you get there, take the briefcase and run inside with the Senator."

"What do I do with the car?" I asked, wide-eyed with nervousness.

"Just leave it in front of the airport. Don't worry.

They'll know who it belongs to." John explained that each senator is issued a small, numbered shield to display on the dashboard of his car. "The police won't touch the car," he promised. "And once you get him there, make sure you wait until the plane takes off. He'd be furious if there was a problem with the flight and you left him stranded."

"Okay," I said. It sounded as if the routine was well-established. "I guess I can handle it."

John lowered his voice and warned, "It's going to be very hairy."

"Why?"

"Because he never leaves when he's supposed to. He'll leave at four-thirty or twenty to five, and you have to fight your way through rush-hour traffic."

I wondered out loud whether the airline would hold the plane for the Senator, if only for a few minutes. John explained that sometimes they would find an excuse for delaying the flight, but they did not like to explain the real reason. All in all, it was far better to get the Senator there on time.

John's briefing was prescient. He was in his late twenties, and did not plan to spend the rest of his life driving the Senator to and fro. I suspected that he was already on the lookout for another job. And no wonder—driving for the Senator was like driving an ambulance on an emergency call.

Shortly after that, Angelique called the mailroom one Friday about 3:45 P.M. to see if I was available to drive the Senator to the airport. "You have to go," she said, sounding as panicked as I felt. "At a quarter after four, be at the steps of the Capitol. The Senator will run down the steps, hop into the car, and off you go. You know the way to the airport?"

"Well, I think I sort of do."

I had the Senator's convertible at the Capitol steps

promptly at 4:15. After waiting for ten minutes, with no sign of him, my suit was wet with perspiration. I decided that I had better call Angelique to report the delay. I knew that there was a phone inside the Capitol doorway, but to use it I would have to step out of view. What if the Senator ran down the steps and hopped into a driverless car?

Seizing the moment, I raced into the building, found the phone, dialed, and sputtered my concerns to Angelique.

"He's running late," she advised. "There's one more vote. It will be another five or ten minutes. Just get there on time, but be careful." How was I supposed to accomplish *both* of these objectives? I wondered.

I stepped back outside. A Capitol Hill police officer was on duty nearby, and I explained my dilemma to him.

"Ah," he moaned with sympathy, "they're all the same." He sketched out a plan: "When I see you go, I'll radio to all the cops along the way. We'll get you off the Hill quickly, but once you get onto the highway you're on your own."

It was 4:40 P.M. when the Senator dashed down the steps, accompanied by Dick Drayne, his press secretary. He threw open the door and said, "Come on, Dick, let's go."

"I'm not going," Drayne protested.

"Dick, get in the car!" the Senator ordered impatiently.

Drayne did as he was told. The Senator jumped into the front seat. I jammed the car into drive and sped off. As we slid easily into the traffic on Independence Avenue, I caught a glimpse of the Senator out of the corner of my eye. He was watching carefully, noting the cooperation of the friendly Capitol Hill police officers who cleared a path for us in the crazed Friday afternoon rush-hour traffic; we blazed through several red lights at the behest of beckoning policemen, and a half-smile on the Senator's face told me that he realized I had done something right.

In almost no time we reached the tunnel that led to the freeway, and on toward the 14th Street Bridge. It was carpeted with wall-to-wall traffic. "Shit!" I muttered.

"Get me there," the Senator commanded. "Get around it."

This, I realized, was where the friendly cop had warned me that I would be on my own. But, in fact, I had a willing assistant driver at my side. "Go up on the right," the Senator suggested, meaning, go up the disabled vehicle lane. *Oh boy.* . . .

Obediently, I spun the wheel and hit the accelerator. The car jumped the curb and slid up onto the apron of the road. We sped ahead with the left wheels on concrete and the right wheels on grass.

Drayne braced himself against the backseat, shaking his head in exasperation, and closed his eyes. The Senator just laughed.

I lurched the car forward as far as I could on the right apron until our path was blocked by a bridge abutment. Then I bullied my way back into the traffic and across three lanes to the left. Now we were in an exit lane that curved up and to the left, toward the 14th Street Bridge. Up ahead, on the far bank of the Potomac, we could see the busy airport.

The Senator was enjoying himself immensely. He eyeballed the thin median strip on our left and calculated that we could squeeze through. "Go up there," he said, leaning forward, pointing. Drayne was now pale, shaking in fright.

I bounced the car over another curb. We had a clear route ahead if I could keep the left half of the car on the median. We sped forward, with the right side of the car dangerously close to the bottlenecked vehicles of frustrated, angry drivers.

Once on the bridge, the Senator informed me that we had to move over to the right lane, to catch the off ramp for the George Washington Parkway. He leaned out of the window and peered to the right, holding up his hand to surprised drivers and screaming *"Now!"* three times, until we had merged into the right-hand lane.

We spun around the off ramp onto grass, to the left of a line of waiting cars. As we straightened out, I hit the accelerator and prayed that the Parkway traffic would give way.

The airport entrance was only a short distance away from us now, and as we careened ahead, the Senator barked out directions to the Delta gate at the North Terminal.

As we reached our destination I jammed on the brakes and glanced at my watch. It was 4:55; we had made it with five minutes to spare! I grabbed the Senator's briefcase and raced after him into the terminal. Drayne remained in the car, unable to move, perspiring.

I couldn't even think about relaxing until the flight took off. Then, as I walked back toward the car, I realized that I was shaking all over. My legs felt like Jell-O. *Did I just do this?* I asked myself. *I can't believe it.*

Drayne muttered, "I will never do this again!"

When he returned from Boston, the Senator informed Angelique that I was now his preferred driver. I would still work in the mailroom, but I would be on standby to shepherd him about Washington.

This coincided with the annual competition for summer internships. Eddy Martin put me on the payroll as an intern, at a salary of fifty dollars per week. At nineteen years old, I was finally on payroll with my political idol and couldn't have been happier.

As the summer moved into high gear, I found myself

spending more and more time at the Senator's residence. One thing that became immediately clear was that my initial impression of the house had been misleading. From the front, it appeared small and unimpressive, but only because the bulk of the structure stretched out to the back and downstairs. A large vestibule at the front entrance opened onto a spacious living room featuring richly textured damask-and-brocade-covered Sheraton and Hepplewhite antiques. Every surface was sprinkled with memorabilia and family photographs. A long corridor led to a large master bedroom, where a deck overlooked the backyard, featuring a spectacular vista of the Potomac. The Senator's private office was attached to the bedroom.

One wing of the sprawling main floor was reserved for the children, with bedrooms for Kara, Teddy, and Patrick, a TV room, and quarters for governess Theresa Fitzpatrick.

The main floor of the house also held a guest room, quarters for Andres, the elderly live-in French cook, who had once worked for the Rothschilds, and a large kitchen and dining room. The library, centered upon a massive stone fireplace, was fashioned of beautiful wood and filled with books. A high-backed wing chair sat atop a gray fur rug near the fireplace, providing a comfortable spot for late-night reading and study. On a small table adjacent to the chair was a white phone, with a list of the family's numbers taped to it.

A stairway led from the library down to an office on the lower floor. At the rear of the office were sliding glass doors that opened onto the yard, below the master bedroom deck. On this lower floor was a large party room. One entire wall of the room was devoted to glass-enclosed bulletin boards where photos were displayed. Famous faces from all over the world mingled with the familiar Kennedy smiles.

Like the Senator's Capitol Hill office, his house, I realized, memorialized his family's history. The Kennedy family's lives were all here. One could not help noticing that so much of the Senator's life had already been dictated by his late brothers, that even if he wanted to do something different, it wouldn't be allowed.

As I walked about this floor, I learned there was also a guest room, laundry room, storage space, and two offices—one for Joan's secretary, Rosalie Helms, and the other for George Dalton, who served as the Senator's majordomo, off-hours driver, and general errand runner.

Rosalie was a hardworking woman with an air of southern gentility. She seemed determined to keep a protective cocoon around Joan; nominally she worked for Joan, but I came to realize that she also kept the Senator apprised of Joan's health problems.

George was a gray-haired military veteran who told me that he had worked for President Kennedy in the communications room of the White House. He was pleasant with me, but sometimes a bit blustery with others. He was a hefty fellow who looked like he had probably played football in his younger years, and he took care of any heavy work around the house. He also handled most of the domestic buying chores. According to George, he and President Kennedy had been best drinking buddies; one never knew whether it was true or not, but it really didn't matter.

As in any large household, there was bound to be "backstairs" infighting, and George and Rosalie were often at odds, trying to one-up the other in serving the family. Sometimes he and Rosalie would both attempt to order a wine supply; invariably they tried to put the Senator in the middle, each wanting him to approve the choice of wines. But the Senator mostly backed off from the controversy, preferring to let the two combatants work out their problems, which they usually did. George also frequently crossed swords with the governess, Theresa, giving the house a real "Upstairs, Downstairs" feel.

Over time, I came to know the Senator's children quite well. Kara was a serious but sweet girl who seemed to take her cue from her mother. When Joan was in a good mood, Kara was bright and cheerful; but if Joan was moody or ill, Kara became distant and somewhat rebellious.

Teddy was timid and introspective. I sensed that much was going on within his mind that he chose not to share with the world. He seemed terribly concerned about his father's safety.

Patrick, the youngest, was a shy, frail child who suffered from asthma that was sometimes so severe he had to be given direct oxygen and a regimen of steroids.

All three seemed like decent, normal kids, and they had a warm relationship with Theresa. She was an Irishwoman, perhaps in her forties, who was clearly devoted to the family and reveled in the role of surrogate mother, which, unfortunately, they needed. Even at my relatively low level within the Senator's office, one couldn't help but pick up vague references to the Senator's wife both at home and at the Hill office. Everyone knew Joan Bennett Kennedy had had a particularly hard time adjusting to life within the dynasty. As one historian later wrote, she suffered a double disadvantage: She was not only not a Kennedy, but not a man, either. And this was, first and foremost, a man's family, a man's house. Anyone could see it.

However, despite problems in the marriage, the Senator tried not to let them affect the relationship he had with his children. Given all the other demands on his time, he would still stop wherever he was, whatever he was doing, and take time out to call them every afternoon. If you happened to be in or near his private office, you could hear him on the office phone talking to Patrick, making animal noises. "Hey, Patrick," he would say, "I'm here with a little doggy, *woof-woof*." Patrick delighted in his father's impressions of horses, cows, ducks, pigs, chickens, and other animals, but Teddy, too "old" for such shenanigans, would often grimace.

The children obviously loved their mother, but her behavior sometimes confused them. Once, when I was in the kitchen, waiting to drive the Senator to an appointment, Joan came in, disoriented and looking disheveled. Her hair, while normally crisp and beautiful, was in disarray, and she had very little makeup on, which would have covered up the deep circles under her eyes. Joan had obviously been drinking. She wanted to make a cup of instant coffee, but she did not know how to turn on the gas range to heat water. Kara seemed especially embarrassed. This was obviously not the first time something like this had happened.

I was concerned for Joan, and I asked Theresa about her. Theresa spelled it out quietly. "I'm sure you've heard stories about Mrs. Kennedy. It is very difficult, but we have to be quiet about it. If she says something strange to you or demands something, just sort of say, 'Yes, Mrs. Kennedy,' then come and get me."

I said, "Fine," but I was very troubled. Even then I was beginning to realize that all was not as it appeared within this great political family. There were chinks in the armor, and, although it wasn't named, there was something called damage control.

Theresa cautioned me further. "Rick, you may see other things that certainly don't seem right. If you have a concern, you can come see me in private, but don't ever raise it with anybody else."

"Of course," I said, puzzled, but too unsettled to ask her to explain.

One Sunday morning when the Senator was out of

town, I arrived at the house to drive Joan and the children to church. When Joan appeared I could tell that she had been drinking and was in no condition to be seen in public. A brilliant line of red lipstick stretched from her mouth toward her eyes; she did not realize that her hand had slipped. Her clothes, while properly sedate for Mass, were sloppily arranged. There was a large run in one of her stockings. I sighed, realizing there was no way she could go to Mass.

"Mrs. Kennedy, I'll take the children to church, you need to go back . . ." I suggested. She looked at me, her eyes registering confusion at first, then annoyance. She mumbled a mild protest but I insisted. "No, Mrs. Kennedy, I don't think it's a good idea that you come today. Why don't you just go back to your room and rest?" She looked from me to the children, who were standing around, shuffling their feet, not saying anything, waiting to see what she would do. And then she went back into the house. I breathed a sigh of relief as I headed off to Mass with the children.

If handling some of the domestic chauffeuring was eye-opening, shuttling the Senator to his extended family members had its moments, too. We would often make the short drive to Hickory Hill, the McLean estate that had once belonged to then-Senator and Mrs. John F. Kennedy. Bobby and Ethel had bought it from them, and Ethel now lived there with her eleven children. Jackie Onassis was quoted as saying of Ethel: "She drops kids like rabbits," and she once produced a caricature of Hickory Hill that depicted kids hanging out of windows and underfoot everywhere.

The Senator had assumed the role of surrogate father, motivated perhaps not only by love, but a sense of obligation. One could immediately see that Bobby's children needed all the attention they could get. I had heard that Ethel was distraught for years after Bobby's death. After spending any time at the Hickory Hill estate, you couldn't miss the chaos resulting from her distress.

The sloping grounds of the estate were impressive, guarded by three-century-old hickory trees, but Ethel's house presented an entirely different picture. Fabrics on a lot of furniture were either worn out or torn. Kids, in various states of undress, ran amok. Ethel scurried about, screaming orders at the top of her lungs.

The kids had adopted nearly a dozen dogs and cats, and these ran about with the same abandon as the children. Some were house-trained, a few were not. Downstairs, I saw cages full of rats and one that held a boa constrictor. The kids, either playing or fighting, screamed constantly. Ethel looked tired. Hickory Hill was definitely a place to visit at your own risk. I was told that once, for a St. Patrick's Day dinner, Ethel used live bullfrogs as a centerpiece. She and the kids still liked to "baptize" guests by pushing them, fully clothed, into the pool.

I was troubled by Bobby and David, who were close to my age. Both seemed out of control. David, especially, impressed me as being only vaguely associated with reality, and he often bore the brunt of his mother's distress about his brother, Bobby, who carried on the fine tradition of Kennedy rebelliousness. It was David who, at the age of thirteen, had been alone in a hotel room in Los Angeles watching his father's victory announcement when the gunshot rang out. He had sat glued to the screen, watching the pandemonium as people tried to save his father's life.

Given the history, one could see why both boys had continual trouble in school—Bobby was at Pomfret, where he insisted on living in an all-black dorm, and David was at Middlesex, where rumors were rife about his drug use. Ethel seemed to be at the end of her rope with both of them. I mentioned my concerns to the Senator, who shared them, and had clearly seen the problems coming for a long time. He knew they needed fatherly guidance, a strong hand to complement Ethel's own, and for a time Lem Billings, the oldest family friend of the Senator's brothers, had tried to fill the bill. But that wasn't working either. The Senator did what he could—attending school functions and other important events in the children's lives—but he had his own family and career to manage, and handling eleven of his brother's children was too much for any man, even a Kennedy. One day, after a conversation we'd had about the children, he grew pensive, as if he knew there was going to be trouble regardless of what he did. It was like waiting for a storm to blow in; there was nothing to do but take cover.

Each year the Robert F. Kennedy Memorial Foundation staged a charity pet show at Hickory Hill, a fundraiser for the foundation's efforts to help disadvantaged teenagers. Ethel had set up the event as a means to carry on her husband's goals with the underprivileged. Guests were invited to bring their own cats and dogs, and players from the Washington Redskins football team organized an obstacle course.

For the 1972 version of the event, Angelique asked me to organize a group of volunteers from the mailroom. Since there was a myriad of details, we worked for several days in advance. I was upstairs at Hickory Hill late one morning, attending to my duties, when Bobby and David appeared, attired only in white jockey shorts, looking as if they had just crawled out of bed, with glassy eyes and dazed expressions. Their shoulder-length hair, Bobby's brown and curly, David's blond and nearly straight, was decidedly bedraggled. They grunted a "Good morning," probably not sure what time of day it was.

Amidst the general din that always filled the house, the oldest son, Joe, calmly walked downstairs, headed for a car, and drove off; he was obviously buying out of the pandemonium.

Ethel's secretary, Caroline Croft, set our crew to work cleaning up the yards and the pool area. Several of my friends began mowing the lawns, and I turned my attention to a garden out back. I grabbed a hoe and began poking at a scruffy-looking plot in a corner of the yard that appeared to be overgrown with a ragged-leafed weed. Suddenly I heard a voice scream at my back, "Rick, Rick, stop!"

I turned to see David, now fully alert and clearly worried, still clad only in shorts, running toward me.

"What?" I asked.

"Just leave that alone," he said. "Don't touch it."

"Why? It looks messy."

"Don't worry," he advised me. "We're putting a fence around it. You could do us a favor. Put a fence around it. But just don't touch it."

"Okay, fine."

David said, "Great, Rick. Thanks." Then he disappeared back inside the house.

I was dealing with the fence when Caroline walked by and remarked, "Oh, they stopped you, huh?"

"Yeah," I said. "What is it?"

"It's marijuana," she answered. "They grow it all the time. And smoke it."

"Oh, great . . ." I moaned, sure my eyes rolled upward. At Georgetown in the early seventies, pot was a fairly constant presence, but it wasn't anything I felt compelled to try. With everything else I was aiming for, the last thing I needed was to try to function stoned.

Still, growing it at Hickory Hill was another matter. It *was* illegal, and even if Ethel's kids were out of control, this was a very public home for the Kennedys, with press and dignitaries coming in and out all the time, but if they didn't see the problem, I certainly wasn't going to raise it.

When Ethel wasn't overseeing her rambunctious brood at Hickory Hill, she spent her summers on Cape Cod, and each year she packed a horse van full of personal effects and sent a driver ahead. This summer she asked if I would drive the van to Massachusetts. I said I would be happy to go. On a beautiful spring Saturday, I headed for my first visit to Hyannis. When I arrived in town, I stopped at a gas station and asked directions to the Kennedy compound. The attendant glanced at my van, emblazoned with HICKORY HILL, and showed me the way.

Since so much had been written in the media about Hyannis to the point where mythology about its size and importance had overtaken fact, I expected to find a huge, luxurious, and well-guarded compound: Camelot behind walls and built with white clapboards. In fact, the home of Ambassador and Mrs. Kennedy did not compare with some of the other extravagant estates in the neighborhood. It sat at the edge of a small cul-de-sac, a street with six houses on it; the structure itself was a rambling one, large and comfortable, but not especially impressive.

When Jack had been President, a sentry house had guarded the end of the street, but that was unmanned now. Ethel owned one of the adjacent homes. The Senator's youngest sister, Jean Smith, and her husband, Steve, had formerly owned one of the houses across the street, but had sold that to another family, unrelated to the Kennedys, some time ago. President Kennedy had owned the house next to Ethel's, and Jackie retained title, although she had her own huge estate on Martha's Vineyard and seldom utilized the Hyannis house. The Shrivers had once owned the house next to the Smiths', but they, too, had sold out and purchased a home a short distance away. The Senator's home was across a bridge on Squaw Island, a white clapboard house on a bluff facing east, overlooking the Atlantic. The "Kennedy compound" was not what it used to be, and not a compound at all.

Nevertheless, I spent a relaxing weekend in Ethel's home, joined by the governess and two of Ethel's children, Joe and Courtney. I met Courtney only briefly. She was gracious and appeared to be a levelheaded young woman. Even though they had their own set of friends and plans for that weekend, I had more of a chance to get to know Joe.

Joe Kennedy's manner was brusque, but underneath the rough exterior there seemed to be a young man with potential. He had experienced his share of troubles in the past, and the press had never been kind to him. Some years earlier, he and the Senator had traveled together to Spain. There, without any training or preparation, Joe had decided to fight a bull. The fiasco resulted in some highly publicized bloody photos.

He had bounced from school to school, achieving only lackluster results. There was some speculation that he suffered from dyslexia, but I did not know whether he was ever tested or treated for it. There was also a great degree of skepticism that he would ever measure up to the family legacy. At Milton Academy he was razzed by upperclassmen and had lashed back in a reckless fashion.

Perhaps his greatest moment, at least in the eyes of the press, had been the poised and poignant manner in which he had greeted and thanked mourners during the extended cross-country train ride that had brought his father's body home from California to Washington, D.C.

Now, a student at the University of Massachusetts, he was eyeing a political career of his own and his future appeared bright. Leaving Hyannis after that weekend, I thought about Courtney and Joe and realized that for all the chaos in Ethel's household, there was still hope for the future. As far as the other children were concerned, I couldn't dwell on their problems anymore. Though they troubled me, I had my own life and assignments to keep on track.

When I registered for my sophomore year at Georgetown, I scheduled my classes either very early in the morning or in the evening so that I would be free during the day to drive the Senator. I gave a copy of my school schedule to Angelique so that she would know when I was available. The Friday-afternoon dash to the airport became so routine that we were able to cut the time to nine minutes flat.

That autumn, we viewed the 1972 presidential election campaign with a mixture of fascination, alarm, and despondency. Richard Nixon carried the Republican banner toward certain reelection against Senator George McGovern and his vice-presidential running mate, Sargent Shriver, the Senator's brother-in-law. Some on our staff considered it a bit of a joke that Shriver was running, for we had higher aspirations; it was an open secret that the Senator wanted to run for the presidency, but this was not the right year. The power of the incumbency was sure to sweep Nixon into a second term; beyond that, the Senator was still battling to regain the political momentum he had lost as a result of the Chappaquiddick tragedy.

Nixon's strength was maintained in spite of the growing level of grumbling concerning the Watergate burglary, which had occurred in June of 1972. The Senator plunged into the investigation in his capacity as chairman of the Administrative Practices and Procedures Subcommittee, a sort of ethics watchdog. On October 12 the Senator obtained approval for the subcommittee to begin gathering evidence concerning the Watergate burglary and related allegations of political espionage and

sabotage. The White House cried foul, pointing out that
the presidential election was less than a month away and
charging that the Senator was out to settle old grudges
and, perhaps, launch himself toward a 1976 candidacy.

I knew, from spending as much time as I did shuttling
him about, that this was not the case at all. He was deeply
concerned with the state of the presidency, and would
have been so regardless of which party was in the White
House. His response to the criticism from the White
House was exemplary. He vowed that his inquiry would
be a "holding action." The preliminary investigation
would be conducted by *both* the majority and the minority subcommittee staffs, and it would take place behind
closed doors. True, the Senator was taking a calculated
gamble. If his investigation took on aspects of a crusade
or, worse, a witch-hunt against the President, Nixon's
forces would surely release a laundry list of "character"
issues about Kennedy—whether true or false—to the
press.

For the time being, the story remained quiet. Reporters hovered, but the Senator maintained his pledge. The
ship leaked no secrets.

On occasion, as I drove the Senator somewhere, he
maximized his time, dragging a pair of subcommittee
investigators along to brief him. I kept my eyes on the
road, but I couldn't help but hear the conversations.
Long before the world knew, I realized that the Senator
had been a victim of one of the "dirty tricks" alleged to
have been conducted by agents for Nixon's Committee to
Re-Elect the President. Back in July of 1971, someone
had apparently utilized facsimiles of presidential hopeful
Ed Muskie's Senate stationery to mail copies of a Harris
poll to Democratic members of Congress. The poll dealt
with the lasting political impact of Chappaquiddick. Everyone knew that Chappaquiddick was the Senator's
Achilles' heel. Arriving on Muskie's letterhead, the

mailer appeared to be a cheap shot by one Democratic
candidate against a potential rival, and it helped to un-
dermine Muskie's chances. It now appeared that it was
Nixon's people, not Muskie, who had sent the offensive
letter. The goal was to clear the field of strong Democratic rivals and thus ensure Nixon's reelection.

In fact, it became apparent that the Senator had been
the initial target of the Nixon camp's campaign of dirty
tricks. In April 1971 Nixon's chief of staff, H. R. Haldeman, had issued standing orders that he should be apprised of any breaking news concerning Ted Kennedy,*
whom they considered to be the major threat to Nixon's
reelection. The Republicans had been trounced in the
1970 midterm elections, and polls indicated that the Senator's popularity, though deeply wounded by Chappaquiddick, was once more on the rise. When the Senator
decided not to run, Nixon simply trained his ammunition
on the available targets.

I was in a unique position to observe the Senator during this time. Everyone else on Kennedy's staff held a
specific area of responsibility and access. My position-at-
large allowed me to kibitz on a staggering variety of
concerns, and my curiosity was far from idle. I was genuinely fascinated by the political process in general, and by
the Senator in particular. I also learned very quickly that
the Senator expected you to keep your mouth shut. But
it would be some time before I realized this had less to do
with matters of national interest than personal issues.

Although the Senator labored diligently to fulfill his responsibilities, he obviously needed and relished the opportunity to relax. His forty-first birthday in 1973

---

*In his book *The Camera Never Blinks,* CBS anchorman Dan Rather
called the Nixon administration's paranoia concerning a Kennedy candidacy "the seeds of Watergate."

provided such an occasion. Steve and Jean Smith threw him a "barn dance" in their New York apartment. To create the proper atmosphere, Jean rolled back the carpet and spread sawdust on the floor. She even arranged for the entrance of a baby donkey—the politically correct symbol—to arrive via the service elevator. The Senator had a great time and roared with laughter as he recounted for me the donkey's accident on the floor of his sister's posh apartment.

It was usually at family gatherings, whether they were in New York, the McLean house, Hickory Hill, or at the Cape on weekends, that one could fully appreciate the way the Senator interacted with his siblings, nieces, nephews, and even his mother. The Senator and his sisters occasionally would bicker, but like many large families, my own included, they were a close-knit clan. Whenever there was a threat from the outside, they knew how to close ranks. Husbands who were non-Kennedys—with the exception of Steve Smith, whom the Senator regarded almost as a brother—and Ethel and Jackie, as widows of slain brothers, and even Joan, were in the second tier when it came to his interaction with his sisters. Joan, though, as far as I can remember, was never around at these gatherings. Acknowledged, yes, seen, no; she was left instead in the care of the staff at McLean. All others, including the family servants, who were considered "adopted" Kennedys, could only get so close. However, one could watch.

As the only surviving son, the Senator was the unquestioned head of the family. His sisters Jean and Pat deferred to him, although Eunice was sometimes willing to take him on.

The Senator's sisters still called him "Eddie." Frequently their conversations resurrected a childhood memory, and cryptic comments flew from one to another, accompanied by spontaneous laughter. It was, I realized, a sort of Kennedy shorthand. Unless you were a sibling of the Senator's, you could never fully appreciate the sidelong glances, the coded references. When you could, almost always the stories involved their mother. When Rose was around, which was usually at the Cape, she tended to join the gathering for a few minutes, then walk out. Although her health was still good then, she was frail and, I gathered, had heard all the stories before. Curiously, they rarely if ever mentioned their father. Of all the family members, the Senator was the one least likely to bring up the past.

I learned a few facts and I filled in some blanks. Before the Senator's birth on February 22, 1932, the baby was in momentary danger of being named George Washington Kennedy—at the suggestion of his fourteen-year-old brother, Jack. But, in fact, he was named Edward Moore, after Ambassador Kennedy's faithful friend and companion. By all accounts, Eddie was a cheerful, loving child, but that basic personality was early on put to the test. His childhood was disrupted by the appointment of his father as Ambassador to England in 1938. From then on he was constantly thrust into new environments. Before he reached the age of thirteen, he had attended ten different schools. It was not the most stable way of growing up, regardless of how glamorous it seemed to the outside world. Privately, the Senator had told friends that after age seven, his life until his teens was a total blank—he had blocked it out. He was reportedly unsure of his intellectual abilities and sensitive to the nickname "Fat stuff" that his brothers had bestowed upon him. But he retained his good humor and his zest for life. His father once remarked, "If he isn't a bright student, he's a good salesman."

When he finally followed his brothers Jack and Bobby to Milton Academy, he was known there as "Smilin' Ed." From his youthful perspective, he saw his older brothers sent out to lead the world. As Old Joe, Jack, and Bobby worked on congressional and senatorial campaign strategies, Teddy trotted off to Red Sox games in the company of his aging maternal grandfather, John J. "Honey Fitz" Fitzgerald, the former mayor of Boston.

The better I got to know the Senator, the more I realized those early years had molded his character. Time passed, and I moved up in the office hierarchy. John Carlin found other work. Now I was the Senator's primary driver and, when not busy with that task, I was given the job of culling through the legislative mail. I took the initiative to ask questions and the Senator gradually became comfortable discussing legislative concerns with me.

The Senator was well aware that he came from a privileged family, and the crux of his political philosophy was that the more fortunate should help the less fortunate in order to bring equality to all facets of society. This was one underlying theme of his opposition to the Vietnam War. He believed, as did I, that our nation's resources were being squandered in a foolish war. We needed to put those lives and tax dollars to work back at home.

However, as he had declared to the war protesters at Yale, he believed in working within the system. He saw government as the strategic tool to bring about social change. To that end, he had assembled one of the finest staffs on the Hill to put his legislative passions into action.

If there was one "cutting-edge" issue that seemed to confuse the Senator, it was women's rights. As a liberal, he supported any new legislation promoting equal opportunities for women. But as a man—more particularly, as a Kennedy man who had been raised with a clear concept that women played a subordinate role in life—he had difficulty putting his liberal principles into practice.

Mary Murtaugh, who was a few years older than I and

one of the Senator's staff workers, attended to his Massachusetts legislative concerns. After she had begun working for the Senator, she impressed him by enrolling at Georgetown Law School. She parlayed her degree into a more than full-time job in the office, working routinely until midnight, sacrificing her personal life in the process.

"At the beginning, it was very difficult," she confided to me. "He wasn't really aware of it, but whenever I brought him a piece of work, he made sure that his *men* checked it out. It rubbed me the wrong way."

But Mary was smart, and her work was good. She never pressed the chauvinism issue with the Senator; she merely let the quality of her performance speak for itself. Using her intelligence and a dry wit, she forged true friendships with the men of the New England fishing community—an important part of the Senator's constituency—and became the unquestioned office expert on issues that concerned them. Over time, she achieved a singular status in the office. Whenever an issue floated about that might impinge upon her area of expertise, the Senator was sure to say, "Let's get Mary's opinion."

"He's definitely trying," Mary said to me. With a sigh, she added, "But it's taking a long time."

3 One night I was on duty late, to drive the Senator to a fund-raising party at the home of the Averell Harrimans, on N Street in Georgetown. The glamorous Pamela Digby Harriman (previously married to Randolph Churchill and Leland Hayward) had assumed the status of the *grande dame* of Democratic party fundraising.

Senate business kept Kennedy on the floor late that day; a series of critical votes was scheduled. I stood outside the chamber, waiting with a briefcase full of paperwork. The Senator chose his moment, when it seemed as if there would be a lengthy hiatus between votes, rushed outside the chamber, and headed for the car with me in tow. As I drove across town through the post–rush hour traffic, he opened his briefcase. I was curious, for I had seen Angelique place a personal letter inside, addressed to the Senator in a distinctly feminine hand. I watched out of the corner of my eye as he ripped open the letter. He noticed that I was watching, and he responded with a sheepish half-smile, but no comment.

When we arrived at the Harriman house, he instructed me to station myself near a phone and call the Senate cloakroom every five or ten minutes, to see if a roll call

was coming up on an issue that was critical to him and
his fellow Democrats. The vote promised to be close.

The Harriman party was accented by the appearance
of several celebrities, and the Senator was gracious
enough to introduce me to everyone, including Robert
Redford, who was considering a run then for the Senate
from Utah.

About eight o'clock, after several uneventful calls to
the cloakroom, the voice on the other end of the phone
informed me that a vote was under way and that the
Senator had eight minutes to arrive before the roll call
ended. I raced to locate the Senator and had to pull him
away from a conversation with a stunning woman. "The
vote is on!" I cried. "They didn't give us any warning."

"Don't worry," he replied calmly. "We'll make the
second call." (If a senator abstains, or is absent during
the first roll call, he can cast his vote as the clerk reviews
the list of those who have not yet voted. Thus, there was
a built-in cushion of time.)

But I did worry, and I dashed back to the phone. The
cloakroom voice told me that we had exactly ten minutes
and fifty seconds before the second roll call.

I ran to the Senator and announced, "We have ten
minutes."

He glanced at the woman, glanced warily at me, and
still he lingered, turning on the charm. It was clear that
I was about as welcome as a mosquito that he'd just as
soon swat away. He kept chatting up the woman. He was
finishing his drink when the cloakroom called *me* and a
voice growled, "Bob Byrd wants Kennedy *here!*"

Again I found the Senator immersed in conversation
with the same woman. "Byrd's calling for you," I reported.

That got his attention. If the majority leader was demanding his presence, then the vote had to be extraor-

dinarily close. He made a quick apology to the woman, then turned to me. "Come on. Let's go!"

We raced outside. The car was parked at the curb, a bit off to one side of the house. I ran for the driver's door, but the Senator directed, "No, no, no. I'll drive."

Oh, my God, I thought. *He's a terrible driver. Is he out of his mind? This is crazy. . . .*

As I hopped into the passenger seat, he was already gunning the engine and he instructed, "You watch on the right side, I'll watch on the left."

I opened the right-hand window and leaned far outside, to get a better view. My hands were shaking, but I tried to keep my voice calm as I called out, "You're okay on the right," or "Watch out for that car," or "Get into the left lane, *now.*" The streets of Washington became a blur. Curbs were barely missed, cars were almost scraped, pedestrians darted out of the way, horns were angrily blown. At each intersection, whether the light was green or red, the Senator barely paused. His foot was on the accelerator, floored, and just as readily available for the brake, determined not to miss a beat.

He negotiated the intricate drive to the Capitol in eight minutes flat. As he jumped from the car, leaving me behind, he called out, "That was good, Rick. We made it." He was very pleased with himself.

With my heart still pounding, I yelled back, "Yeah, but you're *never* driving again!"

He just laughed as he hustled in for the vote, and I realized then that much of his personality was driven by an enjoyment of life on the edge. I came to see, as well, that the Senator was gregarious by nature. Whenever he was in public, and particularly so when he was on his home ground in Massachusetts, he enjoyed mingling with people. This was one part political expediency and one part human caring. He knew there was a mandate to be fulfilled—both his brothers' and his own—and he truly wanted to serve his constituents to the best of his ability, and, to that end, wished to hear their concerns firsthand. Such accessibility, however, had to be managed carefully, otherwise it would get completely out of hand.

Whenever groups of students or others from professional and business organizations journeyed from Massachusetts to Washington, they frequently sought photo opportunities with the Senator. By the spring of 1973, I was often handling the responsibility for these occasions, which meant organizing the group on the steps of the Capitol Building, with another mailroom volunteer ready with a camera. The Senator was usually late, but no one seemed to mind. He would come rushing over, that large, toothy Kennedy grin spreading from ear to ear, and you could see the sparkle in the constituents' eyes, the thrill of touching, as they had probably done with his brothers before him, the legend in the flesh.

On one such occasion I had three groups of constituents ready and waiting for the Senator's arrival. When he approached, I escorted him toward the first group, whose hometown I had scrawled on a piece of paper.

We were still out of the group's earshot when I informed him, "This first group is from Leominster." I pronounced the word phonetically, the way it was spelled, *LEE-oh-min-ster*.

A quizzical look crossed the Senator's face and then his face darkened. His eyes narrowed squarely on me. He asked, "How do you pronounce that again?"

"LEE-oh-min-ster," I repeated, swallowing nervously.

"Ah, Rick, now wait a minute," he lectured. His face registered surprise and disgust. "Uh, if you want to be on my staff—" He grabbed the scrap of paper from my hand, pointed to the name of the town, and asked once more, "What is this name?"

I was thoroughly confused, but I dutifully intoned, "LEE-oh-min-ster."

"Oh, for godsakes . . . Rick, you've got to at least sound like you're from Massachusetts," he said, shaking his head. He lapsed into a colloquial Boston twang and informed me, "It's *LEM*-en-ster." He repeated, "*LEM*-en-ster. It would have sounded ridiculous for you to say LEE-oh-min-ster in front of all these people. I don't have to tell you that they're the ones who keep me in office. Get it?"

I did.

As Watergate began to burgeon into a full-blown scandal that summer of 1973, the Senator urged the establishment of a special committee to be chaired by Senator Sam Ervin to probe more deeply into the abuses. While this was happening, the Senator did his best to separate his public and private lives, but I was now beginning to see both sides of the Kennedy life.

George Dalton, the Senator's jack-of-all-trades at McLean, increasingly found ways to parlay our friendship into getting me to do some of his chores. Often he asked me to pick up something at the store, or to retrieve the children from St. Alban's at the end of the school day. As 1973 progressed, he usually asked, "Rick, are you available this weekend? The Senator has to go to a party on Saturday night." Or, "Can you drive them to church this Sunday?" I didn't mind in the least running errands for George.

And then there was another longtime Kennedy friend whom I periodically drove to the airport. He told me that the Senator's brother-in-law, Steve Smith, had asked the friend to help prepare materials for the John F. Kennedy library, which was scheduled to open in about five years. Smith, working out of a New York office, managed the business concerns of the entire Kennedy clan.

That friend loved to reminisce about the glorious days

of Camelot, and his occasional work for the library, along with other Kennedy friends, gave him many opportunities to share bits of gossip. One day I was totally taken aback when he confided to me what he was doing.

"We're erasing the tapes," he said.

"What do you mean?" I asked.

And that was how I learned well before the rest of the country about the taping system in the Oval Office. It had been installed long ago, by President Franklin D. Roosevelt, and upgraded by President Kennedy; everything that went on in the Oval Office was preserved on tape for the presidential archives. "There is highly sensitive security stuff that we have to erase," the friend confided. "You can never really tell anyone about this, but I'm going through the tapes and erasing anything that shouldn't be heard. There are conversations with some people that we don't want to be on the tapes."

I accepted at face value this person's explanation that certain national security issues had to be safeguarded, and didn't give more thought to the matter until much later.

In May Archibald Cox was hired as Special Prosecutor to investigate the myriad charges of corruption within the Nixon White House. My driving excursions with the Senator assumed a more somber tone, for in addition to his normal burden of paperwork, the Senator's briefcase was now stuffed with dossiers marked "Top Secret." He studied these wordlessly, with a Davidoff cigar clenched in his teeth. Often, at this time, he carried two briefcases, one filled with routine paper, the other locked shut. On one occasion, at an airport security gate, I attempted to assist the Senator by reaching for the locked briefcase. He grabbed it quickly from my hands and snapped, "I'll take that, Rick."

Appearances of corruption within the White House were becoming more and more evident. On Monday,

July 16, Alexander P. Butterfield, former aide to White House chief of staff H. R. Haldeman, testified before the Senate Watergate Committee and revealed the existence of the White House taping system to the world. The Kennedy family—quickly moving to put the correct spin on things—admitted that a large volume of President Kennedy's tapes existed, and that they would be made available when the JFK Library opened in about five years. What they did not say was that a friend of the family had already erased countless "sensitive" conversations.

As that summer progressed, it brought the Kennedy family yet another tragedy. Joe Kennedy was driving a group of friends home from the beach in Nantucket when he lost control of his Jeep. His brother David was badly injured, and one of his friends, Pamela Kelly, was permanently crippled. Press secretary Dick Drayne took the lead in the damage control campaign to manage, as best as possible, the negative publicity. The family, through Steve Smith, arranged a generous cash settlement for Pamela.

Ultimately, Joe was brought before the Nantucket District Court on charges of negligent driving and lectured by Judge George Anastas: "You had a great father and you have a great mother. Use your illustrious name as an asset instead of coming into court like this."

I, like everyone else on staff who knew how the burden of being a Kennedy could wreck one's life, hoped Joe took the words and direction to heart. We had already seen the way some of his siblings were going, and we didn't want the same thing to happen to him. Ethel asked the Senator to have a heart-to-heart with Joe, which he did.

Everyone waited to see if it would work.

4 Lillian was promoted to the position of case-worker and Eddy Martin designated me as the new head of the mailroom. Before she assumed her new duties, Lillian briefed me.

There was a category of mail that never made it into the hands of the volunteers. Lillian screened every envelope before it was thrown into the mailroom mix, and she lectured me on those letters that should bypass the staff and go directly to Angelique. These were simply designated ATTENTION: ANGELIQUE, and Lillian explained that this was how the Senator instructed private correspondents to write to him. These letters were *not* to be opened by mailroom personnel.

Before long I was practiced at recognizing the distinctive handwriting on some of these. Twenty or thirty arrived every month. Many were from relatives; others were addressed in less familiar feminine script.

At the time, I could only guess what and from whom the letters were. Remembering the words of Theresa Fitzpatrick, I realized there were some things better left unquestioned. Besides, I simply didn't have time for speculation—I was busier than ever both at Georgetown and at the office. Eddy made an attempt to phase out my driving duties, but the Senator still preferred to have me behind the wheel and, for some time, I managed to handle both the mailroom and driving jobs.

By now I realized that, as a boss, the Senator had a tendency to pigeonhole people. Others in the know told me that Jack and Bobby had been the same way. Until now, the Senator had never had someone as both driver and mailroom supervisor, but I was determined to find some way to show him that I was capable of more. One way was to figure out how to cut office costs, which would save the government and the Senator money. I had learned various cost-cutting methods as Comptroller of Student Activities at Georgetown, and I knew that the Senator was perennially agitated by the amount of personal funds that he was forced to spend on his office. After doing some research, I discovered that the Rules Committee allowed certain expenditures of which the Senator, and others, were unaware; the committee purposely did not advertise some of these budget items and services, to keep down costs. That, coupled with a long, hard campaign I waged with Eddy to automate the mailroom, and which I was finally given approval to implement, at least forced them to take a second look. I prayed they saw some potential.

Actually I didn't know what the Senator saw, but one day I got a hint. . . .

I was in McLean to deliver a briefcase, and I found the Senator and Angelique working together in the basement office. It was the fall of 1973 and Nixon had defied a Supreme Court order to release his Oval Office tapes.

As I walked in, the Senator glanced up, smiled, and remarked, "Oh, here comes the Archbishop."

With genuine confusion, I asked, "What do you mean by that?"

"You probably never committed a sin in your life, Rick," he quipped, grinning broadly.

I smiled weakly and walked off, but the Senator's comment stuck in my craw. I realized that if I wanted to stay in politics I would have to learn to loosen up.

Shortly after that, Angelique announced her engagement to Dick Lee, a successful businessman she had been seeing. The Senator and Joan invited Senate staffers as well as Angelique and Dick's personal friends to an engagement party on October 15. In celebration of Angelique's heritage, the Senator arranged for a Greek band to perform.

George Dalton asked me to marshal a band of volunteers to park the guests' cars, which I gladly did. At one point during the evening, the Senator stepped outside to thank us for our help and invited us all to join the fun. There were more than one hundred people inside, drinking, chatting, dancing. The Senator, who was thoroughly enjoying himself, made a special point of mixing a supply of daiquiris himself in the kitchen blender.

From across the room, Joan looked beautiful. But up close, her makeup appeared caked and heavy, almost theatrically thick. As the party progressed, Joan's mood went from lively and festive to pensive and depressed. She grew increasingly disheveled. She walked across the room with tottering steps and said something to Angelique. From what I could hear, her speech was slurred. The Senator, who had been drinking a considerable amount himself by now, noticed this, too. "C'mon, Joansie," he implored, putting a firm arm around her, trying to make the best of the situation. "Pull yourself together."

But Joan was obviously not in shape to maintain her duties as hostess. The Senator, realizing this, got a very tight, aggravated, and exasperated expression on his face. He grabbed George, who was walking by, and said very firmly, "Get her out of here." George caught Theresa's eye and the two of them flanked Joan and ushered her off toward the bedroom, practically lifting her feet off the floor since she was in no condition to walk. Joan acquiesced without argument. George and Theresa locked her in for the night, and the party continued, the music getting louder, the drinks flowing even more freely.

The band's featured singer was a very attractive Greek woman. During a break, the Senator sought her out and engaged her in animated conversation. When the band resumed playing, the Senator and the singer hit the dance floor together. It was a slow number and the Senator leaned his body against the woman, pressing her crotch into his. My friend Terry McShane whispered to me, "I know what the Senator wants—"

"No, no," I replied, at first doubtfully, then with more conviction. "No, there is just no way."

Terry gave me an incredulous look. He was a few years older than I, a tough fellow who had served as a Navy Seal before enrolling at Georgetown. His eyes said, *I know what I'm talking about. Grow up.*

I shrugged and repeated, "No way." As I watched them, though, my mouth grew dry. Somewhere in the back of my mind I had the growing and uneasy feeling Terry was right.

It was shortly after that when, upon a clandestine signal from the Senator, George circulated and quietly but forcefully indicated to everyone that the party was drawing to a close. Angelique, as the guest of honor, also communicated this general message by preparing to leave. The Senator stood at the door and offered gracious good-byes to everyone. Our group of volunteers moved back outside to assist the guests with their cars.

Nearly an hour later, when everyone had gone, including Terry and the rest of my parking crew, I stepped back into the house to see if there were any further details to handle. I found myself alone in the party room on the main floor and looked around to make sure that everything was in order. The library had been closed off for the party but now, as I approached, I saw that one of the double doors was ajar. I caught my breath as I saw the Senator on the floor of the library, lying atop the sexy Greek singer. My heart skipped a beat. Instantly I backed away, sure that neither of them had noticed me.

In my haste to retreat to the foyer, I almost knocked down George. I rushed past him outside into the cold night air.

George followed and asked, "Did you see something?"

"Yeah, but I really don't want to talk about it."

George measured his words. "Rick, you know, the Senator really likes you," he said. "The family likes you. You can go far here." Finally he added, "You have to grow up. You can't be—judging. You can't say anything to anybody. If you want to be part of the team, you just have to shut up and go along with it."

George was right, I knew. I had been naïve for far too long. Life was not as cut-and-dried as the priests had counseled from the pulpit. Everything was not black and white, but shaded in variations of gray. And heroes were not saints. The Senator was a man, just like any other. And yet, the image of him being intimate with a woman as his wife slept in the very same house continued to bother me. It was another chink in the armor. As I drove him to several appointments during the next few days, I was sullen and reserved, and concerned that he would pick up on the tension.

Terry McShane counseled, "There are many sides to a story. You don't know all the details of his life. There's got to be a bigger picture. You read the papers. You know what goes on."

Not long after that, George drove Joan to the airport and she left for Europe on vacation.

Soon thereafter, one of the Senator's old buddies flew

in to spend a weekend at McLean. On Saturday I was directed to pick up someone at the house, and when I arrived I was surprised to find a large group of people there. The visiting friend and his wife were partying with another senator and several women I did not recognize. Everyone was drinking and roaring with laughter. More drinks were poured.

Later I asked the governess, Theresa, what was going on. With a slight raise of the eyebrow she explained knowingly, "They're all playing together."

Over a period of time, in bits and pieces, I was educated concerning the private behavior of some of the Kennedy men. The libertine life-style had deep roots, going back to the example of Ambassador Kennedy, whose affairs were legendary. He had even been known to make passes at his son's dates—and had flaunted his affair with Gloria Swanson on a ship to Europe even though Rose had been traveling with him. I could see where the Senator's examples came from. Perhaps the most damaging part of the legacy was that the Ambassador had never been held accountable for his appetites, nor were his sons. In turn, they developed an aura of moral invincibility.

"The men in this family are all the same," Theresa confided one afternoon. "They try to hit on anything in skirts that moves. Why, Ethel's sons, Joe and David, even tried to hit on me."

"What did you do?"

She smiled. "Told Joe to grow up, and David I slapped the daylights out of—how's that?"

As the Watergate crisis propelled forward with Nixon's release of the tapes, a kind of death watch consumed the Capitol and the nation. Nobody, the Senator included, could believe how much profanity was on the tapes, appropriately edited with the cryptic words that fascinated a nation: "expletive deleted."

In the office, my language was changing as well. With more and more pressures, I was easily slipping into "expletives" myself.

I noticed, while shuttling the Senator about, that he wasn't as gregarious as he usually was. The Senator knew Nixon was obstructing justice, but he certainly didn't relish the way the scandal was moving. His real fear was that although it might ruin Nixon, it was going to cripple the office of the presidency far more, and for many more administrations to come, including, I realized, perhaps the Senator's own.

"These are tough times, Rick. Very tough times. And we're all going to pay for them. This will end, but, ah, it will never really end."

Over the next few weeks, as Nixon began sinking further into political quicksand, the Senator was diverted by disturbing news stories indicating that Joan was living her own life, first in Paris, then at some Swiss spa. There were photos of her, partying in a disco, dancing with a European count, sometimes with makeup askew and looking noticeably unkempt. The tabloids relished one particular photo of Joan in a very revealing outfit. The Senator was distressed by the reports. He had tried for ages to encourage Joan to have an outlet other than her drinking. She was a talented musician, had become a member of the National Symphony Orchestra, and occasionally worked with the Boston Pops, but nothing seemed to pull her out of the grasp of alcohol. The Senator tried to focus on her, but he was pulled in a million directions.

Scores of letters arrived in the mailroom, containing clippings of these stories and photos, and comments such as "See what you've driven her to" and "No one in your family is any good, Kennedy."

Photo by photo, story after story, a mirage of conflicting images blurred in my mind. *You can't dwell on the negative,* I reminded myself, echoing George's counsel. *Think about all the wonderful things the Senator has done—and can do—for the country.* In that context, personal flaws seemed to diminish.

5

So much was happening, all at once. It was a week before the wedding of Ethel's daughter Kathleen to David Townsend, and I hustled to assemble yet another group of volunteer drivers. Some in the inner office appeared unusually tense, and I assumed that this was due to the pressure of the approaching event.

Then I received a cryptic message from Angelique, telling me to bring some work to the Senator's house. When I arrived, I found Theresa and Andres in the front hall, holding one another, crying. When she saw me, Andres, who spoke poor English, turned and walked away. I handed the batch of papers to Theresa, with question marks in my eyes.

"Thank you very much," she sobbed.

"Theresa, what's wrong?"

She looked up, tears in her eyes. "We have terrible news about Teddy. He's very ill. He's to be operated on in two days." I was stunned. Teddy had seemed fine and appeared very healthy to me.

Theresa explained that she had noticed a bump on the boy's leg, just below the left knee. Doctors had performed a biopsy and returned the terrifying diagnosis: chondrosarcoma, a fast-growing cancer of the cartilage.

(The Senator said later that breaking this news to Teddy was the most difficult thing he had ever had to do in his life.)

The Senator took a room adjacent to Teddy's at Georgetown University Hospital. My routine suddenly included a daily drive from Capitol Hill to the hospital to deliver a briefcase. The hospital personnel were friendly and accommodating, and somewhat accustomed to handling the special needs of celebrity patients. They allowed the Senator to park his car in the emergency-room lot and utilize that entrance to take a back route up to Teddy's room.

The Senator attended to his work as best he could, but it was clearly not his priority. He spent much of his time on the phone in discussions with the most renowned physicians in the country, soliciting opinions. The consensus was that the leg should be amputated.

Joan flew back from Switzerland to be with her son, and George reserved a room at the hospital for her, separate from the Senator's accommodations.

Rose Kennedy was already booked on a flight from Palm Beach to Washington for Kathleen's wedding. George arranged for a local car dealer to loan us the use of a Ford LTD sedan, and asked me to drive it to National Airport to meet the Senator's mother.

By now I knew the airport personnel well, and they were even more accommodating for the venerable matriarch of the Kennedy clan than they were for the Senator. Mrs. Kennedy appeared fragile, but was dressed well, including her trademark brimmed hat. I was nervous, having read press reports characterizing Mrs. Kennedy as "arrogant" and "stingy."

But when I identified myself and offered her my arm, she accepted with a gracious smile.

As we shuffled through the passenger area, all heads turned. "Oooh, there's Rose Kennedy," someone whispered. The newspapers were full of reports about young Teddy's medical condition, and several people offered words of encouragement.

She seemed a bit hard of hearing, but she was very alert and in full command of herself. When I had her safely ensconced in the rear seat and made sure that the porter had stowed her luggage in the trunk, I slid behind the wheel and announced, "I'm to take you to McLean, to the Senator's house, Mrs. Kennedy."

"No, Rick," she ordered firmly, "to the hospital. Teddy has been through so much. I want to see him."

"Okay."

"I'm just going to lie down," she said. "When we're a few minutes away, tell me." She carefully removed her hat. I covered her with a blanket and drove off gently. From the backseat came the familiar, rhythmic sound of our shared faith. "Hail Mary, full of grace . . ." interspersed with pleas for her grandson. "He is so young, give him strength. . . . Holy Mary, Mother of God . . . Why can't Joan be stronger? . . . Our Father, who art in heaven . . ."

"Mrs. Kennedy, we're about two minutes away."

She sat up, checked her makeup, and replaced her hat.

As we walked through the emergency-room lobby toward an elevator, Mrs. Kennedy responded graciously to everyone, smiling and waving. A door slid open and we stepped onto an elevator that was already crowded with people. A woman patient, on a gurney, was in obvious pain, but her eyes opened wide when she recognized who had just joined her inside the elevator. Mrs. Kennedy spoke softly to the patient and learned that she was on her way to surgery. She placed her hand on the patient's hand in empathy.

The patient told Mrs. Kennedy how much she had loved John and Bobby, and added that she was praying for young Teddy.

Mrs. Kennedy asked the patient's name and promised, "I'll say a prayer for you."

The patient responded, "I know what you are going through, and I will pray for you, too."

On an upper floor, we found the Senator waiting for us outside the elevator. He'd been alerted we were there. He grasped his mother's arm and led her toward Teddy's room. I followed, watching with interest the Senator's genuine attention to every nuance of his mother's voice and gestures. Teddy's face beamed with delight at the sight of his grandmother. I said hello to my young friend, and then left the family alone. After about twenty minutes, the Senator escorted his mother back into the hallway and returned her to my care.

Mrs. Kennedy suggested, "Why don't we stop in the emergency room and I'll go around and speak to people."

She visited with the emergency room patients and their families, offering solace, pledging her prayers. Afterward, we headed back to the Senator's house. That afternoon, when I returned to drive Mrs. Kennedy to the wedding rehearsal dinner, she took time from her prayers to ask me, "Teddy has suffered so much. Why does he have to go through this?"

She did not expect an answer, nor did I offer one.

Later that evening, during the return drive, she said softly, "I don't understand why Joan just can't stop drinking so much. She is such a lovely girl, but she just has never been able to control it. If she could control it, her life and the children's would be so much better."

Terry McShane drove Mrs. Kennedy to Kathleen's wedding, for it was my responsibility to chauffeur the bride. I picked up Kathleen from her home at Hickory Hill, along with the precious cargo of her Oleg Cassini gown, and sped toward Holy Trinity Church. In the meantime, George brought the Senator and Joan from the hospital. We met at a preset rendezvous point near the university. The Senator, in formal attire, jumped from George's car into mine and we rushed to the service.

The church was packed with celebrities, including John Kennedy's rumored old flame, Angie Dickinson, as well as Art Buchwald, Joe Califano, and singer Andy Williams, who, more often than not, could be found at Ethel's side as her escort.

At one point before the ceremony, Jackie Onassis swept into the church, trailed by a small entourage. Every head, except a few in the family, turned. The famous face, the famous smile, added the extra touch to the wedding that immediately stamped it a full-blown Kennedy affair.

The Senator, performing yet another duty of the surrogate father, gave away the resplendent bride, but I knew that his thoughts were with his son.

Later, when I drove the Senator from the reception at Hickory Hill back to the hospital, he said, "Rick, I want you to take care of my mother. She asked for you."

Mrs. Kennedy remained in town for several days after the wedding, and I drove her wherever she wanted to go. She visited an Elizabeth Arden salon and went to dinner at Pamela and Averell Harriman's house. *Johnny, We Hardly Knew Ye,* by former JFK aides Kenneth P. O'Donnell and David F. Powers, had just come out in paperback and she asked me if I knew Kenny O'Donnell. I said no. "Well, I'm really upset about some of the things he said," she declared. She told me that O'Donnell and Powers had mentioned that Jack sometimes jumped into the White House pool for a nude swim. "He shouldn't have put in something like that," she complained, still concerned about protecting her dead son's image.

When I took her back to National Airport at the end

of her visit, she pulled $150 out of her pocketbook and handed it to me.

"Oh, no, Mrs. Kennedy," I demurred. "I really don't—"

"Well, just give it to charity," she said.

Teddy's recovery was remarkable. During the surgery, a cast had been made from the diseased limb, from which a temporary prosthesis was shaped. Not too many days after his surgery he was walking with the aid of therapists, parallel bars, and the unwavering encouragement of his family. Eventually, Teddy was fitted with a more sophisticated prosthesis, fastened to his leg by suction and by a belt secured to his waist. Teddy's spirits were remarkable and he was pleased to learn that his leg had been used for research. He amused himself by drawing Christmas cards and cartoons for friends and family.

The Senator kept a steady stream of Teddy's friends coming into his room, determined that the boy wouldn't sink into depression. Joan and he had a few words about just how many visitors he should have, her feeling being that quiet rest was the best possible prescription for his recovery. The Senator disagreed and naturally won out. Between the two of them, they were also trying to deal with Teddy's siblings. Patrick was still young and didn't really have an idea as to how serious his brother's problems were, but Kara did. She began to worry that somehow her brother's cancer was transmittable. She was assured that it was not.

Teddy's room was inundated with flowers and presents. Artist and family friend Jamie Wyeth drew a farmhouse scene especially for Teddy. Toys arrived from all over the world. The Senator advised him to keep a few of the gifts, but to donate the remainder to other children in the hospital.

The Senator drove Joan and Teddy home from the

hospital, and I followed in a car filled with presents and flowers. In McLean, Teddy laughed as I, with my arms full of gifts, pretended to lose my balance, threatening to plunge into the fountain in front of the house.

A few days later I received a hand-drawn card from him, thanking me for my help.

While all of this was happening in the Senator's personal life, events of momentous consequence were occurring elsewhere in Washington. In late November we learned that a mysterious eighteen-and-one-half-minute gap was found at a critical juncture on one of the Nixon tapes. Knowing that there were deletions on the Kennedy tapes caused me some distress, but I tried to rationalize that there was a clear difference. The Nixon erasures were surely political—an obvious and illegal attempt to obstruct the progress of the Watergate investigation. The Kennedy erasures, I believed, were simply personal. My conclusions on the subject were strengthened when someone at the office said, "The Senator should come out and really knock them on the tapes," and he took the advice and made a number of speeches criticizing Nixon on the subject.

Still, the entire episode was vaguely unsettling. I was sure that the family friend who had done the erasing was acting under the direct orders of Steve Smith, but did the Senator know the friend was editing his brother's tapes? On some level he had to be aware of what was going on. After all, this person spent many weekends in Boston at the library. Surely they talked. But it's possible they didn't—sometimes, I realized, the Senator preferred to be officially "unaware."

One day, out of concern, I finally said something to Theresa.

"Don't get into it," she advised quickly. "Forget it.

Don't ever mention it to anybody. You are better off to shut up and never say anything."

One Monday, the friend, just in from Boston, grumbled that he had had a really tough weekend. "We had to erase a couple of hours of tapes," he said, " 'cause Marilyn was on the phone with the President. Boy, the things they talked about. . . ."

At the time, I decided not even to ask who Marilyn was. Besides, there were other things to think about.

After Teddy's surgery, the family seemed determined to make a fresh start. Joan resolved to stay home, but even at McLean, I rarely saw her with the Senator. If he was around, Joan was usually sequestered in her bedroom. They rarely ate together and hardly ever dealt with the children together. When she was with him, she appeared subdued and obedient, more like a daughter than a wife.

As for the Senator, he diligently tried to plan his family time more carefully than before. Lew Wasserman, the head of MCA, Inc., which owned Universal Studios, and who was an old friend of the Senator's father, sent over prints of new movies so that the family could screen them in the basement projection room. The kids invited friends over and we provided popcorn and soft drinks. Often the Senator started "the show," and then left the children to enjoy it as he attended to business.

During the weeks and months that followed the surgery, the volume of letters—augmented by telegrams, flowers, and gifts—flowing into the Senator's mailroom increased greatly. Our Washington staff could not handle it all, so additional volunteers were added to the Boston office. Each week we shipped them several huge canvas bags full of correspondence, for sorting and acknowledgment. Teddy composed a brief thank-you note that was printed in quantity and used as a standard reply.

In early March 1974, the Senator enlisted the aid of

Dr. Phil Caper, who was on the staff of the Senate Health Subcommittee, which the Senator chaired. They coordinated a brainstorming session in McLean attended by experts such as Dr. Hugh H. Fudenberg of the University of California at San Francisco, Dr. Emil Frei III from Boston, Dr. James F. Holland from New York's Mount Sinai School, Dr. Kent C. Johnson, Jr., of the Armed Forces Institute of Pathology, and Dr. Joseph Ballant of Georgetown University Hospital. After a four-hour meeting, the consensus was that Teddy should participate in a new, still-experimental course of chemotherapy to attack any remnants of the malignancy. Every third Friday I drove the Senator to National Airport, where either George or Theresa met us with Teddy. No matter what the Senator's mood, he was always upbeat in Teddy's presence, for he knew that the boy would already be dreading the ordeal. Father and son flew to Boston to spend the weekend at Children's Hospital Medical Center, where Teddy endured injections of methotrexate—a drug so toxic that additional shots of antidote were needed. The Senator slept on a chair in Teddy's hospital room, and did all he could to help. Already schooled in administering allergy shots to young Patrick, he learned how to give the antidote to Teddy himself, so that they could spend less time in the hospital and return home on Sunday instead of Monday or Tuesday. The side effects of the chemotherapy were severe, including nausea and hair loss. The Senator made occasional remarks to me about how strong Teddy's spirit was, but I knew that the boy wavered between periods of optimism and deep gloom.

The tension of the continuing treatments ate into the family's resolve. Kara was jealous of the attention lavished on Teddy and, understandably, felt guilty about it at the same time. Everyone was walking on eggshells.

After a time the treatment site was moved to Georgetown University Hospital, and we set up a "buddy system" so that Teddy would never be alone. I volunteered for duty, along with George, Theresa, and Louella Hennessy, the longtime family nurse from Boston. We also recruited Teddy's cousin Joey Gargan, who flew in from Massachusetts, and friends from St. Alban's, including Senator Tunney's son, also named Teddy, and a youngster who went by the nickname of Broadway Jackson.

Friday afternoon until Sunday, we stayed with Teddy in four-hour shifts, to keep up his morale and help him through the bouts of nausea. The Senator pulled the eight-hour, all-night shifts.

I enjoyed the duty, for I liked Teddy and admired his courage. As we watched TV or played Monopoly or Scrabble, he rarely complained about the IV dripping poison into his veins.

Over time, I saw Teddy's spirits rise, and his personality mature. He changed from an introvert into an extrovert, determined to address life in a more aggressive manner.

One day, while Teddy was continuing his chemotherapy, and after Rosalie took Joan out for the afternoon, Theresa said to me, "You have to help me search."

For what? I wondered, but I followed her. To my amazement, she headed directly for the master bedroom and began rifling through drawers. "Check the closets," she commanded. "Look for any pills; clean them out." We found bottles of liquor and vials of Valium stashed at the very backs of dresser drawers and stuffed between the mattress and the box spring of the bed.

Because the Senator did so much entertaining, liquor was a staple in his house. Theresa decreed that the liquor was now to be kept locked away from Joan, and we would attempt to inventory it carefully.

On an afternoon soon after that, the Senator, with

briefcase in hand, directed me to drive him to a location on K Street, near George Washington University. When we arrived, instead of hopping out of the car, he remained seated, immersed in his work. He glanced up briefly and requested, "Let me know when Joan gets here."

A few minutes later George drove up in Joan's car, a white Pontiac convertible bearing the Massachusetts license plate USS1. "She's here," I advised.

The Senator closed his briefcase, exited from the car, and joined Joan on the sidewalk. Together they disappeared into an office building.

We repeated this procedure once a week. On the third or fourth such occasion the Senator felt the need to explain. As Joan arrived, driven this time by Theresa, he said to me, "We're having some counseling." He opened the door, put one foot onto the pavement, then turned to add quietly, "I don't know if it will help."

As I was about to see, it didn't.

The Archibald Glover estate was an immense tract of land on the northern edge of Georgetown that retained enough open space to accommodate sheep and donkeys behind its ten-foot-high stucco walls. On a few occasions I drove the Senator to an exquisite little house at the edge of the estate. It was known as the Gatehouse and was the former residence of the estate's groundskeeper, but it had been fashionably remodeled.

The first few times we visited the Gatehouse, I waited in the car as the Senator busied himself inside. I was curious as to who owned this beautiful residence, but did not feel bold enough to ask the Senator. Instead, when I found an opportunity, I asked George. He replied curtly, "A friend of the Senator's."

Before long, "The Ear," an irreverent and popular gossip column in *The Washington Star,* reported that the Senator was carrying on a romance with socialite Paige

Lee Hufty. This was another rumor of the type that Lillian characterized as "trash." Indeed, Dick Drayne issued a response for the Senator, denying any truth to the story.

The next time we visited the Gatehouse, the Senator took me aside and introduced me to the owner, Paige Lee Hufty. She was a gracious and highly attractive woman who made sure that I was comfortable and had something to read as I waited downstairs while she went upstairs with the Senator.

It was, I decided, the way of the Kennedy men. I'd heard Bobby had been the same way. And by now, everyone knew about President Kennedy.

The Senator's relationship with President Kennedy's family was decidedly more distant than it was with Ethel and the Hickory Hill clan. He regarded Jackie Onassis as a very good mother, and was careful to respect her privacy. He cared so strongly about her welfare and that of John, Jr., and Caroline that when Jackie decided to marry Aristotle Onassis, the Senator had worked out the initial financial arrangements.

Jackie and her children journeyed to Washington, D.C., for important occasions, but spent most of their time in New York. She kept her distance from most of the extended families, opting not to subject her children to the Kennedy fishbowl more than absolutely necessary. But there was another reason as well. Jackie found the behavior of most of Ethel's brood all but intolerable. David was now almost completely immersed in drugs, and Bobby was part of a destructive triangle that included Christopher Lawford and Lem Billings, Jack's old friend, who was also partaking in drugs. Even the Shrivers tried to keep their children away from Ethel's.

So Jackie stayed in New York, managing most of her affairs through her own office there, but the Senator was always ready to provide whatever assistance she requested.

On one occasion I was elected to provide the help. Angelique reached me by phone and announced, "You're going to have a guest."

"What do you mean?" I asked.

"Christina Onassis is coming into town. Jackie just called and she wants somebody very special to show her around. She's never seen Washington."

I met the famous heiress at National Airport, thinking, *My gosh, this is a woman who is worth hundreds of millions of dollars, and I'm supposed to drive her around town in my VW Beetle?*

But I found her gracious and an easy conversationalist. She smiled when she saw my car and said, "It's so cute!" She was only slightly older than I. First we drove to the Senate, where Kennedy took a few moments off the floor to greet her. Then I took her around the rest of Capitol Hill to show her how the system functioned.

I gave her the standard tour of the city, including the Supreme Court building, all the monuments, the Smithsonian Institution and, of course, the Kennedy graves at Arlington National Cemetery. As we drove past the White House, Christina sniffed, "It's not very big. You know, Jackie always bragged that it was a big house. It's not that big."

Christina seemed very pleased by that.

Each day, after an early class, I headed for the Hill. Later, if the Senator's schedule allowed me a bit of spare time, I zipped back to Georgetown to study.

As we drove about Washington the Senator—who was one of the busiest people I had ever known—asked me, "How do you do it? How can you be doing all of this at the same time?"

I shrugged. The answer was you *do* it, but you don't

necessarily do everything as well as you might. My guess was my academic record was affected by the time I devoted to the Kennedys, but there was no doubt in my mind that it was worth it.

People began to comment that my mannerisms were starting to mirror those of the Senator. And indeed they were. The force of his personality seemed to imprint itself on anyone who spent a great deal of time with him. The right hand, jutting forward for emphasis, the speaking style, unfinished sentences punctuated by uhs and ahs, the quick grin, and the nearly perpetual motion had all become part of my posture.

I took it as a compliment. It was several years before I learned there was a big downside to being too much like a Kennedy.

6 The House Judiciary Committee approved three articles of impeachment against President Nixon.

On August 9, 1974, the office was filled with rumors that the President was finally going to resign. Like the rest of us, the Senator was relieved to see him go. The Senator had a great deal of respect and admiration for Vice President Gerald Ford, but Ford was no political star. And so almost immediately after Ford was sworn in as President, pressure mounted on the Senator to make a run for the Democratic nomination in 1976.

One of the negative considerations was that his Senate term would expire the same year and he couldn't run for both offices. For the time being, he pointed himself toward a Senate reelection campaign, but he kept his options open.

At an early fund-raising gala for the Senate campaign, I met many of the Senator's key supporters, including historian Arthur Schlesinger, the Dunfeys of the Boston hotel chain, lyricists Adolph Green and Betty Comden, and Lauren Bacall, a good friend of Steve and Jean Smith. Barbara Walters was there, escorted by Mort Zuckerman, but the Senator seemed determined to avoid her at all costs.

Also there were the Senator's good friends Jamie and Phyllis Wyeth. Jamie's father, Andrew, was the renowned painter, and Jamie, a charming, handsome man in his late twenties—sporting the Senator's style of curly, unkempt hair—was somewhat involved in the political scene as a member of the National Endowment for the Arts. Wyeth once described his pet pig, Baby Jane, as having "Kennedy eyes with white lashes, darting, not missing a trick." His wife, the former Phyllis Overton Mills, a beautiful heiress of the Du Pont family, was a remarkable woman. In 1968, just prior to their marriage, Phyllis was paralyzed in a car accident. She fought her affliction doggedly, and had become a tireless advocate for the rights of the handicapped. Taller than Jamie, and extremely thin, Phyllis managed to maneuver on crutches with a decided air of elegance. The Senator was a partner with her in working for the appropriate legislation to improve the lives of the disabled. The Wyeths' main residence was a farm in Chadds Ford, Pennsylvania, in the fashionable Bucks County area, but they also maintained a New England home, not far from the Kennedy compound, and an apartment at the Watergate in Washington. I gathered they lived fairly separate lives. Phyllis spent much of her time in Washington, and Jamie remained in Chadds Ford.

At the fund-raiser, numerous people made pointed references that they were happy to contribute to the Senator's political fund, but made it clear that "it's really for the presidential campaign."

The Senator wanted to run. "Did you see the poll?" he asked me whenever new figures came out, reflecting either his own popularity or Ford's declining ratings. "What do you hear? Ricky, what are the kids saying on the campuses?" But his key question was, "Do you think Teddy is strong enough?"

Although Teddy was making slow but steady progress,

the family still worried about him. In addition, they were also concerned about Patrick, whose asthma had gotten far worse, and Kara, who had, at least once that I was aware of, run away from home. The Senator also suspected Kara was sporadically trying drugs but so far didn't have any hard proof. And so he brooded about his children.

And then there was the "problem" of Joan.

Joan had taken the first tentative steps toward acknowledging, to herself and to her family, her substance-abuse problems. She had checked into the Silver Hill Foundation, a rehabilitation center in Connecticut, hoping for anonymity, but the family was unable to keep the news from leaking to an increasingly inquisitive press. Things got worse for Joan when, after leaving Silver Hill, she was arrested for drunk driving and sent to an alcohol rehab unit at a New York City hospital, where she remained for almost a month.

The Senator seemed at a loss as to what to do with her, and when conversations came around to her when we were driving, he would usually sigh, as if suffering from battle fatigue.

Beyond Joan was the specter of that tragic night of July 18, 1969, when the Senator had driven his Oldsmobile off Dike Bridge on Chappaquiddick island, leading to the death of his passenger, Mary Jo Kopechne, a woman whom he had been partying with at a cottage nearby. Far worse than the accident itself, in the eyes of the nation, were the Senator's subsequent actions, which nearly indicated criminal irresponsibility. As Mary Jo Kopechne lay dead underwater, Ted Kennedy had changed clothes back in Edgartown, made an appearance in his hotel lobby at 2:30 A.M., trying to create an alibi, and then made seventeen phone calls from his hotel room, none of which were to the police, who were notified almost seven hours later, and almost ten hours after the accident.

The Senator studiously avoided this topic on most occasions; when he had to comment upon it, he held to his oft-repeated statement that his actions in the wake of the accident were "irrational and indefensible and inexcusable and inexplicable," but he offered no further illumination. Much as he would have liked to forget Chappaquiddick, he could not. He had to assess its potential impact upon voters. In the office, the consensus seemed to be that any residue would be washed away by the stain of Watergate; the Republicans were in no position to sling mud. Earlier in the year, as the fifth anniversary of the 1969 tragedy had approached, there had been some discussion as to whether or not Kennedy should call Joseph and Gwen Kopechne, the parents of the victim; he and the staff had decided not to do so.

It did not take the Senator long to sort out his options regarding a bid for the presidency; the family was still reeling from the emotional effects of Teddy's surgery, and Joan was not up to the pressures of a presidential campaign. The timing was not right. On September 23, 1974, the Senator announced publicly that he was withdrawing his name from any consideration as a candidate for the '76 presidential nomination. Almost immediately after that, talk in the office and among the family was that Sargent Shriver was thinking about stepping into the ring.

When I asked the Senator about the possible candidacy, he simply rolled his eyes, making it clear he thought Shriver had very little chance of getting the nomination. But how much could he really say? After all, Eunice was his sister, and probably the most morally sound of all the Kennedys, thanks to her deep religious beliefs. She was one of the key players in the creation of the Special Olympics, which allowed retarded children an opportunity to compete in their own Olympics. One day we were en route to a board meeting of the Joseph P. Kennedy, Jr., Foundation at the Special Olympics office on K Street, with the Senator sitting at my side in the car, Eunice in the back.

"Eddie, did you have to do that?" Eunice asked the Senator.

"What?" he asked in response, trying to get through some paperwork in his briefcase.

"Disclose your financial records?"

The Senator glanced at his sister and grimaced. With a tone of resignation in his voice, he reminded his sister that he had cosponsored some of the reform laws enacted in the wake of Watergate, designed to promote more integrity in government. The Senator had made his 1973 federal income tax return available to the Boston newspapers. The world now knew that his trust income from the previous year had been $385,995.

Eunice pressed on. "I understand that, Eddie. I know we're in a kind of witch-hunt political environment, I understand the *reasons,* but still . . . it's a little dismaying. Everybody poring over our records, digging up how much the Kennedys really have. Honestly. It's bad enough as it is. Everybody thinks we're rich," she complained. "The worst thing about it," she joked, "is that the foundation [the Joseph P. Kennedy, Jr., Foundation] staff is asking for a raise."

The Senator threw back his head and laughed.

Even Eunice saw the humor in her words, but she protested, "I'm serious. I'm serious, Eddie. They are all asking me for raises. What am I supposed to do? I'm telling them you are the rich one, I'm not."

The Senator laughed again. "Ah, Eunice, the things you have to worry about . . . right, Rick?"

I smiled, but didn't answer. I knew he was right. He had a lot of other things to worry about, and in 1974, so did I, mainly where was I going from here? In the spring of 1975, I would graduate from Georgetown. I was happy, for the moment, with my role in the Senator's office, but what else could I do within the Senator's office and beyond?

The Senator himself answered part of the question by approving my promotion as office manager. I would also continue to supervise the mailroom. In my new capacity, I began dealing with the Senator's brother-in-law, Steve Smith, who managed the Kennedy family office in New York, known as the Park Agency, Inc., located on the thirtieth floor of the Pan Am Building. Smith came from a Brooklyn family that was wealthy in its own right, thanks to a fleet of tugboats. In his late fifties, the gray-haired Smith was sometimes abrasive, but unquestionably brilliant. Although the Senator was president of the agency, Smith handled the day-to-day operations, and he was highly effective at overseeing the maze of investments. His staff included eight accountants and two former Internal Revenue Service agents.

But it was Steve who was considered to be a shrewd and effective businessman. Through Smith and his protégé, Joe Hakim, the agency handled nearly all personal financial matters for the family members, including the preparation of tax returns. Keeping track of the movement of money via an IBM System 3 computer, Hakim now had the bulk of the family assets in real estate investments (largely in Florida and Texas), stocks, bonds, tax-exempt securities, and oil and gas enterprises. Since 1945 the key asset had been the twenty-five-story Chicago Merchandise Mart, featuring showrooms and exposition space for various retail industries. Estimates of the total family fortune ranged between $330 million and $500 million. The agency also supervised the activities of various charitable concerns, such as the Joseph P. Kennedy, Jr., Foundation, the John F. Kennedy Library, the Robert F. Kennedy Memorial, the Park Foundation, and Special Olympics, Inc.

Jackie Onassis's children were far wealthier than others in the clan. The Ambassador's final trust, set up for the grandchildren in 1959, provided approximately $10 million for the children of each family, but its details resulted in an unequal distribution. The late President left behind only Caroline and John, Jr. On the other hand, Robert Kennedy sired eleven children and each was entitled to receive a comparatively small sum. Additionally, Caroline and John could count on inheriting considerable holdings from their stepfather, Aristotle Onassis, who, though rumors were rife about the state of his marriage to Jackie, adored her children.

In contrast to Jackie, whom the press had clocked at spending up to $7 million a year of Onassis's money, the Senator's income—especially for a family of means—was relatively modest. His expenses, which were always high, constantly threatened to spin out of control. This naturally concerned Smith. Whenever he had a suggestion for the Senator, he usually offered it mildly at first; if necessary, he grew firm. He usually got his way with financial matters.

"The Senator says we have to save on costs," Eddy reported. "Do something."

After studying the office setup, I made several recommendations regarding the staff. One of these concerned a committee staff worker who seemed, based on his position and experience, to be seriously overpaid. I suggested that we consider letting him go.

The Senator's eyes grew wide with alarm. "Oh, er, no, no . . . no, that's just not possible, Rick." He explained that the man had been with him a long time and he felt a great deal of loyalty toward him.

I pressed again, but he refused even to consider it,

which I found strange. It was such an obvious way to cut costs, but I let it go.

Over time, we were able to reduce the Senator's personal contribution to the office budget from about $100,-000 annually to $30,000. As a bonus, work flowed more easily from one sector of the busy suite to another, and I was handed the additional job of dealing with some of the Massachusetts legislative work.

The more I had a chance to see the Senator interact with his colleagues on the Hill, the more I was impressed with his efficiency at accomplishing his business. He had an ingratiating personal style that caught newcomers off guard. He possessed a charming sense of humor that always found a way to poke fun at himself, rather than others. Many people, especially in the press, had suggested over the years that the Senator was not particularly intelligent. I found, however, that he had an amazing grasp of the pertinent issues and was very bright. While President Kennedy was graceful and eloquent, and Robert fiery and impassioned, the Senator was a natural trouper for liberal causes. He tried to carry forth the ideals of his brothers, of his party, while at the same time assembling the proper amount of courage to take strong stands on controversial but important issues of the day, including abortion, gun control, and health care.

He was a tireless public servant who did his homework. Unfortunately, this sometimes had detrimental effects on his own personal health, namely the constant pain in his back, broken in nineteen places in the 1964 private plane crash. Often this was nearly debilitating by four or five in the afternoon, so he would routinely head to the Senate baths, one of the perks that has recently become a target among voters angry about government spending. Located in the Russell Building, the ornate spa was reminiscent of the Roman baths of old. Lush green ferns flourished in the humidity, and marble accoutrements added to the members-only atmosphere. The sole domain of United States senators, the baths were guarded by two huge, intimidating masseurs known as the Johansson brothers. They were expert at rejuvenating the Senator and sending him off refreshed to whatever dinner or reception was scheduled for the evening.

Later, back home, he reviewed the briefing book for whatever hearing might be coming up the next day—the Senator attended over one hundred such hearings a year—and then fussed over paperwork until about midnight.

By morning, he appeared refreshed and ready to go again.

And he was always on the go. As time progressed, the Senator became even more in demand as a speechmaker. Jim King worked in the Senator's Boston office as the advance man. But demands for the Senator in the Washington area had accelerated as well, and so it seemed logical to groom another advance man to handle the local appearances. When the Senator agreed to speak at a Democratic party function in nearby Baltimore before three thousand people, his political adviser, Paul Kirk, said to me, "Why don't you do the advance work?"

I drove to Baltimore a few weeks prior to the speech to meet with the organizers of the event. I discussed every detail I could think of with security personnel and a police representative. Maryland state troopers agreed to meet our car at the District of Columbia line and escort us to downtown Baltimore.

As we were driven to Baltimore on the designated evening, I found myself very nervous, for I knew that both Kirk and the Senator would pay close attention to see if I had handled everything properly. I was pleased to see a state trooper waiting, as planned, at the Maryland line. We eased in behind him and headed north on Interstate 95.

The evening ran smoothly. Security procedures clicked into place. Dinner was acceptable and the Senator presented a fine speech; the crowd lavished its applause.

Afterward, the Senator cornered me and ordered gruffly, "Get into the car."

Uh-oh, I thought. *Where did I screw up?*

During the first few minutes of the ride back to Washington, the Senator lectured me at a staccato pace. "An advance man can make you or break you," he said. I slumped in my seat as he enumerated my mistakes: The head table was set up in such a way that too many people could move across in front and try to chat. "I didn't have a chance to go over my speech," he complained. He lectured me on the need to set up the hall with natural barriers between the dais and the crowd; all politicians consider this, but a Kennedy, in particular, must separate himself from the people as unobtrusively as possible. If the citizenry had unlimited access to the Senator, he would never get anything done. Finally he discussed the route we took out of the room, through the hotel hallway, back to the car. "I saw a quicker way," he said. "You shouldn't have made that right turn." We could have saved a few precious seconds and, once more, reduced the Senator's exposure.

I knew that the Senator was correct on every point, and I figured I had blown my chance.

The car dropped me in Georgetown before heading for McLean. As I exited, the Senator smiled, held out his hand and proclaimed, "Rick, you did a great job!"

I mumbled faint words of thanks and went to sleep that night totally confused. In the morning, I sought out Kirk and asked, "Paul, did I screw up?"

"No, you did a terrific job," he declared.

"But there were so many things that he didn't like."

Kirk explained. "Rick, he pointed out those details for a reason. You'll never meet a better advance man than Ted Kennedy." Kirk reminded me that the Senator had performed the job during his brother Jack's presidential campaign. "He knows exactly what he wants and exactly how everything should be," Kirk said. "He's just giving you pointers so that you won't make the same mistake again."

And so, in addition to my other duties, I became the Senator's new Washington-area advance man.

Graduation finally rolled around on May 17, 1975. Many of the Kennedy staffers came to the commencement ceremony, and the Senator himself sent a warm note of congratulations. My parents were pleased, and I was amazed to learn that I was the recipient of numerous honors, including the Dean's Citation for "outstanding contributions . . . to the welfare of the school."

After the ceremony, as we sat in the town house I had just rented on 36th Street, directly across from the university entrance—my first home away from my parents—my mother asked, "How did you find the time to do all this?"

My father, beginning to become resigned to the fact that I was still working for the Senator, asked, "What's next?" Luckily or not, neither of us knew.

7 Teddy's rehabilitation had gone well, but he still vacillated between moods of determination and despair. The Senator wanted him to look to a future with optimism, and to that end, provided a specific goal. The past few summers, Teddy had taken a trip with some of his schoolmates, supervised by one of the teachers from St. Alban's. "This summer we're going to do another trip," the Senator promised his son.

As it happened, no one from St. Alban's was available to chaperone a student trip during the summer of 1975, so to keep his promise, the Senator decided to plan a private tour for Teddy and three of the friends who had helped him through his chemotherapy sessions: Teddy Tunney, Joey Gargan, and Broadway Jackson.

It was Theresa who first hinted to me that the Senator wanted me to accompany the boys on the trip. She warned, "It's no small thing, taking four boys, almost teenagers, across the country."

About a week after Theresa spoke with me, I was at the Senator's house when he called me into the library and asked if I would do the trip, which would take six or seven weeks. "Ah, you'll be on your own with them most of the time, Rick, but Tunney and I'll fly out to join you for some of the weekends." The Senator and Tunney were known as "the Dads" to the boys and their friends. He emphasized, "I really want you to do this."

"It sounds like fun, but what about my work at the office?"

"We'll arrange something with Eddy to see that the mailroom is covered. And as for driving, we'll get somebody else. It's about time, anyway."

The Senator, Teddy, Angelique, and I spent weeks organizing the details, making sure we had a full schedule of activities for four rambunctious boys. The more time I spent with the Senator the more we enjoyed each other's company. He was letting his Kennedy guard down more frequently, sometimes assuming the role of father/older brother instead of Senator/employer, giving advice, and more often than not making barbed jokes, trying to get a rise out of me. He was beginning to see that I was breaking out of my "archbishop" mold and opening my eyes to a bigger world. He got a kick out of that.

As the relationship between the Senator and me began to grow, George Dalton, his majordomo, became increasingly hostile toward me. I genuinely liked George, but there was nothing I could do. My job was to serve the Senator.

And so I did.

Teddy Kennedy, Teddy Tunney, Joey Gargan, Broadway Jackson, and I flew to Colorado and rented a station wagon for the first stage of our trip. We spent a day in Aspen, then headed toward the old mining town of Silverton, to what was supposed to be one of the highlights of our trip, a journey on the Butch Cassidy and the Sundance Kid train, which would take us to the very spot where the legendary outlaws had jumped off a cliff in order to evade a tenacious posse. The train was supposed to let us off in the wilds, where we would camp for the night. But we drove into cold, freezing rain—at this altitude, we even saw a few summer snowflakes.

Our car bogged down in mud, and by the time we freed it—with the help of some friendly lumberjacks—we were all sopping wet and freezing. Teddy said, "Hey, Rick, let's forget this and head for the sun."

"Your father is going to be furious if we don't stick to the schedule," I told Teddy.

"We're so cold!" Teddy countered. "Let's just find someplace that's warm."

One of the other boys muttered, "It's just a damn train."

Fine. We turned the car around and headed for our next scheduled destination, Mesa Verde National Park, on the border between Colorado and Utah, where a tourist campground had all the amenities. We checked in and pitched our tents on adjacent lots, one for me and one for the four boys. After the boys took hot showers, Teddy made his obligatory daily phone call to his father and, with a wink directed at me, said into the phone, "Look, Dad, we're going to be heading for a really isolated spot, so we're not going to be able to call for a few days, okay?"

The boys climbed into a nearby stand of trees and framed some Polaroid snapshots that appeared to show us in the pristine wilderness. Teddy slipped them into an envelope and sent them home. "He'll think we're really roughing it." He laughed.

Sometime during the evening, as I read a paperback in my tent, I realized it was far too quiet in the tent next door. Sure enough, the boys had secretly swiped a six-pack of beer from my tent and were feeling no pain. *The Senator's going to kill me,* I thought. I confiscated what beer remained and gave them a quick lecture, which they heard while doubled over in fits of giggling.

Teddy made his way very well through most of the

trip, parts of which—like the river raft ride—were pretty rigorous. I tried to be solicitous of him, but the Senator had made it clear Teddy was going to have to learn that no matter how difficult things could be personally, life must go on. I knew the objective and tried to treat him like the other boys, but I couldn't pretend that he was the same. He was aware of his leg and so was I. Sometimes I helped him wrap the stump, because he was still bothered by considerable itching. More often, when I was wrapping it, he would stare at the space below, where the rest of his leg had once been. My heart went out to him. Once he did become obviously depressed and frustrated, and I drew him aside and gently lectured, "Cool it. You just have to deal with it."

He remarked wistfully, "I know, Rick. . . . I just wonder what the future will be like."

On one occasion, a kindly older couple, recognizing Teddy, approached him in a friendly manner. Teddy was used to this, of course, and he usually handled it well, but on this occasion he was gruff. "Can't you just leave me alone?" he growled.

I overheard this, and sat him down for a private talk. "Teddy, you've got to understand: You're representing your father, and this is important. You have to be pleasant. You shake their hands, say hello, and then we'll go on. It may be a hassle, but it's part of who you are."

Teddy nodded, feeling contrite. He sought out the couple, apologized, and signed an autograph for them. From that point on he faced every adventure with the legendary Kennedy resolve, taking everything that came his way head-on.

We moved on to Utah, where we visited Robert Redford's rustic estate, Sundance. The actor was in Hollywood, on the set of *All the President's Men*, which we would see when we were later in Los Angeles, but his wife, Lola, took great care of us.

By the time we hit Lake Tahoe, "the Dads" were on their way to join us for a few days; we were booked into two plush condos at the edge of the lake. Our hostess was a comely young woman.

The Dads arrived on schedule, and everyone looked forward to an active weekend of swimming, boating, and hot-air ballooning.

The boys struck a deal with their fathers. If the Dads would do the grocery shopping, the boys would cook a Friday-night meal. I went along as Senator Edward M. Kennedy and Senator John V. Tunney swept down on a Lake Tahoe supermarket, probably their first visit to a supermarket in years. It was as if they had landed on another planet. No one else in the store was shopping; every eye fixed on the two men as they blundered through unfamiliar territory, crashing their carts about, knocking things off shelves, complaining about the prices, and trying to understand the labels. They grabbed armfuls of cookie boxes of every variety, had a tug-of-war with an entire leg of lamb, and seemed totally perplexed by the vegetable section. Tunney tossed a fistful of loose tomatoes into the cart so forcefully that they splattered against the wire mesh, creating a mess. The Senator eyed the frozen food section and dove for cartons of ice cream. We returned to the condo with a barrel of groceries, very few of which would make a decent meal.

As I took inventory in the kitchen, I decided that the only recourse was to help the boys whip up a batch of spaghetti.

As we labored in the kitchen, the pretty woman who had shown us the condos appeared at the front door with a girlfriend in tow. By the time we had the pasta ready, the two women had paired off with Kennedy and Tunney and popped the cork on a bottle of wine.

Broadway Jackson and Joey Gargan nudged one another and giggled, out of the adults' earshot, "Uncle Ted's going to have fun tonight."

Teddy overheard this, and his face fell. He watched his father chatting up one of the women, drew me aside, and moaned, "I hope Dad doesn't, you know . . . do something."

"They're just relaxing, having some fun," I said reassuringly. "Don't worry, nothing's going to happen." But by now Teddy knew what to expect.

After the dinner, which was surprisingly good and seasoned with a generous supply of laughter, the Senator suddenly announced, "All right, Rick, time to get 'em outta here."

Just like that.

I took the boys next door and packed them off to bed. But through the open windows I could hear—and I knew they could too—the foursome in a hot tub on the nearby lakeshore, carousing well into the night.

The boys were up early the next morning and happened to be outside when the two women emerged from Kennedy's condo. Young Teddy glanced in their direction, then just turned away, silently suppressing his pain. Head down, he kicked at something imaginary on the ground. At that point he seemed more vulnerable than at any time since the chemotherapy had ended. The women, totally oblivious to the Senator's son's mood, waved at us, saying, "Bye-bye!"

Teddy muttered something unintelligible under his breath about the women, but I got the drift. I put my arm on his shoulder and said, "Come on, let's get this place cleaned up."

The sadness in Teddy's eyes reminded me of a similar scene I had witnessed some time earlier. One Friday when Joan had been away for the weekend, George Dalton asked me to drive to National Airport to meet Margaret Trudeau, wife of the Canadian prime minister. I waited for her at the gate, recognized her instantly, and introduced myself. During the drive to McLean, I realized that she planned to spend the entire weekend with the Senator and I felt decidedly uncomfortable. Whatever understanding the Senator and his wife had about their marriage was their business, but there were children around.

After I delivered her to the Senator's door and turned to leave, I caught a glimpse of Kara staring out of the window of her room with a melancholy expression on her face. It was at that moment that I saw the profound loneliness of the Senator's children. They were captive to their mother's alcoholism and continual absences, captive to their father's sexual flings, and most of all, captive to their name. They would never be able to escape what they were. It was a haunting image, and one that I tried to shake off.

But the Senator's children were not the only ones imprisoned by their family history. We kept hearing gossip in the office about Ethel's children. There were increasing rumors that Bobby and David were sinking fast into full-time drugs. Children of the other families were coping better, but Jackie always seemed to have a sixth sense as to when to keep John and Caroline away from the more rebellious members of the clan.

"Jackie likes her distance," the Senator said once, "but I can certainly understand why. . . ."

And yet, Jackie was determined that the President's children know their legacy and see the governmental process up close. That summer, Caroline Kennedy and a friend became interns in the Senator's office and, after the boys and I returned from our trip, I got to know her. She divided her personal time between the Senator's home in McLean and Hickory Hill, and didn't seem fazed by the pressures and craziness that beset some of the others. She was rather shy, a bit reserved, but she performed her tasks well, fit in easily with others, and played an impressive shortstop on our softball team.

It was my task to coordinate the activities of the interns, and I kept her busy, treating her the same as the others. To give the interns the "flavor" of the Hill, we rotated their jobs from week to week. Caroline worked with Carey Parker, helping to research legislative issues, but she also approached the more mundane tasks, such as mailroom duty, with enthusiasm.

She rarely, if ever, spoke about her father, and when someone would comment about their admiration for the President, she would graciously say "thank you" and change subjects. But her absent father was very close to her heart. One day as I drove her to a softball game she said, "Oh, Rick, can we turn here?"

We drove slowly past 3307 N Street, NW, in Georgetown, and she smiled wistfully. "I remember this from when I was here with my father."

No, I decided, these children will never forget who they are, which was both a blessing and a curse.

The Senator's race for reelection was coming up in 1976 and he was already looking ahead. Though his challenger was considered little threat, the Senator was determined to capture 70 percent of the state vote, solidifying his mandate.

"I'm going to ask my nephew Joe to run the campaign," he said one day as we were driving to National Airport. Bobby's eldest son, a fresh graduate of the University of Massachusetts, would be the front man, officially designated campaign manager. But the Senator knew that Joe did not have the background to handle the business details of a campaign. "Can you go up there and take care of the financial stuff and set up the office?"

The Senator had a special agenda for me. He appreciated the way I had brought the office budget into line and he suggested it would be nice to run a campaign that did not end up in the red. This seemed like a pipe dream; we were still holding occasional fund-raisers to work off the debt from Bobby Kennedy's presidential campaign in 1968.

Still, I would have been crazy not to accept, and so I did. Shortly before we reached the airport terminal, the Senator changed the subject abruptly. "Rick, what do you really want to do?" he asked. "I know that you don't need to work here. What are the things you want out of life?"

There was little time for me to reply, for we had arrived at the gate. I mumbled a vague response, but the truth of the matter was, I wasn't sure. And it didn't seem important. I was just happy to be the new budget director and administrative manager to the Committee to Reelect Edward Kennedy.

Before work could begin on the campaign budget, there were some domestic issues in the Senator's life to resolve. A battle for control of the Senator's household, where ill feelings had been brewing for some time, was heating up. Theresa Fitzpatrick and George Dalton fought constantly. She complained that George ordered with no regard for cost. When the Senator complained about the size of the household bills, George pointed out that everything was expensive. He blamed Rosalie for excessive spending and she, in turn, blamed him.

George probably felt underpaid and underappreciated, but it was not my position to deal with that. When Andres, the longtime cook, retired and moved back to her native France, her replacement, a graduate of the Boston Culinary Institute, quickly allied with Theresa. It was getting more and more like "Upstairs, Downstairs."

To complicate matters at McLean, Joan was back in the picture. Out of rehab, Joan seemed to be managing her drinking problem with some degree of success and, sober, she was more willing and able to assert herself. Her face wasn't nearly as puffy as it had been—at times it had been so bloated she had looked as if she were on steroids—her clothes were more neatly worn, and her makeup wasn't quite as heavy as usual. I could measure the degree of her health by her determination to deal with the domestic turmoil. She announced that she wanted to create a "clean slate," to bring the McLean budget down to sensible proportions and, at the same time, eliminate or at least reduce the tension and bickering.

The Senator avoided personal confrontations whenever possible, so he assigned Eddy Martin to straighten out the mess. Eddy, in turn, forced me into the picture. "We gotta do something," he moaned, obviously not looking forward to it.

In consultations with the Senator, we decided that all three of the veteran household employees had to go, but this presented an extremely sensitive dilemma, for Theresa, Rosalie, and George were privy to all the secrets of McLean. Somehow we had to find a way to move them on—yet keep them happy.

We decided to take things slowly. Theresa would go first; we would deal with Rosalie and George later.

We convinced the Senator that he had to do the dirty work himself and rehearsed him for the difficult moment. He stammered through several trial runs and seemed exasperated at having to pull the plug himself. Eddy suggested it would be better for the Senator and the employees to wait until after the holidays.

He nodded, relieved to be delaying the firings. But then, to our shock, he jumped the gun. Just before Christmas, he gathered his courage, tossed back a few drinks, and plunged into the distasteful task. He sat down with Theresa and mumbled: "Uh, Joan's here more now, and uh, the campaign's coming up and, uh, well, you know, the kids, they're, uh, getting older and, well . . ."

Theresa looked totally confused. So he blurted out that "I, ah, have authorized an extremely generous severance payment for you and have made arrangements for, ah, you to join the office staff as assistant to Dick Berliner [who had replaced press secretary Dick Drayne sometime earlier]. That is, ah, if you want it."

Theresa sat there with her mouth open, shocked. And then the Senator announced that he really must be off to Aspen for the family's annual Christmas vacation.

Theresa was devastated—and furious about the timing. She spent the holidays at the McLean house alone, but after the holidays she seemed resigned to her new fate. For a time she moved in with our new mailroom supervisor, Mary Carney, and attended to her new duties.

Joan took the initiative in searching for a new governess, someone who could be more of a friend to the older children, and who could get along with Rosalie and George.

We all prayed she would find someone . . . and fast.

Early in 1976 I rented a Boston apartment and set to work organizing the Senator's reelection campaign. Bookkeeper Kay Mulcahy and I devised a secret plan to stash $200,000 of campaign money in a special account, known only to her and me. We figured that if Joe Kennedy or the Senator or any of the other key campaign workers knew that the money was available, they would find some way to spend it. So we decided not to tell anyone else about the $200,000 unless we faced a fiscal crisis.

Joe Kennedy had a rough edge. His manner was brusque, so one of my major concerns was to tone down his style. Joe had distanced himself from the family as a defense mechanism, and generally avoided drugs. There was evidence that the 1973 Jeep accident in Nantucket, which had crippled his friend Pam Kelly and left his brother David with a legacy of pain, was a turning point for Joe. Since that time, he appeared to have settled to his tasks, heeding the advice of the Nantucket judge who had advised him to use his illustrious name as an asset. He had completed his college degree, then volunteered at the Daniel Marr Boys Center in South Boston, where he taught working-class boys the genteel art of sailing. Now he seemed ready to assume a preordained position in the family's political life. Cardinal Cushing called the Senator's appointment of Joe as his campaign manager "a most powerful vote of confidence." The more I got to know him, the more I liked him. He was a strapping fellow with long, curly hair, and he seemed reasonably levelheaded. He was surprisingly frugal in his habits. Amazingly, he still wore his father's hand-me-down suits, but Bobby had been a slightly built man, and the suits appeared shrunken on Joe's bulkier frame. This was no way for a campaign manager to look, so I took him to Filene's basement to buy a suit.

Throughout the campaign, Joe joked about the other family political race that was under way; Sargent Shriver, having lost the 1972 election as McGovern's vice-presidential candidate, was now waging his doomed campaign for the presidency. Once Shriver had announced, the Senator told Eunice he had to remain neutral publicly, but would do whatever he could privately. If the Senator ever did do anything to help behind the scenes, we didn't see any evidence of it.

Both Joe Kennedy and Rick Grogan, a bright young Wall Street businessman who was helping out, panted with enthusiasm when a gorgeous young woman walked into our offices one day to volunteer for the campaign. Long, jet black hair curled down below her shoulders.

She had previous campaign experience and we quickly put her to work running the phone bank. Joe and Rick immediately set off on a more-or-less friendly competition to win her affections.

One day I was at the phone bank to deliver some files and we fell into an easy conversation. I asked, casually, if she would join me for a drink after work. She agreed and we spent a pleasant evening together. The next time I saw the Senator he couldn't resist commenting, "Joe's told me that you've got the best-looking girl in the whole place." *News travels fast,* I thought.

The Senator and Joan chose this time to purchase an apartment on Beacon Hill in Boston that served as an official home base for both of them; in reality, it was a place for Joan to live an increasingly separate life, even though the official word was that she was simply "dividing her time." She had made the decision to concentrate on staying well. Her mother had died that year of alcoholism, and perhaps her death was a wake-up call for Joan to renew her efforts to remain sober.

Since Joan had chosen to deal with her problems by shuttling between Boston and McLean, this meant forgoing certain public appearances with the Senator. Others were often called to fill in, to lend an aura of support at crucial moments. Occasionally invitations were extended to Jackie Onassis so that she, Caroline, and John could participate in various campaign functions. These were always low-key approaches; no one wanted to pressure Jackie. If she agreed to send the children to Boston for an appearance, she set strict ground rules, for she did not want them to miss their school obligations; the visits were infrequent, brief, and all business.

Caroline always greeted me with a smile and a friendly, "Oh, hi, Rick," and John was extremely polite. Jackie shepherded them carefully through the scheduled events, speaking in the whispery, breathy voice that she was famous for.

The routine was always the same. After a campaign speech by the Senator, Jackie, Caroline, or John might say a few words to the crowd, then adjourn to a reception line. The occasions served more as photo opportunities than anything else. Caroline and John handled the duties with poise.

Jackie, always reticent about public appearances, maintained a special wariness now. She had been recently widowed for a second time, and *The New York Times* had made a great deal out of reports that Onassis had been on the brink of filing for divorce. It was the Senator who had accompanied Jackie to Onassis's funeral and who, in the middle of the motorcade, caused Christina—who had been in the car with them—to stop the car and bolt out in tears, when he reportedly told Christina that it was "time to take care of Jackie."

The scrutiny of Jackie following Onassis's death was relentless. Understandably she had no desire to face press inquiries concerning the Onassis estate, and the Senator did everything he could to shield her during these events. But on some level, we also knew the motivations were politically based—less attention on Jackie at these events meant more attention for the candidate.

The reelection campaign ran smoothly. We were so confident of an impressive victory that we returned to Washington prior to the election. On the Fourth of July, I celebrated the holiday in three different cities. In the morning we watched the festival of the Tall Ships in New York Harbor and then we flew to Philadelphia for a noontime parade. We ended up in Washington that night to attend a party that staff member Mandi Carver threw on the rooftop of her apartment building on Connecticut Avenue. When the Senator walked into the party, I noticed Mandi's eyes brighten, and a flash of suspicion crossed my mind. I wondered whether Mandi's gaze reflected mere campaign excitement or a message of earned intimacy.

None of your business, I reminded myself.

By now the affairs of the Kennedy men had become legend. Just as the press had been climbing all over Jackie after Ari's death, so, too, were the papers exploding that year with reports of President Kennedy and a beautiful dark-haired woman named Judith Campbell (now Judith Campbell Exner). *The Washington Post* had just broken a story of what it termed "a bizarre White House episode," and further investigations raised evidence that Campbell was also involved with Mafia figure Sam Giancana, who, in turn, was involved with the CIA in plots to assassinate Castro.

Campbell was apparently introduced to both Jack and Ted Kennedy by Frank Sinatra in February 1960, during the presidential campaign. Soon after that, it was said that Jack and the woman had begun an extended love affair. This had all occurred during an era when the press obligingly turned a collective blind eye to a politician's dalliances. But that era was over, and now it was alleged that Judith Campbell had carried on love affairs with Chicago-based Mafia boss Sam Giancana *and* President John F. Kennedy simultaneously.

Washington—and the rest of the nation—was captivated by the stories, but I tried, wearily, to shrug them off. I couldn't believe that President Kennedy would have jeopardized national security like that, but, as I was beginning to see in my dealings with the Senator, there were cracks in the Kennedy façade.

When all was said and done, the Senator garnered nearly 75 percent of the vote against his challenger that year, 5 percent more than his original goal. His nephew was at first furious and then incredulous when he learned that I had withheld $200,000 of the campaign money.

The Senator was genuinely thrilled—as was Steve Smith. My assignment had been to break even; a $200,000 surplus was unheard of. We used a portion of that for town meetings, parties for campaign workers, and for extra caseworkers for the Boston office, reducing the surplus to around $70,000.

As his famous uncle went on to yet another term in the Senate, Joe seriously considered running for a congressional seat from Massachusetts. Instead he set out on his first business venture, the New England Energy Coalition, a discount oil company. He asked me to come to work for him, and the offer was appealing. But I declined, for I suspected that my star was on the rise in Washington.

8 Angelique asked me to buy a copy of the new book *My Story*, by Judith Exner. It was 1976 and the book was making headlines. I brought it to her, and happened to be in the office when the Senator came in. He eyed it like a target and, without comment, picked it up and took it into his office.

I read my own copy with ambivalent feelings. A great deal of Exner's story was holding up under scrutiny. For the family, it was a particularly exasperating moment in their history. Prior to the book's publication, word was that Eunice had been especially upset by the charges about the President—after all, it was the first time the country had had a front-row seat in Jack Kennedy's bedroom—but the Senator had assured her that the allegations simply weren't true.

And then the book hit.

Exner said that Frank Sinatra introduced her (then as Judith Campbell) to both Jack and Ted Kennedy, as well as Peter Lawford, in the Las Vegas Copa Room. After watching the live show, the party went to the lounge for drinks. She sat next to Ted and, after a few drinks, he "leaned over to ask if I would show him the town." She agreed. She was flattered that Ted seemed to want to know everything about her. The questions apparently did not flow both ways; Exner claimed that she had no idea that Ted was married. He also, she said, lacked his older brother's sophistication and charm. "He was the baby brother," she wrote, "walking in his older brother's shadow."

Late that night, Ted escorted Exner to her room. He requested the key, unlocked the door, and bowed as she entered. He attempted to follow, but she stopped him abruptly, in the entranceway. Ted was insistent, and Exner warned, "I know you wouldn't want me to lose my patience."

"Oh God, no," Ted said, laughing, "that's the last thing I want you to lose." He agreed to say good night, but added, "You can't blame a guy for trying."

In fact, he was not yet through with his quest, diligently trying to persuade her to fly with him back to Denver, where he was working in the campaign. When this didn't work, he phoned her several times from the airport, still trying. What he did not know was that it was Jack himself who had caught Exner's eye. The two began a love affair that lasted even after Jack was in the White House.

On one visit, Exner wrote, the President asked suddenly:

> "Have you heard from Teddy?"
> That stopped me. "You mean your brother?"
> "Yes. Has Teddy called you?"
> "Of course not," I said. "You should know that."
> "Well, I just wondered."
> Jack never forgot what Teddy had tried in Las Vegas. Several times when we were in bed he said, "Boy, if Teddy only knew, he'd be eating his heart out." I think he got a big kick out of the fact that he had succeeded where Teddy had failed.

I tossed the book aside and went about my business. As much as I wanted to believe the allegations were "trash," as Lillian used to say, part of me wondered how much had been rewritten over time by the family to create the dynasty they'd wanted. I remembered the family friend erasing President Kennedy's tapes . . . the spin they constantly put on Joan's "problem" . . . the euphemisms used to describe David and Bobby Kennedy's substance abuse. . . .

Judith Exner's story brought back the entire controversy concerning the assassination of President Kennedy. It now appeared that Giancana had been recruited by the CIA to assist with various plots against Castro, and the whole thing smelled very suspicious. Congress held extensive hearings on the subject. The Senator had his own team of investigators nose into the story, and he studied their reports carefully, but he kept his own counsel. Using his own investigators, however, was interpreted by some of us as an expression of less than full confidence in the official reports. Somewhere in the back of his mind, the Senator still had questions. In public, he held to the family's traditional response concerning a possible assassination plot: that there had been a proper investigation and that they supported the conclusions of the Warren Report.

Through private conversations over the years, I knew that several of the children had different opinions. Joe Kennedy tended toward the conspiracy theory, and he believed that whatever group was responsible for the death of the President had also killed his own father, Robert.

The Senator's children were more reticent with their thoughts. Once, when I was watching television with Teddy and a group of his friends, a news report came on concerning the long-standing assassination controversy. I jumped up to change the channel.

Teddy didn't say a word, but it was obvious that he, like I, was quite happy to watch something else.

• • •

Early in 1977, Angelique submitted her resignation as the Senator's personal secretary. Since her marriage, Angelique had led a dual life, continuing to work for the Senator in Washington and commuting to Boston on weekends to be with her husband. It was a grueling schedule. Concurrently, Paul Kirk, the Senator's political adviser, spoke openly about leaving. Almost every day, Eddy Martin said he wanted out. But we were used to Eddy's grousing and considered it the natural fallout of the pressures and frustrations of the job.

"Would you want to take my place?" Angelique asked me one night over dinner at a small French restaurant.

"What?"

Susan Riley had mentioned to me that she'd heard I was being considered for the job. It seemed like a long shot. I was *very* young for such a responsible position, and there were scores of capable people with far more seniority; this would be a gargantuan leap. In addition, the job of personal secretary had always been held by a woman, and the Senator was a traditionalist in these matters. But despite Susan's hints, I was too stunned to say anything else.

"Yes," Angelique continued, "it's come up in discussions that the person the Senator is most comfortable with is you. Certainly you know everybody." Discretion, she emphasized, was a prerequisite. Beyond that, she believed that Eddy would not be able to bully me and he wanted nothing to do with the Senator's personal life. "You'll have Connie for the typing and Sarah for the letters and Chris for the appointments. You just coordinate everything. Would you want to do that?"

I thought for a moment. The Senator and I were comfortable together, and he knew that he could trust me. Without hesitation, I answered, "God, yeah! That would be great."

"Okay," Angelique said. "The Senator was wondering if you'd want to do that. So tomorrow he'll talk to you."

The next day the Senator asked, "Did Angelique talk to you?"

"Yeah," I replied.

"Well, ah, what do you think?" I could sense that he was wondering if he could really replace Angelique with a man.

"I think it could be great, but I have some concerns. I've graduated from Georgetown and I'm thinking about going on for a master's. I don't want to be just your personal secretary."

"I can understand that," he said.

"And I still want to keep my office manager responsibilities. I've got my degree and I want to put it to work. How about calling me your executive assistant?"

He thought about that and realized that the cosmetic change in the title allowed him to sidestep his sexual stereotype of a "secretary." And if the feminists complained that he did not have a high-level female assistant, well, he was used to parrying those thrusts. "That's great," he agreed. "No problem with that. Talk to Angelique about when to announce it." He smiled and leaned back in his rocking chair.

Angelique seemed genuinely happy for me, even with the title change. She demonstrated her trust by revealing to me the combination that would unlock the secret file cabinet that stood adjacent to her—my—desk.

The following Friday we commandeered the Senate Caucus Room for Angelique's going-away party, and the Senator gathered the staffers and told them of the appointment. The Senator made the new office structure clear to the inner staff. Sarah Milam, who ghostwrote much of the Senator's correspondence, appointment secretary Chris Capito, as well as Angelique's secretary, Connie, were to report directly to me and I would report to the Senator. The exception was Eddy Martin. I assured him that I would defer to him on all matters regarding politics and legislation.

Try not to let this go to your head, I repeatedly told myself. *The quicker the rise, the faster the fall. You're now in the position of authority with some highly competent people, most of whom are older than you. Keep things in perspective.*

This was more difficult than I realized. Tom Brokaw did a feature on the "Today Show" about the Senator's new and very young aide. *The Washington Post* and *The Boston Globe* noted my appointment. When I went home for the weekend to visit my parents in Connecticut, both said they were very proud, but showed it in different ways. Mom delighted in telling me that her friends had seen me on television. She was beaming. Dad was delighted I had demonstrated the abilities to get the job, but he was naturally more hesitant.

Later, Dad drew me aside and said, "Listen, you're in a very important position. I hope that you think about it and realize why people act the way they do toward you." *Right,* I thought. This was a man, I reminded myself, who had had a long-standing animosity toward the Kennedys in particular and Democrats in general. I was soaring too high to worry about landing on solid ground. And I was, unfortunately, too busy to dwell on the deeper implications. Years later I would look back and wonder why I hadn't listened to my father more carefully.

But Dad was not the only one who wondered about my job. Eddy Martin glanced at me slyly one day and asked, "What are you doing this for? You certainly don't need to work here."

"What do you mean?" I responded. "I love working here." Yes, I was blessed with a comfortable family, but I wanted—needed—to make my own way through life. I was one of eight children and my parents rightly expected each of us to take care of ourselves. I asked, "How would you know whether or not I need this job?"

He replied enigmatically, "We just know."

I was a bit perturbed by this. My parents were not extravagant people. We were comfortable, thanks to the success of Dad's business. Mom was a socially conscious person, active in volunteer work. She instilled in us a sense of duty, to help those who were less able to help themselves. In fact, she demanded that we take an active role in the betterment of people's lives—do the greatest good for the greatest number. I tried to live up to that while growing up, and during summers got enormous pleasure from working in a camp for underprivileged children.

No, Eddy, I thought. *This is my chance to work with a great man to help him accomplish worthy goals.* In that sense, the work was critical to me.

My ambition was to do the best possible job for the Senator. I did not want a single detail to slip through the cracks. From this moment on, I tracked my activities for the Senator in a simple spiral-bound steno pad. We met first thing every morning and then several additional times during the day. He issued instructions at a mile-a-minute pace as I scribbled furiously in my pad.

One day he commented, "Hmmm, do you take shorthand?"

"No," I replied, "I just write fast."

My notes reflected the incredible pace of the Senator's life, encompassing much of his daily schedule, personal and professional. When one notebook was filled, I started another. I did this throughout my time as the Senator's personal assistant, except for portions of the 1980 campaign.

I am a pack rat by nature, and I saved each of these notebooks; I still have them today.

As I settled into my position, the Senator's associates quickly learned whom to contact. The first time Suzie Chaffee heard me answer the Senator's private line she giggled, "Rick? So you're in the hot seat now. Oooh, this is great!" I had known the Olympic skier for some time, originally meeting her at National Airport when she had flown in to meet the Senator. After that, when she was in Washington I'd escort her to various functions. Frequently, unless Joan was coming in from Boston, Suzie would spend the weekend with the Senator. Naturally I put her through. I was learning quickly that very few calls from women didn't go through.

I had been in my new position for about a week when a package arrived in the mail, a box about five inches long and an inch thick. A handwritten notation on the brown paper wrapper identified it as coming from a physician; it was addressed to "Senator Edward M. Kennedy" and marked PERSONAL—ATTENTION: ANGELIQUE. It resembled a cigar box, and I assumed that it was a supply of Davidoff cigarillos, the Senator's favorite brand.

Already I was learning how to deal with the Senator's personal correspondence. If a letter came in from a family member, I opened it, reviewed its message, and brought it to the Senator's attention. Obviously personal letters went unopened into his briefcase; often he showed them to me after he read them. But this box did not fit into either category. Since it was addressed to Angelique's attention, and since I was Angelique's replacement, I decided to open it. I pulled off the brown wrapping paper and found a small cardboard box. Inside the box, covered with a cottony mesh, were about two hundred large yellow capsules.

"What is this stuff?" I muttered.

I examined the contents more closely. The side of the box was labeled AMYL NITRITE.

Confused, I called Stu Shapiro at the Health Subcommittee, which the Senator chaired. Stu was a physician, and I asked, with what I hoped sounded like benign curiosity, "We had a discussion and somebody raised the subject of amyl nitrite. What does it do?"

"It's used to revive heart patients," Shapiro said. He explained that when you snap open a capsule and hold it under someone's nose, it acts somewhat like smelling salts, resuscitating the patient with a jolt.

"Thank you very much," I said, trembling. I hung up the phone and faced one of my worst fears: *Oh, God, he's sick. Senator Kennedy has a heart condition and I'm one of the few people who know about it. . . .*

Alarmed, I decided that I should at least find out the full details of any medical problem the Senator might have. I checked his address book and discovered the name and phone number of the physician listed there. I called him immediately, introduced myself, and asked, "Am I supposed to use these things? I know they're for a heart condition—"

"No, no, no," the doctor interrupted. "It's something else." He hesitated. "Look—don't worry about it."

"Oh. Okay," I mumbled.

Discreetly, I checked and learned that the doctor had been friends with the Senator for years.

Now I was even more confused. I locked the box in my desk.

That evening, a secretary in our office who was dating a college friend of mine brought a few of her friends over to my place. I knew that some of them had been involved in the drug scene at Georgetown and waited—until after drinks—to ask as casually as possible, "Does anybody here know about amyl nitrite?"

"Poppers," one of my guests snickered. "They're called poppers. You can smell the stuff in the discos.

They smell like dirty socks. People crack them open and put them under their noses. It gives them a rush."

"You're kidding,"

"No, it gives you a real rush while you're dancing—and it's great during sex."

The next morning I walked into the Senator's office. "This box came for you," I said. I opened it and showed him the contents. "I actually thought you had a heart condition or something and called the doctor."

"A heart condition?" The Senator roared with laughter. "That's rich. . . . Well, Ricky, you handled that one pretty well. From now on, you can open anything that comes in for me," he said. He grabbed a handful of the poppers from the box and gave them to me. "Here you go. Try 'em," he suggested. "It's time you lived a little, Ricky. Go out, find a girl, have a good time. I'm taking the rest with me to Aspen for the holidays." There was a twinkle in his eyes, and I knew what would happen in Aspen.

Live a little? Go out, have a good time? In other words, loosen up, just as he had hinted in the past. Before I could do a slow burn, I realized he was trying to give me a friendly message: I was still too straight for his liking. If you worked for him, you had to learn to be more . . . flexible. Maybe he had a point.

I had just turned twenty-four. Less than a year earlier I had been a college student. Now I was at the right hand of one of the most powerful senators in America. Things were moving very quickly. . . . It was, for this Catholic boy from Connecticut, heady wine. I was realizing a dream of actively participating in governmental service, but that didn't mean I couldn't have fun. God knows the Senator certainly did. And the last thing the Senator needed was an "archbishop" running his personal affairs. Or, as I would later discover, maybe that's *exactly* what he needed. . . .

That weekend my friends and I went to a Georgetown club called The Third Edition. I was dancing upstairs with a woman when I pulled a popper out of my pocket and snapped it under our noses. We inhaled deeply . . . and almost instantly burst into laughter. The popper was powerful—the rush was immediate and strong, but short-lived.

It wasn't until years later, when I began to write this book, that I realized that it was at that moment, in that club, that I crossed a moral boundary . . . one small step, a snort of amyl nitrite, and my system of values changed. In some ways I'm sure it was to please the Senator, to show him I was just as hip as he was; in other respects it was a longing to be an adult and party like an adult. Washington is nothing if not a town of competitors, of who can outdo the other. It is an environment that breeds excess, whether it be drugs, alcohol, sex, or power.

My friends schooled me quickly. There were various types of poppers out there, some of which were nonprescription varieties sold in head shops, or right in the discotheques, with names like "Rush," "Bolt," and "Locker Room." But prescription amyl nitrite was considered to be the best and cleanest way to generate a great high.

And so I began to loosen up, but it had to be reserved for the weekends since we were extremely busy. Mixed feelings had floated around the office ever since Jimmy Carter's inauguration in January of 1977. The fact that the Democrats had finally recaptured the White House was bittersweet. The Senator, of course, was pleased to have a party man in power, but it also meant that, if he was to be an obedient party loyalist, eight years would pass before he had any chance at the office himself.

As his executive assistant, I was the Senator's personal aide, and officially there was no reason to include me in political and legislative meetings, but I wanted to get around the Senator's tendency to pigeonhole people, so I included myself, simply barging in and taking a seat at the table. At first I was a silent observer, but gradually I ventured opinions on various issues. After a time, no matter who called a meeting, I tended to be the one who organized the agenda and made sure the appropriate people were there. Before long I was in the mainstream of the Senator's political life, and I found it to be both exhilarating and exhausting.

The new schedule almost wiped out my personal life. There were only twenty-four hours in a day, and I learned quickly that the Senator expected me to be available during all of them. I happened to be at his house one day, sitting downstairs with him and Joan—one of the rare moments when I saw them together. Since she had been living in Boston, Joan had been in a treatment program at McLean hospital, outside of Boston, but her success there was sporadic at best. Today, though, there were no puffy eyes or heavy makeup. She was sober when Teddy bounced in from school, said hello, and sped off to his room.

The Senator, who had quickly gotten a look at his son, turned and said with alarm, "Oh, my God, Joansie, did you see him? He's got an earring."

Joan seemed concerned, too.

The Senator's face grew worried and he turned to me. "Uh, Rick, do you think he's . . . you know, gay?"

"I don't really know," I said, "but I think earrings are sort of becoming a rage now. All the high school kids are having their ears pierced. It doesn't mean he's gay."

"Oh, my God . . ." the Senator repeated, shaking his head. "I think he might be gay. I mean, it's not the worst thing that could happen. We have numerous friends who are gay, but, well, you know . . . it's just so much easier if you don't have to go through all that. . . ."

"I don't think you have to worry."

The Senator instructed me to check out the earring phenomenon. I called some of my friends, who explained that although St. Alban's was more exclusive than a normal high school, it was populated by a more-or-less average group of teenagers. Boys with pierced ears and earrings were now considered hip.

The Senator seemed quite relieved.

I was now swimming nicely in the inner office, but it wasn't long before I realized doing a good job had its pluses and minuses. One night in the midst of a quiet dinner party with friends, a rare evening to relax, the Senator called, clearly agitated. He had been driving himself to a museum benefit when another car clipped his Pontiac. His first thought was not to call the police, but to call me. This was a typical response mechanism on his part. Avoid outsiders. Control it from within.

"Was anybody hurt?" I asked, bracing myself.

"No, it's just a fender-bender," he replied, still clearly upset.

"Where are you?"

He gave me the address, on Connecticut Avenue, near the State Department. "Ricky, come get me," he ordered. I issued a quick apology to my guests and drove to the scene.

The accident was not serious, and it was clearly the other driver's fault. However, by the time I obtained the insurance information, provided the police with necessary details, arranged for the car to be towed to a repair shop, and drove the Senator home to McLean, my dinner party was ruined.

Late that night I wondered, *Couldn't he just handle it himself?*

I realized that although the Senator enjoyed interaction with people, the circumstances of his life obviously distanced him from uglier details. It was a lot easier to slip out the back door and have somebody else clean up the mess. I was now that person. It was *my* job, and he had just reminded me of that.

9 The voice on the Senator's private line said, "Hi, Rick, I'm Barbara Logan. The Senator gave me this number and said I should ask for you."

"Hi," I responded.

"Is the Senator there?"

"No, but if you'll give me your number, I'll have him get back to you."

"Okay."

Later, when I told the Senator about the call, he smiled and said, "She's a wild one. You'll like her." He explained that Barbara was a Florida woman he had met at a social function. "She's coming into town for the weekend," he announced.

"Oh, yeah?" I responded warily.

"She's bringing a girlfriend with her, too," he said, raising his eyebrows knowingly.

"Yeah?"

"They want to see the Senate."

"You're going to bring them here?" I asked in a voice full of doubt. While discretion was part of my job, it seemed to be fairly responsible to question bringing a "wild one" to Capitol Hill. "How are you going to pull this one off?" I asked.

"I don't know," he muttered in resignation. "I tried to persuade her not to, but she wants to come to the Senate. What am I supposed to do?" He paused, then detailed his strategy: "I'll have them come in and ask for you. Barbara's brother is picking them up at the airport and driving them here. Give them a tour of the Senate and my office and get one of the volunteers to take them to the Senate chamber. When they come back, you take them out to dinner." I knew that the Senator had several important receptions to attend that evening. "Later," he said, "I'll call you and you can come over with the girls."

"Fine," I agreed. I knew that Joan was away, but I was still dubious. The children were all living with their father and though they were growing older, they were still impressionable.

When Barbara next called, I detailed the plan and warned, "This has got to be very toned down."

On Friday, I offered a silent prayer: Please don't let them be flakes.

Receptionist Melody Miller was not amused when Barbara and her friend, Lori Dawson, bounced into the office and announced airily, "We're Rick's friends. From Florida."

Over the office intercom Melody singsonged, "R-i-i-i-ck, Bar-bie's here."

When I laid eyes on the women I moaned inwardly. It was March in Washington, a month that carries the legacy of winter, yet here were the two visitors, Barbara and her friend, Lori, in filmy, bright-colored, spaghetti-strapped sundresses that left little to the imagination.

Barbara, a stunning brunette, probably in her late twenties, with a toned, athletic body, stood nearly five feet ten inches tall. You could not miss her presence. Lori was shorter and perhaps younger, a dark-haired beauty.

I gave them a brusque tour of the Senator's office, attempting to ignore the knowing leers of my coworkers, and then suggested with faint hope, "You don't really want to go over to the Senate, do you?"

They giggled and said they did.

I recruited a volunteer from the mailroom to squire them to the Senate chamber. When they returned, they announced that they were going to Barbara's brother's house in Virginia to change clothes. Thank God. They'd call me and drive over to my town house in Georgetown.

No sooner had they left the office than my phone rang. It was the Senator, calling from the cloakroom. "Can you believe it?" he asked. "Jesus, they wore *sundresses.* Every senator's eyes turned up toward the gallery the moment they walked in. Half the Senate had hard-ons."

I learned that evening, as Barbara and Lori sat in my home, why they were so bubbly. Barbara's brother had, indeed, picked them up at the airport, but he had deposited them at The Foundry in Georgetown. This was a spot I had only recently recommended to the Senator, for it featured private dining booths upstairs, where the waiter wouldn't disturb you unless you pressed a call button. The Senator had checked it out and, apparently, recommended it to his visitors. The women were already high when they sauntered into the Senate gallery.

Now they wanted to go back to the same spot for dinner, so I called and reserved a private booth. During the course of the evening, one of the bartenders joined us and chatted with the women as if he were an old friend. Barbara introduced him as Richard. He was young, tall, mustachioed—quite full of himself—and clearly on the make.

Trying to score with the women, he produced a vial of white powder and offered it around. I'd seen cocaine before, at school parties, but avoided it.

Now, here it was—again—in front of me.

Barbara was obviously practiced in its use. She pulled a single-edged razor blade from her purse and used it to separate the coke into thin lines, about two inches long. When the lines were ready, she tempted, "C'mon, Rick. This is how you do it." She rolled a hundred-dollar bill into a thin cylinder. Then, using it like a straw, she inhaled one line of the fine white powder.

She offered the hundred-dollar bill to me, but I said, "Uh, no, no . . . that's okay, I'll pass." I gulped, instead, at my scotch and soda. The alcohol only underscored my panic. I tried to think rationally. Even though I didn't do it, pot seemed relatively harmless. The very smell of it never appealed to me. Poppers seemed safe enough, especially if the Senator's doctor friend was supplying *him* with them. But cocaine was a different matter. Sure, it was becoming the drug of choice for those who could afford it, and everyone said it didn't produce a hangover and was nonaddictive, but I wasn't so sure. To me, it seemed like a serious drug. Not heroin, at least, but still heavy-duty and more importantly *very* illegal.

This is a disaster, I thought, putting my head in my hands for a moment while the three of them snorted away. *We can't have the Senator mixed up with two coked-out women.*

I nervously tossed back a couple more drinks, but repeatedly declined the cocaine.

After dinner, we returned to my town house, and I was glad to get away from Richard and his free-flowing drug. Barbara studied my record collection. I had dozens of albums that I had never removed from their plastic wrappers, being too busy to listen to them. She found a new Fleetwood Mac album and cranked up the volume on my stereo.

Here in my own home, off the streets and away from the leering presence of the bartender, I was finally able to unwind.

"It's time you lived a little, Ricky," the Senator had said when he'd given me the poppers.

The women were full of life. Barbara proved to be a very intelligent woman, but she seemed to apply her mind with full force to the social scene. She told me about her failed marriage. For several years, she and her highly successful husband had lived an extravagant life-style, working their way to the edges of the jet-set crowd. Throughout that time, they had had an arrangement that allowed each to have their various sexual adventures.

Suddenly the doorbell rang. I answered it and, to my horror, found Richard on my stoop, inviting himself in. Within moments my coffee table was covered with thin white lines of cocaine. *This is quickly turning into a nightmare,* I thought. I was supposed to keep these women on ice until the Senator called. . . .

"C'mon, Rick," Barbara coaxed once more. She produced the crinkled hundred-dollar bill from her purse, snorted a line, and handed the "straw" to me.

I looked at the lines, and heard him again, in the back of my mind, saying, *"It's time you lived a little, Ricky."* With several scotch and sodas under my belt, caution deserted me.

It was another moral line I was about to cross, a line bigger than simply doing poppers. I certainly wasn't the "archbishop" anymore; I didn't know what I was.

I continued staring at the line of coke. . . . They were waiting for me.

What the hell, I thought. *At least we're safe here in my own home.* Following Barbara's example, I pinched one nostril closed, inserted the hundred-dollar bill into my other nostril, bent low to the table, and sucked in a line of white powder. I felt an immediate rush of energy and euphoria, much as I had with the popper, but this was more intense. And it wasn't a bad feeling. Life was still okay, and I was okay.

When the Senator finally called and asked me to bring the women to McLean, I was fortified with coke and scotch and sodas and thought, *Why not just continue the party there?* But I had to find some way to lose the bartender. *No way is he coming to the Senator's house,* I thought. I cornered Barbara and told her the situation. A few minutes later she told Richard that her brother had called, worried about her, and she had decided to head home. The bartender, his sexual fantasies shattered, decided to make an investment in the future. He handed the women a small supply of cocaine and left.

We headed for McLean.

Despite the amounts of alcohol I had consumed, I didn't worry about my ability to drive; I felt a strange sense of omnipotence. My only concern was that Kara, Teddy, and Patrick were asleep in their wing of the house.

It was after 11:00 P.M. when we entered quietly; even Barbara and Lori knew a certain amount of decorum was required. The Senator greeted us, wearing a sport shirt with an open collar and a pair of casual slacks. He invited us into the library, closed the sliding doors, and uncorked a bottle of wine for the women. The Senator and I preferred scotch. Barbara sat at one corner of the blue-patterned sofa, in front of the wood-grained coffee table. Lori sat at the other end and pulled me down to sit between her and Barbara. The Senator dragged his favorite blue wing-back chair close to the coffee table, close to Barbara. We slipped off our shoes, sipped our drinks, and talked. With Barbara, conversation was easy. She chattered on about her plane trip, her visit to the Senate, and our dinner that evening. With a laugh, she announced that she and Lori had "corrupted" me.

The Senator laughed, but didn't ask how.

After a time, Barbara pulled the packet of cocaine out of her purse, found her razor blade, and began to prepare four lines on the coffee table.

The Senator sat back in his chair and observed her

actions without comment. Our eyes met briefly, and we shared a fleeting moment of silent communication. I was searching his face to see how he would respond, and I realized that he was watching me for the same reason.

The hundred-dollar bill circulated around the coffee table. Barbara went first, followed by Lori. Then the Senator accepted the hundred-dollar bill, leaned over, and snorted one of the two remaining lines of cocaine. I did the last line.

The party continued at a higher energy rate from that moment on. The drinks flowed. We tried to keep the laughter subdued so we wouldn't wake the children.

We snorted another round of coke.

Our revelry continued for about an hour. Then the Senator excused himself to use the bathroom, just down the corridor from the library. A few moments later I glanced up to see him framed in the doorway. His expression said, *Come out here, Rick. I need to talk with you.*

Barbara and Lori were laughing about something, and didn't notice when I rose from the sofa and stepped out of the room.

The Senator and I stood next to the balcony railing, near the stairway leading to the basement offices, when he whispered hoarsely, "Go."

"Okay." I pulled my car keys out of my pocket.

"But go—" He wrung his hands together, searching for the words to get his message across to me. He thrust a finger in the direction of the women and blurted out, "with her!"

"Go with the girls?" I asked, fairly buzzed.

"No!" He lapsed into muffled laughter. "Go," he repeated. Again his fingers twitched. His eyes were bloodshot and dilated. He put an arm on my shoulder and turned me so that I was facing the women. Barbara and Lori were unaware of our Abbott and Costello routine. "With *her*," the Senator said, pointing. Still, I could not understand, until he spelled it out. "Not Barbara," he said, exasperated and rolling his eyes.

"Lori? Where am I supposed to take her? She's staying with Barbara's brother."

"What, are you stupid?" the Senator asked. "Take her to your house."

Lori and I tottered off, arm in arm, and somehow made it back to my town house.

The phone woke us early the next morning. The voice on the other end sounded a bit harsh and jolting, but I realized that everything seemed jolting this morning. It was Barbara calling, and she wanted to talk to Lori. In a stupor, I listened to Lori's end of the conversation.

"It was incredible," Lori reported.

Lori was quiet for a moment and then she winked at me and quipped with exaggeration, "I think Rick's the Marathon Man. He wouldn't stop all night."

After the call, Lori and I dressed slowly and eased into the blinding glare of the sunlight, in search of breakfast. George drove Barbara from McLean to meet us.

Over coffee, Lori, who was a political activist, said knowingly, "You know, Ted's not the only one who knows how to play hard. Honey, I know Gary Hart *real* well. We had this torrid affair. He still calls me all the time . . . trying to come back for more, I guess."

My head was pounding, both from my hangover and Catholic guilt. *Please God,* I implored the ceiling, *just get these women out of my life.* It was not to be, for the remainder of the weekend loomed in front of us. Fortunately the Senator was busy that day, and I was relieved to learn that the women were, too. They were having dinner with Barbara's brother that evening.

The rest of my Saturday was mercifully quiet. Attempting to subdue my conscience with work, I attended to a myriad of details concerning the Senator's life.

By Sunday afternoon I had recovered somewhat. As I

picked up Barbara and Lori and drove to McLean for a tennis date, I found my guilt slowly diminishing. I had survived, the Senator had survived, and the girls had survived. The women weren't as outrageous as they had been, and were actually fun to be with. Life, in fact, seemed pretty good.

We arrived in McLean to find that the children were out somewhere with the governess. Barbara and Lori played poorly and my own tennis skills were average; the Senator was an accomplished player, and I could tell he was somewhat frustrated by the lack of competition. Afterward, he whipped up a batch of daiquiris in the blender and we sat outside in the springtime sun, drinking and chatting.

When the children returned, the Senator calmly introduced Barbara and Lori as friends of *mine*. The children, though polite, looked at the women suspiciously. They hadn't bought their dad's line. They'd been around him too long. They knew the score.

On Monday morning, the Senator wouldn't discuss business until he had savored the aftertaste of the weekend. Like two bad boys from school, we compared notes on the women, but shied away from any mention of cocaine.

"Well, Ricky," the Senator laughed, "you've graduated from being the, uh, Archbishop to becoming the Marathon Man."

He laughed again when I reported Lori's comment about her having an affair with Senator Gary Hart. "I'll bet she has," he clucked.

Not long after that, the Senator and I happened to encounter Hart on the floor of the Senate chamber. The Senator flashed a mischievous grin at me and said to Hart, "You know, Gary, Rick is a good friend of Lori Dawson."

"Oh, really?" Hart said, wide-eyed.

In an instant, he was gone.

One Saturday not long after that, I was out at the Senator's home, double-checking his schedule for the upcoming week. He had a sudden thought and drew me toward his private office, just off the master bedroom. "Come on in, I want to show you something," he said.

He displayed his private desk, and pointed out locked drawers. Then he took me to a closet in the room and showed me where the key was hidden. As he unlocked the center drawer, he instructed, "Rick, if anything happens to me, clean out this desk and throw everything away." He pulled open a side drawer and I glanced inside. It contained stacks of private correspondence, assorted mementos, and a wooden cigar box.

The Senator repeated, "All of this is what you have to destroy."

10

"The Senator's expenditures are getting way out of hand," Steve Smith said to me one day over the phone in 1977. "Have you seen the printouts, Rick? What does he do with all that cash?"

I knew, but I certainly wasn't going to say. Discretion intervened. "Let me look at the figures, see what we can do to get things under some control, okay?"

Smith seemed mollified for the moment, but I knew his concerns were legitimate. The Senator's annual trust income may have been lavish by normal standards, but he was not very adept at managing it, and his expenses were high. It was once said of Jack Kennedy that trying to talk to him about personal finance was "like trying to tell a nun all about sex," and the Senator exhibited the same naïveté. He could be extremely frugal; instead of buying a new pair of sneakers, he might have his old ones resoled. But he would visit Louis of Boston and drop several thousand dollars on clothes in the blink of an eye.

And as Steve Smith had noticed, he was capable of going through cash in an astounding fashion. Often, as the weekend approached, he handed me a check drawn on his personal account at Boston's Freedom Federal Savings and asked me to cash it at the Senate bank. The checks were for three or four or even five thousand dollars' worth of cash, and there were reasons for him to carry such large sums. If a woman was coming in for the weekend, for example, he wanted to pay for her trip, but discretion demanded that he not leave a record on a charge card. He never seemed to worry about his bank balance; if he was ever overdrawn, the bank would call Steve Smith in New York and the Park Agency would cover the deficit immediately.

Each month we received a statement from the agency, detailing the money paid out for the Senator's Washington and Boston offices and the McLean household.

Periodically, Steve Smith or his young assistant, Joe Hakim, who was taking over more and more of the nuts-and-bolts management duties, raised questions with the Senator about various categories of expense. Because of some of the cost controls I had instituted, the office budget had become more manageable, but the Senator's household expenses were still extraordinarily high. Finally he said to Eddy Martin, "Rick's done such a good job on the office budget, let's have him look at the house." Eddy agreed.

"Look," the Senator complained to me, pointing to a printout from the agency, "we spent five hundred dollars on toilet paper!"

I studied the account records intently and began to make recommendations.

I was amazed to realize how much he spent on gardening. He kept an old man on the payroll as a full-time gardener and, due to systematic raises over the years, now paid him more than $40,000 annually, plus benefits. When we added the costs of supplies and part-time assistants, the Senator realized that he was spending more than $100,000 every year just to maintain the grounds of his home. Since the gardener was approaching retirement age—he was nearly blind as well—I persuaded the Senator not to replace him; instead, we contracted with a professional gardening service and saved about $30,000 annually.

But this wasn't the Senator's biggest expense problem. He had abdicated control of his household account by giving both George and Rosalie authority to sign checks. This led to waste, perhaps inevitably. George, for example, had written a check for about five hundred dollars for a shipment of wine, but the Senator could not remember asking for such expensive wine. "Look," I said, "Rosalie thinks she is running the house." The Senator acknowledged this with a nod. "George thinks he is running the house."

"Ummm," he sighed, sitting at his desk, placing a hand on his cheek in resignation. A look of pain crossed the Senator's face. He knew it was time to do something about Rosalie and George.

In short order we restructured the checking account so that the Senator would be forced to monitor every household expense. There was no other choice, but it caused a lot of animosity.

As the tension increased, so did the Senator's concern for his privacy. "Well, what do you think?" he asked me in the office one day. "What happens if we get rid of Rosalie and George and all of a sudden one of them runs to the press? Do you think there is any way we can have them sign something to prevent them from discussing things?"

"I'll check into it," I said, making an entry in my notes. I asked around, gathering opinions from Paul Kirk, Joe Hakim, and Steve Smith. The consensus was that we simply could not structure an agreement that would be binding in court. Finally, the Senator decided that the best way to ensure continued discretion was to provide Rosalie and George with generous severance allotments, as well as sterling recommendations for future employment.

Rosalie went first. She was angered and bitter, but she kept her own counsel. Terminating George was a more delicate matter. He was as loyal as a puppy dog, to the family in general and to the Senator in particular. We did not wish to alienate him; we simply wanted to encourage him to move on.

In New York, Joe Hakim arranged financing so that George could purchase a couple of service stations; he became very successful.

George was not replaced. Instead, I assumed most of his duties.

One night after a particularly grueling day, I sat in a bar with a friend, a Senate Judiciary Committee staffer. Since the night at the Senator's house with the two girls, I had gradually made a concerted effort to relax more. Relaxing in the pressure-cooker atmosphere of Washington, as I had witnessed with the Senator and others, meant having a few drinks and maybe hitting the dance clubs, where poppers—and more—abounded.

"Do you do coke?" my friend asked casually, more curious than anything else.

I looked at him, worried that somehow he could see the truth. I thought about how I was changing in this new, fast-paced, high-octane environment . . . and had decidedly mixed feelings. Why was it that just months before, people still viewed me as an innocent, and now this relatively new acquaintance found it easy to talk to me about drugs? Was I simply growing up, leaving the naïve Roman Catholic–boy image forever behind? Or was the Senator's hungry appetite for life rubbing off on me? It really didn't matter, I was still the same old Rick deep down inside. Or so I quickly told myself.

"Yeah, I've tried it," I admitted, not giving the details.

Since that first encounter with the Senator, Barbara, and Lori, I'd found coke helpful in loosening up on the weekends.

My new friend leaned closer. "Well, Rick, if you ever need some, I can get it for you."

Tepidly, I began making small buys through an intermediary, and I was careful never to conduct any of this business on Capitol Hill, although once you're even partly familiar with the drug's use, you sometimes pick up a sixth sense about who else is a user, even if the signs are no more overt than simply a runny nose. And in the Capitol, I noticed, there seemed to be a number of young people—and even some well-known congressmen and senators—who had a disproportionate series of "colds" and runny noses, even out of season. There were also a number of lawmakers who were conservative Republicans by day, railing on the Senate floor about stiffer drug laws and the ills of drug users, who were coke users by night. This I knew from my own connection, who was more amused by the hypocrisy than anything else. I chalked it up to all the pressures we were under and the emerging, more lenient times.

For a time the vivacious Barbara, worrying little about decorum, called the Senator at home almost every night. The Senator made it clear to her that this was unwise, and so she soon switched tactics and began to call the office nearly every day. "Ricardo," she teased, dubbing me with another nickname, "Lori says hi. When are you coming to Florida? Lori wants to go out with you again." *No kidding,* I thought. As if to drive the point home, Lori had sent me a photo of herself, clad in a skimpy outfit, with a come-and-get-it look.

Barbara was not content with photographs. She flew into Washington frequently to see the Senator and didn't want her family to know that she was in town, so she became my houseguest.

"You take care of it," the Senator directed when I asked about her travel expenses. I charged Barbara's airline tickets on my American Express card and sent vouchers to the Park Agency, requesting reimbursement for "personal expenses." These were paid without question.

At first, Barbara was convinced that the Senator would divorce Joan and marry her. Joan was spending almost all of her time in Boston at this point, rarely seeing the children, and sometimes falling "ill" for days on end. We tried to monitor her activities through the Boston office, and we knew her struggle with alcohol was getting rockier, not better, often requiring several weekly visits to her psychiatrist. The Senator seemed resigned to the fact that she would probably never change, and unloaded his feelings on Barbara, who took the candor as a sign of impending divorce.

Barbara badgered me with calls, talking over the possibility of moving to Washington, of what life would be like with the Senator once Joan was out of the way, how the children would respond to her as a stepmother, and on and on. I sighed, and listened, but limited my responses.

"Barbara called five times today," I complained to the Senator.

He laughed ruefully. "She's hooked, Ricky . . ."

"She's considering moving here," I warned.

That got his attention. He looked up and, very seriously, said, "Take care of it."

The next time she called, I counseled, "I think the situation is more difficult than you realize. Politically, a divorce could be very damaging to him, and there's also the religious issue . . . don't get your hopes up."

Eventually, Barbara faced the reality of my advice. She

realized she was going to have to accept no more than occasional interludes with the Senator. At least for the moment, she was willing to settle for that, but she was clearly in love with him, and she grilled me for information about other women in his life. "What do you mean he's not going to be home tonight?" she would ask. "What's he doing? Is he seeing somebody? Is there somebody else? What's going on?"

"Barbara, I can't give you the details of his schedule," I said.

"Come on, come on."

"It wouldn't be right," I replied. "I work for him, remember?"

"He's screwing somebody else," she pouted. Well, Barbara knew that two could play that game. If the Senator was going to run around and not crown her full-time mistress, she'd get back at him. I was the person she decided to use to make her point. One night at my town house, when we had been drinking and doing a few lines of coke, Barbara put the moves on me. She *was* alluring and incredibly sexy, no doubt about it, but I had qualms about sleeping with my boss's girlfriend, no matter how transitory she was in his life. She was undaunted and I, naïvely, didn't realize the game's objective. Finally, with too many scotch and sodas and a little too much coke under my belt, I gave in. Before I knew it we were in bed together.

When Jack Leslie, my housemate and current coworker whom I had known since college, saw Barbara emerge from my room the following morning, he raised his eyebrows and shook his head.

The irony was, nothing had happened. The effects of the alcohol and coke had pretty much negated that possibility. Still, Barbara took almost wicked delight in taunting the Senator about the night she "slept with Rick." I really had to laugh at this point. . . . If he only knew.

Barbara had no qualms about phoning me at home late at night. Almost by necessity, the two of us became friends and, at least from her perspective, confidants.

One Saturday Barbara spent the entire afternoon at the McLean house, but the Senator had an appointment for the evening, so it was my duty to take her out for dinner before returning her to McLean later. It was cold outside that evening, and she wore a full-length fur coat. She was high on cocaine and giggled uncontrollably throughout the short drive. Tonight, I realized, she was going to be a lot to handle.

When we were out on the street, walking in twilight toward the restaurant, she said, "You haven't looked at my dress."

Uh-oh, I thought. *It's probably really low-cut.* "I'm a little afraid that I'm going to be surprised," I admitted.

"You *are* going to be surprised," she teased.

"Barbara, what's going on here?" My eyes darted about to see who was looking.

There, on the Georgetown street, she threw open the front of her fur. Underneath, she was totally naked. "That's just a preview of what I'm going to do later . . . for my baby," Barbara announced.

"Well, I'm not taking you to the Senator's house naked," I snapped, pulling her coat shut. I drove back home and Barbara humored me by donning a filmy slip. She kept her coat on during dinner.

It was very late when we arrived in McLean. We knew the children were at home, but we were sure that they would be in bed by now. The Senator had instructed us to come around to the back and up the deck to the door opening onto his bedroom. He promised to leave it un-locked.

Despite a considerable intake of both alcohol and co-caine, I managed to maneuver the car into the driveway quietly. Barbara and I tiptoed around toward the back of the house. Admonishing each other with "Shhh," we crawled through brush and shrubbery and scrambled up the rough wood stairs leading to the deck. I was concerned that the children would see or hear us, and Barbara couldn't stifle her giggles. When we finally reached the Senator's bedroom door, I shoved Barbara inside and onto the bed. She had already shed her fur coat by the time I beat a hasty retreat. At least she was his problem now, not mine.

As the Senator later related, they had a "pretty wild time" and then Barbara went off to Florida. Not long after that, though, she was on her way back to Washington. Knowing this, he instructed me, "Have her call our friend." It was then that I realized that he was using Barbara as an intermediary to get cocaine for him; she arranged the buys through Richard, the Georgetown bartender.

On June 12, 1977, the Senator stood in a muddy field on a peninsula in Boston Harbor, in a run-down area of the city known as the Dorchester section, for the ground-breaking ceremony of the John Fitzgerald Kennedy Memorial Library, now planned as a $12 million modernistic structure fashioned of glass and concrete, designed by renowned architect I. M. Pei. Jackie Onassis was there, too, along with Caroline, John, and Rose.

President Kennedy had long ago chosen a site near the Harvard Business School where he wanted the library. But the family had run into opposition from the citizenry, who complained that the area was already congested, so the new site was chosen. Putting the best face on it, Jackie declared that it was a "place more lonely and windward, more epic in scope."

In his speech, the Senator promised that the library would "be more than just a collection of documents under glass. It will also be a very personal memorial, a link between the future and the past." His voice cracked as he predicted that the materials in the library would describe his brother's "life and works in ways that will make him come alive for future generations." He asserted that the library "will tell the kind of man he was."

In fact, I was gaining my own view of the late President, which was not the portrait the family painted. One of my duties was to pack up old files, the Senator's legacy of material from the Camelot days, and ship them to Steve Smith, who was then supposed to forward them to the library. To do this, I had to sift through the contents of the locked file cabinet in the inner office, adjacent to my desk. One drawer held a supply of PT-109 tie clips and Kennedy silver dollars. Another drawer held court documents regarding Chappaquiddick.

Here, too, was a three-inch-thick stack of summaries of portions of President Kennedy's Oval Office tapes, the material that the Kennedy family friend had worked with some time ago. Some were transcriptions of unedited tapes, accompanied by edited versions, with sections blacked out. By comparing the two, I could see what it was that had been excised. They were all personal conversations. Several of the passages were calls from Marilyn Monroe. One was a long, romantic conversation with the woman then named Judith Campbell. I glanced at only a few of these. Some of the conversations were fairly erotic and steamy. It would have taken hours to read them all, but none of them seemed to involve presidential business. Without further thought, I packed up the stack of transcripts and sent them on their way to Smith. I never learned whether all—or some—of the material arrived at the library.

As I studied the contents of the file cabinet, I also found a number of love letters, written in a feminine hand, signed "M." The script was unmistakable to my eyes; this was the handwriting of staff worker Mandi

Carver. When I found the right moment, I asked the Senator if he had a relationship with her.

"Yeah, but that's over and done with," he replied.

Well, not quite. It was a relationship, I learned, that ebbed and flowed. In periods of social drought, the Senator was quite likely to call Mandi and attempt to rekindle the relationship, sometimes at the expense of her current romance. Mandi was intelligent as well as beautiful, but the Senator, with his charismatic charm, quick wit, and Kennedy self-assurance, seemed to be her weakness. The power of his personality was like a black hole—once you were sucked in, there was little chance of a way out, so strong was its gravity. As with most of us in his office, we wouldn't have wanted out anyway. Loyalty kept you going along for the ride.

As time passed, I realized that Mandi was not alone among the women in the office who carried a torch for the Senator. A number of other women who worked directly on the staff or in the committee offices all spent their share of private time with the boss.

After seven years with the Senator, political adviser Paul Kirk resigned his post and joined the Washington office of Sullivan & Worcester, a Boston-based law firm. For the time being, the Senator did not replace him. Rather, he remained close to Kirk, calling him frequently for advice.

Administrative assistant Eddy Martin also made good on his desire to quit, accepting President Carter's appointment to a HUD post in Boston. It was a measure of the Senator's esteem for both Kirk and Martin that he took the news graciously, if regretfully. When others left the Senator's employ, he often harbored a grudge. Earlier in the Carter administration, when his former advance man, Jim King, had gone to work for Carter, the

Senator had gone ballistic, and still refused to have anything to do with King.

Eddy's departure opened a vacancy for the AA position. It was the ultimate staff job, and one that I would have been crazy not to want. Sure, handling the Senator's personal life was an immense challenge, but it was far different from being involved in his professional life, where you could really make a contribution to various types of legislation, issues, and goals. It was also an opportunity to fulfill my mother's directive to do the greatest good for the greatest number. There were a great many parts of the good Roman Catholic boy still intact.

The Senator was hesitant, concerned about my still-tender age. He also didn't want to lose me as his executive assistant.

"I can do both," I assured him. "And we can give Connie more responsibilities in the personal area."

He said no, and I realized that I was still a victim of his tendency to pigeonhole people. He was very comfortable with the work I did as office manager and executive assistant, and did not want to make any changes in those responsibilities.

Finally I said to him somewhat belligerently, "Okay, see if you can find somebody else who could do a better job."

He reviewed applications and interviewed several people. He seriously considered Rick Grogan, whom he had met through Joe Kennedy during the Senate campaign. "How about if I bring Rick down from New York?" he suggested to me. "You still have all the office and the personal stuff, and Rick will just do the political stuff."

"You know I want the political stuff," I answered honestly.

Eventually, and much to my chagrin, he named Kenneth Feinberg as his new AA. Feinberg was a brilliant lawyer, a former federal prosecutor in the Southern

District of New York, who had been working on the staff
of the Judiciary Committee at the critical task of reform-
ing the nation's Federal Criminal Code. Feinberg approached the job with zeal; his intentions were good, but
he lacked a measure of Eddy's diplomatic finesse. Whenever the Senator had told Eddy to do something *now*,
Eddy had been street-smart enough to dish out the necessary carrots along with the commands, in order to moti-
vate his subordinates. But if the Senator told Ken to do
something *now*, within moments the office was likely to
be filled with screaming.

As that summer of 1977 progressed, with its typical
Washington high heat and humidity, making all of us on
Capitol Hill swelter in even our lightest suits, the Senator
became involved with a woman named Paula, a Capitol
Hill staffer. I spoke on the phone with her several times
a week, and often arranged lunchtime liaisons in the
Senator's private office.

The private office was in the Capitol building, near the
Senate floor. In this Congress, the Senator had achieved
enough seniority to rate one of these special suites, which
was really a small hideaway just off the rotunda. There he
could escape for a private meeting or even lock himself in
for a nap. Although Angelique had decorated it before
she left, the Senator thought it was too stuffy, and preferred an easier, more casual style. So it was redone and
featured a comfortable sofa, several chairs, a dining
table, and a bar.

Paula was particularly concerned about keeping the
relationship discreet, and that was just fine with the Senator.

One morning the Senator called me from the Senate
cloakroom and said, "I want you to go meet somebody
and bring her over to the private office."

I assumed that he was talking about Paula, and I wondered why she needed an escort. "Can I send somebody else?" I asked. "I have a lot of things to do."

"No, no, you have to do it yourself," he said. "I told her you'd be meeting her. Now this is what she looks like. She has dark hair and she's *very* big up top." So it wasn't Paula. Now I realized why he wanted me to handle the errand personally. "Bring her over to the private office and find out what she would like for lunch," he said.

I met the young woman on the street, at a corner of the New Senate Office Building, and when I first saw her, I thought that she didn't seem the Senator's type. He usually preferred tall blondes, reminiscent of a younger, healthier Joan. This brown-haired summer intern—a college coed who could not have been much older than eighteen—was attractive, but no knockout. The Senator was right on one point, however; she was extremely well endowed.

"Hi, I'm Rick," I said, trying not to sound wary.

"Hi," she replied, flashing a disarming smile, showing beautiful teeth.

"I'm going to take you over to see the Senator."

We engaged in small talk as we walked. She spoke animatedly about her summer job, and seemed delighted about lunching with the Senator in his private office. I had her settled in, with the food on the table, by the time the Senator appeared. I let him in and excused myself, locking the door behind me, thinking, *Another one bites the dust*.

As I walked back to the office, I thought about the sheer number of women who moved through his life. For any man it would have been an impressive number, but with the Senator's responsibilities, schedule, and time demands, it was amazing to me that he could juggle it all.

One way he kept his energy up was, increasingly, through cocaine. My own intake had accelerated parallel to his, though I tried to limit it to weekends. The Senator never tried to hide his usage from me. Far from it. Time and time again he'd ask Barbara to "get in touch with our contact," meaning Richard the bartender, or, if Richard didn't have any, my own connection.

The drug helped him, as I thought it did me, keep on top of an ever-demanding social life. The Senator maintained the proverbial little black book of names and phone numbers, and it was crammed with entries: Amber, Annie, Bonnie, Carla, Cindy, Claudia, Debbie, Felicia, Florence, Greta, Hillary, Janice, Jo Ellen, Kathy, Laura, Libby, Margaret, Mary Ann, Maureen, Nancy, Nicole, Norma, Patti, Peggy, and Stephanie. To name a *few*. Since it was my job to coordinate the Senator's travel plans and social engagements, I bought my own black book and copied the essential data.

The women were a scattered assortment of types, mostly blond, some quite smart, others simply bimbos who liked the high times and fast life. Some were professional women, others were professional flirts, bouncing from one powerful person to the next. Some were truly wonderful women who happened to fall under that fatal Kennedy spell. Margo Frye, for instance, was a staff aide on one of the Senator's subcommittees who moved in and out of the Senator's life. She, like a number of the others, also shared his growing passion for cocaine.

One of the most consistent but least demanding of his girlfriends was Helga Wagner, yet another stunning blonde, who owned a shell jewelry store in Palm Beach. She had met the Senator in 1967 at a cocktail party at the Palm Bay Club. At the time, she had been married to Robert Wagner, vice president of American Eastern Company. The Wagners divorced in 1970, but Helga remained one of the Senator's closest friends. She called me every week or two to check his schedule, to see when and where they might be able to meet. Sometimes they would rendezvous in Florida, sometimes in New York.

Helga held a different status from some of the Senator's other companions. She and the Senator were longtime friends, sometimes lovers, sometimes not. He would call her every now and then just to talk things over; in fact, Helga said she had been one of the people he had phoned during the first nine hours after the Chappaquiddick accident. Helga seemed to have no illusions that she might become the second Mrs. Kennedy. Like so many others before—and after—her, she could only expect so much as long as he was married to Joan.

The business of the Senator was still the Senate, and I watched—now from a closer vantage point than ever—as he applied his finesse to his work. At issue was the Criminal Code Reform Act of 1977. The Senator knew that the bill meant a great deal to a leading conservative on the Judiciary Committee, Senator McClellan of Arkansas, and he also knew that many of its provisions were simply unacceptable to liberals. Acting on the principle that some reform of the criminal code was better than none at all, he huddled with McClellan and hammered out a compromise. He persuaded McClellan to address several potentially repressive changes in existing criminal codes—those issues that most troubled liberals. McClellan agreed to drop these and add some liberalizing reforms, and the Senator, in turn, agreed to try to sell the package to his liberal colleagues.*

As the delicate negotiations unfolded, it became a classic exercise in political compromise and illustrated the Senator's philosophy that it is better to accept the possible, rather than fight for the perfect. My respect for him as a lawmaker had never been higher.

• • •

*The Federal Criminal Code was adopted by the U.S. Senate on January 30, 1978, by a vote of 72–15.

"Hello," I answered the Senator's private line, never knowing what to expect.

"Oh, hi, Rick," the soft voice replied. "This is Mrs. Onassis. The Senator said I should give you a call."

I had to concentrate in order to catch her words. Although we had met only briefly during the reelection campaign, she sounded as if she remembered me.

"I talked to him last night at home," she explained. "It's about my housekeeper. She's got a problem with her visa."

"What's the problem?" I asked.

"Her time is up, and they're not going to extend it. Do you think you can do anything?"

"We'll get right on it and see what we can do," I assured. "Can you give me the details?"

"Could you call Nancy Tuckerman? She'll fill you in."

"Sure," I said.

I phoned Jackie's secretary and copied down the necessary information. The housekeeper was from Central America and seemed to have a legitimate case for the renewal of her visa, which would allow her to live and work in the United States.

Every senator and congressman receives such requests for assistance. But our office was swamped with them, for the Senator chaired the Subcommittee on Refugees. We had a caseworker in the Boston office, Matilda, who was assigned to shepherd applications through the offices of the Immigration and Naturalization Service. Normally, the process consumed several months. But in this instance, Matilda and I expedited the matter. I had the housekeeper's file delivered to Boston, Matilda quickly arranged for a temporary card, and soon thereafter a new green card.

"Oh, Rick, thank you so much for your help," Jackie said when she called back.

"You're welcome," I said. "Anytime."

"Okay," she replied, taking me at my word. "You're going to get a call from my sister. Her housekeeper has a similar problem."

That day, Jackie's sister Lee Radziwell called and, once more, Matilda and I swung into action.

On Saturday, October 1, 1977, Georgetown University honored Rose Kennedy by presenting her with a Doctor of Humane Letters, Honoris causa, for her leadership in care of and research on the mentally disabled. The citation read in part: ". . . knowing one of the children to be mentally retarded, she chose, unlike so many of her contemporaries, not to hide the fact. Rather, she turned this affliction into the occasion for beginning a crusade on behalf of all other similarly afflicted. . . ."

The citation was also an acknowledgment and honor to Rosemary Kennedy, the Senator's sister, who lived in a Wisconsin nursing home. At roughly the same time, the family, working through the Park Agency, established a research institute at Georgetown University Hospital for the study of the prevention of birth defects. The family viewed this as one alternative to abortion.

That issue was one of the most perplexing that the Senator faced. He was clearly a liberal Roman Catholic, who believed in the laws of the Church, but also in the right of free choice. Over the years, he had developed a compromise position, declaring that he was personally against abortion, but was in favor of a woman's right to choose. He claimed that he wanted to discourage abortion in general, but he was against a constitutional amendment banning it and he favored federal financing of abortions for indigent women. It was a difficult fence upon which to sit, and there were many times he wished the issue would go away.

His lukewarm stance did not satisfy pro-life proponents, such as Terence Cardinal Cooke. On occasion, the

Senator met with Cooke at the Cardinal's residence behind St. Patrick's Cathedral in New York. The Cardinal, as a conservative, clashed with the Senator on many points, but Kennedy often emerged from such meetings with the single comment, "Well, he certainly doesn't like me on the abortion issue."

The Senator's sister Eunice was also very involved in the right-to-life movement, and the subject sometimes led to heated debates. She argued, "Eddie, you know it's been proven that life starts at conception."

"No, Eunice," he countered, "it isn't proven."

It seemed inevitable that the issue would eventually impact upon the Senator's personal life.

Here was a public proponent of equal opportunities for women who frequently relegated women to trifling positions in his private life. In the great game of sex, they were convenient playing pieces.

Shortly after Barbara returned home following one of her visits to the Senator, she called the office on the private line. I picked up the extension at my desk and heard Barbara insist that she had to talk to the Senator *immediately.*

"He's not here," I said. "Wait a second." I hit the hold button, moved into the Senator's office, and closed the door behind me. Then I sat at the Senator's desk and resumed the conversation.

Barbara said, "Ricardo, I'm late. I'm worried. I don't know what's going on."

I thought: *I can't believe this woman is talking to me about this.* Out loud, I asked in a tone of incredulity, "Don't you two take care of this?"

"Well, I was on the pill, but I got screwed up, and, oh, I'm not sure. . . ."

She chattered on. *Yeah,* I thought. *You got screwed up all right. This is all we need.* Finally I said, "Well, I hope you're taking care of things."

"Yeah," Barbara replied.

When I reported the conversation to the Senator, he rolled his eyes in disbelief.

Barbara called me frequently over the next few days, at the office and at my home, invariably late at night. I was sure that she called the Senator at home also, despite his reluctance to speak to her there.

Listening to her chat on and on, I learned more than I had ever wanted to know about female reproductive biology. Finally, after more than a week had passed, she declared, "False alarm. We're safe. Don't worry."

I relayed this news to the Senator, and he responded with a deep sigh.

11 "Come over to the Senate," the familiar Massachusetts voice demanded on the other end of the
phone.

I glanced at my watch. It was already well into the
evening on a Friday. Why did the Senator want to see me
now?

I found him in his office with Cindy Marks, a woman
whom he had met the year before in Palm Beach. They
had established a long-distance relationship. I did not
know how far it had progressed. Now she had traveled to
Washington to spend some time with him.

He wanted me to meet her, and, when I did, I found
her to be stunning. She stood about five feet six inches
and was slim and shapely, with shiny auburn hair. The
three of us shared a drink together in the office and then
I returned home, but I found that I could not keep my
mind off her.

I was surprised when she called the next day from
McLean. The Senator and his family had flown to the
Cape for a brief visit, and he had invited her to use the
house for the remainder of the weekend. She was on her
own now, and wanted to talk. I suggested that we meet

at The Foundry, and reasoned that she probably wanted to discuss the Senator.

I was right. Over a drink, Cindy said, "The Senator says I can talk to you about anything. He trusts you, so tell me the truth. If I get involved with him, what's going to happen? I'm thinking of moving here; I'm sure I can find a job. What's this going to do to me?"

I had to be honest. "It would be a difficult relationship," I pointed out. "He's married. Don't expect anything. If you are moving here for him, forget it."

We moved on to other topics. Cindy seemed to accept my advice, and decided to move without consideration of her relationship with the Senator. She wanted to know more about Washington and asked me to show her the city. I drove her around for several hours, showing her the usual sights—the monuments, the Smithsonian, the Kennedy Center.

We spent an enjoyable evening together that included dinner and dancing, and she surprised me by saying, "Rick, *you* were the one I was really attracted to last night."

I was flattered and surprised, since she had just spent the night at the Senator's house, but didn't really know whether to believe her; people often tried to ingratiate themselves with me simply to be closer to him. Still, she appeared sincere, and I wondered where it would lead. If I got involved with her, how would the Senator react?

I didn't have much of a chance even to think about it because near the end of 1977 the family received an official invitation to visit the People's Republic of China; the Senator would be one of the first official visitors since President Nixon had opened relations between the two countries. He decided to add a side trip to Japan, to visit U.S. ambassador Mike Mansfield. The trip was scheduled to begin on Christmas Eve, and couldn't have been better timing. This year, the Senator could not pack up the entire family and its traveling entourage and fly off to Aspen. My mandate was to reduce his expenses, and I realized that by forgoing the annual jaunt we would save thousands of dollars.

Joan was pleased for other reasons. Here was a chance for a traditional, if early, family Christmas at home. She had been dividing her time between the fishbowl of Washington and the apartment she and the Senator had in Boston. When she wasn't in either place, she was traveling or at the Cape. Unfortunately, she was still not having success with her treatment. In fact, there were a great many holidays when nobody saw her at all—not the Senator, the children, her friends, or other family. Joan opted, instead, to be alone with her problem, which inevitably led to more drinking. But the China trip was one she anticipated with pleasure, becoming more lively, taking an active interest in the planning, trying, even briefly, to be her old self. It was tough, I knew, for alcoholism is a disease, not something you can turn off like a faucet. The hardest part in dealing with addiction is admitting there is a problem, and Joan had not reached the point where she truly believed the problem was bigger than she was. However, preparing for the trip and the holidays in general helped her, for a time, to gain control over her drinking. The Senator liked to include other family members in important events, so, in addition to his three children, he invited his sisters Eunice, Pat, and Jean to come along, as well as Caroline Kennedy and Ethel's son Michael.

We had less than a month to prepare, and our office buzzed with work. Our new appointment secretary, Joanne Reagan, coordinated our efforts with the State Department. One of my tasks was to arrange visits to McLean from scholars conversant in the history, politics, and general culture of both China and Japan. On several occasions, the family had as many as four of these experts over for dinner and a lengthy seminar-style conversation. Often they were joined by State Department experts and our in-house foreign policy adviser, Jan Kalicki, who happened to be a specialist on China.

We went over the itinerary in detail. On December 28, 1977, the Senator would visit a hospital at a people's commune in Peking and, later, play table tennis. Then it would be on to Shanghai for two days of studying the local health-care, energy, and legal systems. From there, the party would train to Han Cho for a boat ride on a scenic lake and a visit to a Buddhist temple.

Finally, after a frantic month of preparation, I saw the family off on a plane, accompanied by a group of reporters. They were to be gone for a blessed ten days, and I hopped a flight to Connecticut, to spend some time with my parents and enjoy a late, but quiet, Christmas.

Upon her return from China, Joan exhibited recurrent symptoms of her drinking problem. With increasing frequency, the Senator rushed into the office and grumbled, "Let's get Sister Hargrove on the line." She was the president of Manhattanville College, Joan's alma mater, and had long maintained a status as Joan's friend and adviser. Both the Senator and his wife loved and respected this fine woman, and she tried her best to help. After speaking with her, the Senator would say, almost desperately, "We gotta do something." Sometimes this meant a meeting or a phone call with Dr. Hawthorne, the therapist in Boston.

Periodically we searched Joan's bedroom for contraband, just as Theresa Fitzpatrick and I had done years before when Theresa saw the drinking get out of control. Aware that we were on the lookout for vodka and gin, Joan took to buying mouthwash with a high alcohol content. We cleaned out her supplies whenever we could.

As Joan's problems became increasingly public, the

Senator urged her to acknowledge openly her chronic difficulties in order to stave off further innuendo. To some, this seemed like the first real step toward recovery, but it was her husband's idea, not hers, and, within a few weeks, we were spiriting more bottles out of her bedroom.

The consensus seemed to be that Joan could not handle the pressures of her existence in Washington; she considered making a fresh start, back in Boston. Instead of shuttling back and forth between the two cities, Boston would become her permanent home. At least until she could get well. The city was more private, the people less prying, and perhaps the decreased exposure to the press would help her. The Senator did not push her on this. He knew that it had to be her decision. When she decided to move permanently to Boston and enroll in courses at Boston University, he was supportive.

Kara, Teddy, and Patrick would remain in McLean, not so much choosing their father over their mother, but more to stay in school with their friends. While they were all sad that she was making another city her home, they hoped that it would be the best thing for her. And so they went to visit their mother on most weekends.

Joan set about to restructure her life. She busied herself by redecorating the apartment. Along with Ted's cousin Sally Fitzgerald, she became involved in activities at the Tanglewood Music Center in the Berkshires.

Sometimes the Senator journeyed to Boston to participate in therapy sessions with Joan and Dr. Hawthorne. He was usually tight-lipped concerning these meetings, but once, when I was with him in Boston for the weekend, he voiced his frustrations. A local newspaper had proclaimed that Joan's problems were the result of her husband's philandering, but the Senator pointed out angrily that Joan's mother had been an alcoholic, and fumed, "The fact of the matter is, she had a problem before I ever married her. Sister Hargrove says she had a problem back in high school—and I'm being blamed for this!"

Meanwhile, in Washington, there was a variety of issues for him to confront, both in his immediate family and his extended family. Kara began dating Michael Richardson, the son of former Attorney General Elliot Richardson, a key figure in the Watergate "Saturday Night Massacre." The Richardsons and the Kennedys were neighbors, both in McLean and on the Cape. But they were *Republicans*.

"Ricky, do you think this is trouble?" the Senator asked, holding his palms against his head.

"Michael's a good kid," I replied.

The Senator smiled at his own fatherly concern and quipped, "I'm going to have to say something to Elliot."

A more serious problem surfaced when, in the middle of one afternoon, the Senator and I arrived unexpectedly at the McLean home. We heard loud rock and roll emanating from the kids' wing of the house, punctuated by the laughter of several teenagers. Then we both scented a suspicious odor. "What is that?" the Senator asked.

The question was rhetorical, since we both knew it was pot. The Senator thought out loud: "Should I go back in there and throw everybody out? Should I, ah, sit them down and talk to them about it? If I confront them, ah, they're just going to hide it from me in the future." For several moments he couldn't decide what to do. Then he brightened and half-suggested, half-ordered, "Why don't *you* go back and talk to them, Rick?"

I refused immediately. The Senator seemed quite willing to push the limits of my duties, but I drew the line here. When I left the house, he was still debating the wisest course of action.

In the office the next day, he told me that he had had a "chat" with Kara and Teddy. He told them, first of all, that he did not think they should be smoking pot. Second, he did not want them smoking it in the house.

"What did they say?" I asked.

He looked sheepish and admitted, "They sort of laughed."

Was it any wonder?

Ethel Kennedy had money from her own side of the family (the Skakel fortune came from Great Lakes Carbon Corporation), but she, like the Senator, had trouble keeping track of her expenses. Her major problem was disorganization. On regular occasions, Steve Smith traveled to Washington to lecture Ethel on her spending habits. Each time the situation stabilized, but only temporarily.

I was frequently on the phone with Joe Hakim at the Park Agency, asking something like, "Why haven't you paid Ethel's grocery bill? I got a call from her grocer, who says he hasn't been paid in months."

Hakim would check the records and report back, "We never got the bill. If we don't get the bill, how can we pay it?"

Creditors called constantly, including Ethel's gardening service and a plumber. One man raged, "She owes us eleven thousand dollars. It's been a year and we're gonna sue!" There was nothing to do but handle each situation individually.

In his role as surrogate father, the Senator exhibited growing concern over Ethel's children, particularly Bobby and David. After he was busted in Hyannis Port for possession of marijuana, Bobby ran off to California, where he was reportedly seen on the Berkeley campus asking strangers for handouts. I helped arrange treatment for him at McLean Hospital and, as time passed, he appeared to be on the road to recovery.

David, plagued by chronic back pain as a result of the

1973 accident in his brother Joe's Jeep, became addicted to painkillers, such as Demerol and Percodan, and those were the legal drugs he was addicted to. Everyone was worried about him, too.

As far as the younger children were concerned, discipline and supervision were major problems. As a result, Ethel had difficulty retaining household employees. She called me one day and wailed, "Rick, I'm desperate. I need to get a governess." This task added greatly to my agenda, for I was still trying to find a professional governess for the Senator's children. Joan had not been successful in her search. Since the Senator had fired Theresa Fitzpatrick, several women had attempted the job, but no one had lasted. In Joan's absence, it was even more important than before to find a surrogate mother.

After conducting numerous interviews, I found a wonderful woman to recommend to Ethel, a nurse who had worked previously at Georgetown University Hospital. But after only a few weeks on the job, she called me at home, late at night, crying, complaining that the kids had planted a pet snake in her bed. I drove to Hickory Hill, spirited her away from the madness, and checked her into a hotel for the night. She was history.

"This is ridiculous," I complained to the Senator.

"Let her handle it from now on," he advised.

Eventually, Ethel's former secretary, Caroline Croft, who had now joined the Senate Administrative Practices and Procedures Committee staff, recommended Gretchen Geiger for the job. Gretchen was blessed with a personality that allowed for trauma to slide off her back, and she settled in at Hickory Hill and managed to relate well to Ethel as well as to the kids. They soon dubbed her with the affectionate nickname "Grouch."

The Senator was impressed with Grouch and asked her if she knew of anyone who could fill the same position at his home. Grouch mentioned her sister, a registered nurse, was available, and the Senator contacted her immediately.

Grouch's sister, Carol, came with impressive credentials and an abundance of common sense. Carol was attractive and charming, a perfect combination. The Senator liked her immediately and so did the children. I was pleased as well, for she was able to assume many of the household management tasks that I had inherited from George.

Despite the improvements, Hickory Hill remained a zoo. The kids obtained a pet pig, which ran amok and exhibited a nasty habit of defecating whenever and wherever it chose. Time solved this problem, for, after the novelty wore off, no one thought to feed the pig and it died of starvation.

Some of Ethel's children had come to regard Uncle Ted, who was supposed to be their role model, as a bit of a joke. To be sure, they respected him as an effective senator, but they knew that he drank a great deal and enjoyed a party with as much gusto as anyone. Spending time around the children, you'd hear comments like "Uncle Ted had a great time last night; he really tied one on."

In truth, we all knew that the Senator indulged himself too much, but there was great reluctance to confront him over the issue. He worked hard—damn hard—and he seemed to need to relax with just as much vigor. One of the physicians who served as staff director of the Health Subcommittee was the only staffer who ever raised the issue with me. On occasion, usually at an official function, he drew me aside and said, "Rick, you've got to tell him to stop drinking."

"It's not my place," I replied, thinking it would be hypocritical of me anyway, since I was playing very hard, too, rarely missing my scotch and sodas, and rarely missing some lines of cocaine. But the doctor didn't need to know that.

Cindy Marks accepted a job offer with an architectural firm in Washington and moved to nearby Arlington, Virginia. We began to date one another regularly, and I realized that she was one of the few women I had been involved with who could understand the pressures of my schedule. She was a professional herself. She knew that I did not have much free time, and, in fact, her schedule was likely to be as erratic as mine.

The Senator knew that Cindy and I had become friends, but that was all he knew, and he sought to use me as a conduit of information to further his own romantic aims. He often called late at night to ask, "What's going on with Cindy?"

"She's seeing other guys," I replied, not telling him that she was at my side at that very moment.

"Hmmmpf," he'd usually reply, clearly agitated that there was one woman the Kennedy charm was not working on. This was such a rarity that it only frustrated him further. You could almost hear him scratching his head on the other end of the line, trying to figure out where he had gone wrong. I didn't have the heart to tell him she was no longer interested, but Cindy had no compunction in telling him. From time to time he called her at the apartment to ask her out, but she spurned his overtures, saying thanks, but no thanks.

He wouldn't say "Hmmmpf," but she could tell he was totally perplexed.

When Jack and I moved into a house on Beecher Street, we threw a housewarming party. We invited scores of friends and coworkers, including the Senator. Cindy wondered how he would react to see her at my side. "We'll just be honest," I decided. "We'll just tell him what's going on."

Indeed, the Senator was very surprised to see Cindy at the party, which was in full swing when he arrived. He eyed her, then eyed me. You could almost hear his mind churning, putting two and two together. It was an awkward moment. The next day at the office he teased me about it.

I didn't respond, but tried to direct his attention to business. But my nonresponse answered his question. That was all the motivation he needed. Like a determined hunter going after his prey, he pursued Cindy even more aggressively than before, and he enjoyed a singular advantage: He controlled my travel schedule.

I took the precaution of warning her, "He's going to put a move on you. Just tell him no."

Over the next few weeks he pestered her with phone calls. "The more I see you, Rick, the more insistent he becomes."

Now I was getting slightly aggravated by the game. This was a woman I cared a great deal about. Yet the Senator's attitude was that it was a contest . . . and he was determined to win. Maybe it went back to the competition he'd endured with Jack and Bobby. In the Kennedy family it was winner take all, both in politics and in the bedroom.

On several occasions Cindy planned a quiet dinner for two, went to a great deal of trouble and effort, only to have me call and cancel at the last moment, due to pressing business. We tried to work our way past this strain, but before long it grew into an impossible situation. Her frustrations escalated as my unavailability, thanks to the job, escalated. Though we still cared for one another, it was becoming extremely difficult for both of us.

The Senator sent me to Boston to attend to details concerning the JFK Library and, while I was away, he invited Cindy to the McLean house. She was lonely, depressed over our relationship, and, perhaps in retalia-

tion for yet another absence on my part, finally accepted.
When I returned to Washington, she was both irritable
and upset, unhappy with herself, with me, with Washington, you name it. Something had clearly happened when
I was away. I had to probe to get the truth, but finally she
broke down and told me she had gone out to McLean.
Seizing the opportunity, he had poured on the Kennedy
charm, playing it to the hilt. They'd had some drinks,
done some coke, and ended up in bed. Listening to her,
I thought, *Big surprise, huh?* I could have written the
script in advance. I knew every move he made with
women; his modus operandi rarely varied.

My second thought was, *I've been a total jerk, and he's
an even bigger jerk. . . .* I was furious with myself for
letting it happen, and with the Senator for instigating it.
He had stepped over the line and I realized that this was
typically a Kennedy move. He possessed some sense of
being unaccountable for certain actions, not out of arro-
gance per se, but out of his upbringing. Life was a game
that Kennedys were expected to win any way they could,
normal rules of competition notwithstanding.

Deeply disappointed, I said to Cindy, "That was a
stupid move."

To myself I said, *There is no way I can pursue this now.*

The next morning, when I saw the Senator, the strong-
est comment I could muster was, "Well, I think you just
screwed up my love life."

He brushed this off with a casual laugh. This time, he
was the one who turned the discussion to the business of
the day.

12 The Kennedy charm and legendary prowess

had finally won Cindy over. Our romance was now finished. But Cindy and I both decided that if we weren't going to be lovers, we were definitely going to remain close friends. Since I was working day in, day out with the Senator, this decision made it easier for everyone.

The Senator's relationship with her quickly escalated into a very serious love affair. I was probably as surprised by this as he was, because she was the first woman in a long time who seemed to hold a spell over him. Knowing her as I did, it was easy to see just how quickly one could fall. Cindy was smart, devilishly funny, beautiful to look at with her long auburn hair, but more than that, she was special. The Senator, too, had fallen hard.

For a while, they were cautious about signaling this evolution of their relationship to the Senator's children. But Cindy spent a great deal of time at the McLean house, and the kids, all bright and knowledgeable, knew the telltale signs. Besides, you didn't have to be a rocket scientist to see the chemistry between their father and his "friend."

Although the Senator made at least a token attempt to hide his relationship with Cindy from his children, he didn't have any qualms concerning his mother. On a weekend visit to Palm Beach, Rose and I happened to be in the kitchen when the Senator and Cindy burst in through the back door. They were clad in bathing suits and left a trail of water on the floor. After pulling cold drinks from the refrigerator, they linked arms, laughed, and ran back out to the pool.

Rose, with resignation in her voice, said to her cook, Nellie, "Oh, Teddy and his girls . . . what can a mother do?"

Rose was a wonderful woman who certainly knew better than anyone what her children were capable of, but she was getting older and it seemed almost disrespectful to throw it in her face. Later, I pulled Cindy aside and said, "You know, his mother's been through a lot. Did you really have to parade around in front of her like that?"

Cindy casually dismissed my concerns. "Oh, Rick, Ted tells her everything. She knows."

Well, I doubted he told her *everything,* but who was I to argue? The children discerned the truth, of course. By this time, Kara and Teddy appeared to have little hope that their parents would reconcile. They loved their mother and visited her frequently in Boston, but they knew she was ill, and certainly didn't need the pressures of children around as she tried to recover. Regarding their father, their attitude was that Dad was, well, just Dad. They knew that this was not his first affair and probably assumed it would not be his last. But, moreover, they genuinely liked Cindy, and she was genuinely fond of them.

How long the Senator would stay enchanted with her was another matter. He was often like a child in a candy store, grabbing women like so many bags of M&M's, never having enough. Cindy was just as aware of this as I was—his appetite for sex, like his thirst for good drink, or his desire for some good lines of coke, was sometimes insatiable.

There was, for example, Barbara to consider. She complained to me via long distance, "I'm not supposed to call the house anymore. What's going on? Who is that woman? What's she doing there, Rick? She doesn't work there."

I knew that she was talking about Cindy, but I was tempted to ask, "Which one?"

Barbara muttered, "I'm not putting up with this shit anymore. I oughta tell him to go fuck off."

Despite her initial animosity, Barbara liked Cindy the moment they met. It happened one weekend when Barbara was in Washington for a visit. The Senator was busy on Saturday afternoon, so Barbara came into Georgetown to have lunch with me, and found Cindy at my home. I wasn't feeling well, and, when I begged off, the two women decided to go out together for lunch and a bit of shopping. They borrowed my car, promising to return it by evening.

Evening came and went, but the women did not return.

It was about 1:30 A.M. when the phone rang. I answered and heard a voice ask for Barbara.

"She's not here," I answered groggily.

"Oh, Rick, it's Warren," the voice said casually.

"Well, hi, Warren."

"Can you have Barbara call me? I'm at the Carlyle in New York."

"Okay."

He gave me the number and hung up.

Cindy brought the car back late the next morning, whipping it into a parking space, then storming into my town house, furious. Slamming the door, she railed about how she was going to dump the Senator and then if he was lucky, maybe he would drop dead. I finally got her to calm down, then asked what had happened. As she detailed why she was so mad, she became increasingly distraught.

"Barbara and I went shopping and then stopped for a drink. We had a lot of champagne. I had a real buzz on, and the next thing I knew, we were driving over to the Senator's. He was in a good mood, ready to party. So we drank some more, did some coke, and . . . and, well, then—I ended up in bed with them *both.*"

I rolled my eyes. Two at once? Definitely a kid in a candy store. Cindy and I talked about the experience, and the more she talked, the more she thought she'd overreacted. By the time Barbara showed up, Cindy's mood had softened. They actually started giggling about the previous night, now two old friends instead of rivals. Cindy, who had first balked at an open-end relationship with the Senator, was changing before my eyes. Maybe we were all changing too quickly, I thought.

As I tried to sort out my thoughts, I told Barbara, "Someone named Warren called you from New York."

"Oh, that's Warren Beatty," she said. I was too numb at this point to register surprise. I grumbled, "Well, first of all he woke me up at one-thirty in the morning. And second, how did he know my name?"

"Oh, I told him all about you," Barbara said, grinning.

She called Beatty at the Carlyle and arranged to meet him in New York. To my utter surprise, Cindy decided to go with her, two fast friends.

The Senator's orgiastic behavior continued; Cindy remained acquiescent about the Senator's penchant for pulling another woman into the scene, but ambivalent. "I don't have anybody to talk to," she complained to me over the phone one Sunday morning as I was toasting some English muffins. "I just have to talk to somebody, Rick. If I can't get it out, I'll just explode. . . ."

"Fine, go ahead," I replied, trying to be empathetic.

"It was absolutely wild this weekend. I can't believe he—he invited Kitty Brewer over."

Neither could I. "Oh, really?" I asked. Kitty Brewer was a woman from Rhode Island whom he had met on a boating vacation.

Cindy said, "Yeah. He has her over. She's nice enough and all, but the next thing I know, we're all in bed together. At first, I resisted it but, you know, when you do a lot of coke and you're drinking and stuff like that, everything just falls apart." The Senator had encouraged Cindy and Kitty to give him "a show."

I counseled, "Well, you make your decisions. You could've said no, Cindy. And even with coke and everything, if that's something you're not interested in, you better make it clear to him."

"You're right," she agreed, feeling better.

Within days, Kitty called me, too. She had tried to reach the Senator at McLean, but could not get through, so she phoned me at the office to try to track him down. She was an intense person by nature, but she was especially upset this day. Knowing the answer, I asked why.

"Cindy was there the *whole* weekend," she moaned. "I didn't know Cindy was going to be there. Well, we drank, we partied, and you know how he is. . . . One thing led to another. . . ."

I told her the same thing I had told Cindy. She was responsible for her own actions; she could say no.

Not that a no would have deterred the Senator. If somebody wasn't interested in playing, there was always somebody else to call upon.

The Senator appeared to be assembling a harem, and besides his increasing penchant for three-ways, he told me he had to have something he'd discovered in Aspen.

There, the Senator had been introduced to the wonders of the Jacuzzi. Aside from the enjoyment factor, the heat and pulsating water soothed his back. Now he informed me he would not rest until he had his very own hot tub installed on the back deck of his home. When I asked the New York office if we could write off the costs as a health-care expense, I was advised, "You've got to get a letter from a doctor, saying that it's necessary for his back." I got the letter. I don't know whether they ever took the deduction.

The contractor suggested that we cut a recess into the deck so that the tub would be installed below the surface. The Senator could then ease himself into the hot water without stepping up.

There was no question that the hot tub provided much-needed therapy for the Senator's back. But I knew that he had other uses in mind, too.

"I need the black book," the Senator said suddenly one morning at the office. He was searching for a European phone number—one that was not listed in my own version of his private directory. "Go out to McLean and get it. It's in the top right-hand drawer of my desk."

The errand frustrated me, for it would take at least an hour, but I dutifully drove out to the Senator's house. Carol Geiger, whose professionalism and discretion had indeed made her an ideal choice as the new governess, let me in. She went about her tasks and I entered his private office, located the hidden key, and opened the desk.

The black book was not in the upper right-hand drawer, so I opened the other drawers and searched.

The second drawer on the right held a box of poppers. In the bottom right-hand drawer I found an old wooden cigar box. Curiosity getting the better of me, I glanced inside, wondering what private treasures the Senator had squirreled away. Here I found a small brown plastic vial, full of white powder. There were several sheets of paper, their corners neatly folded; I knew this was the way to stash and carry small amounts of cocaine. Here, too, was a "bullet," a plastic-and-aluminum cocaine dispenser. When you tap one end of the bullet, it releases a dose of powder into the tip, from where it can be snorted through a hole.

"This is what you have to destroy," the Senator had instructed me earlier.

By now it wasn't any surprise to find a drug kit locked away in the Senator's desk. But why, I wondered, was the bottom of the cigar box littered with rice?

When I had a chance, I asked Cindy.

"Rice soaks up the moisture," she replied. "It keeps the coke dry." Cindy told me that she had given the bullet to the Senator as a gift. She explained that it was a handy travel tool, allowing you to carry a supply of cocaine unobtrusively so that you could snort it at your convenience. "No mess, no hassle," she said.

Soon after that, Cindy presented me with my very own bullet. I stored it in an empty checkbook box in my desk at home, along with a supply of coke and a liberal dusting of rice.

Juggling the Senator's personal life was one of my key jobs, and certainly the hardest one, but I was also still the office manager. There were moments of great happiness—such as seeing a Kennedy-sponsored bill passed—and, by the same token, moments of true sadness. For years Mary Murtaugh had devoted sixty or seventy hours of her week to the Senator's business. The effort had paid off by gradually lifting her to a level of prominence and trust in the Senator's mind, but she had paid a heavy price by ignoring any chance at a social life. Now the office was abuzz with the happy news: Mary had a boyfriend. There was a bounce in her step, a glint in her eye.

One day Mary chattered excitedly to anyone who would listen about her plans for the evening. She and a friend were double-dating; they were going to a play at the Kennedy Center.

That night, after the play, the foursome returned to Mary's home for a glass of wine. Mary mentioned that she had a slight headache and excused herself to get an aspirin.

A few seconds after Mary had disappeared into her bedroom, the others heard the sound of a fall. They found Mary on her bedroom floor, dead. An autopsy determined the cause of death to be an aneurysm.

Everyone at the office was stunned. At the funeral, the Senator presented a moving eulogy. The suddenness of her death affected him deeply. Afterward, he privately told me, "You know, Rick, you gotta live it to the fullest."

I knew better than anyone that he certainly intended to do that. But my job was to try and rein him in a bit. . . .

Sometimes when the Senator and I were together at an official function, I caught him eyeing a woman and I'd whisper in a friendly but firm way, "No, not now. . . . It's not the time."

"Ah, come on, Ricky," he'd say, frowning.

"Just keep it in your shorts," I'd whisper.

As much as he didn't want to hear it, he knew that it was wise counsel.

That's not to say he always heeded my advice. Trying to keep him reined in was often like trying to keep a bull from charging a red flag. One of my tasks was to review the applicants for internships. We had about a dozen of these jobs to parcel out each summer, and there were some basic requirements. For example, the Senator preferred that one of the interns be a good tennis player. We hired one intern, not because he was a brilliant Harvard student, but because he was on the tennis team there.

One summer, we offered one of the intern positions to

the son of CBS newsman Roger Mudd, who had called to request the opportunity for his boy. We were happy to oblige. Mudd was not only a neighbor, a fellow resident of McLean, but he had far more personal ties. He was the one who had escorted Ethel Kennedy through the crowd to the side of her fatally wounded husband in Los Angeles. In ensuing years, he was a regular participant in the RFK tennis tournament.

I remember the summer that the Senator asked me in an idle tone if a young woman named Pam Farmer had applied.

I rifled through a stack of paperwork, found the name, and reviewed the application. Unlike most of the applicants, who were college students, this girl was still in high school.

"Yes," I answered, "but I discounted her. She doesn't have the background."

"Well, I want her put in the running," the Senator said.

I eyed him suspiciously and asked, "Where is she from?"

She was from Mobile, Alabama. "I met her recently," he explained. "She's going to be in town next week and I want you to have lunch and interview her."

And so I did. From the moment I laid eyes on her auburn hair and her appealing features I said to myself, *No, we're not going to get involved with this one.* Over lunch I asked her, "How did you meet the Senator?"

"In a restaurant at the Cape," she replied in a southern drawl as thick as molasses. "He kept callin', askin' me to go out for a drink." She explained that when she finally agreed to meet the Senator at a bar, she brought her parents along with her. . . . I almost laughed out loud. I could just imagine the look of consternation on the Senator's face when this southern-fried dish's parents showed

up. "He looked a little surprised," she admitted inno-
cently, "but we had a drink and that was that."

I could see the writing on the wall, though. I tried to
be pleasant, but I was feeling more like a pimp than a
senatorial aide. I asked, "How old are you?"

"Sevuunteen," Pam drawled.

She was sweet, naïve—and much too talkative. She
chattered on for a time about her boyfriend back home
in Mobile; they were planning to be married after she
graduated from high school the following year. She
seemed to feel that her experience as a cheerleader qualified her for this job.

Near the end of our meal, I asked, "Where are you
staying this weekend?"

"I'm having dinner with Ted tonight and then I'm
going back home."

I scrawled numbers onto a piece of paper, handed it to
her, and said, "Okay, this is my telephone number. If you
need any help or have any problems, please call me."

I did not hear from her until a few days later, when she
phoned from Mobile and announced that "Ted" had
told her to call me to arrange an airline ticket for her. She
was going to meet him at the Cape that weekend.

As soon as I could, I collared the Senator at his office.

"Are you sure you know what you're doing?" I asked.

"Yeah, don't worry," he reassured. But there was a
familiar grin on his face.

"She's awfully young," I warned. "And I'm not so sure
she's going to keep her mouth shut."

The grin spread to a full-blown smile.

"I don't think she's intern material," I snapped, exasperated.

He retorted, "I'm the boss."

I spent much of the following summer keeping Pam,
our bubbly teenage intern, under control. She fell head
over heels for the Senator rather quickly and, just as

quickly, became upset and jealous about his other relationships. She turned to me as a confidant, freely admitting that she and the Senator had slept together, and detailing how the Senator had turned her on to coke and the joys of poppers. The only time she balked was when he tried to get her into bed with himself and another woman at the same time.

"That was just too much," she whispered in her southern drawl.

Pam's fiancé, a tough college wrestler, was justifiably suspicious of what was going on in Washington that summer; whenever he called, all Pam could talk about was Ted this and Ted that. I could just see the tabloid headlines: SPURNED WRESTLER STALKS KENNEDY. Perhaps to allay his fears, the Senator invited him to fly up from Mobile for a weekend. I asked Pam where he was going to stay.

She replied, "Oh, well, you know, the Senator said for us to stay at the house."

"Oh, yeah?" I asked with irony.

"Oh, yeah," she said, missing my sarcasm. "We're gonna play tennis and go swimming."

Don't bet on it, Scarlett. I know him a lot better than you. Saturday afternoon, the Senator suddenly called me at home and ordered, "Keep him away from me!" *Oh God,* I thought, *my facetious scenario is coming true.* The guy was a jealous lover. I wanted to ask the Senator what was going on, but he was too apoplectic to talk. Instead, he slammed down the phone. Before I even tried to speculate, Pam and her boyfriend were at my door, seeking refuge. They were clearly angry at one another, as well as at the Senator.

Something had happened. . . .

Damage control, I instructed myself. *Above all else, you've got to protect his image. That's your job.* I invited them in and coaxed them to talk, offering them nonalco-

holic drinks and trying to be friendly. But I could draw
only a few details from them. They had all gotten into the
hot tub together, relaxing with drinks in their hands.
Everything was going well. They were laughing, there
were more drinks, a couple of hits of coke from a bullet,
and then . . .

"It got—difficult," said Pam.

Her boyfriend glowered.

"That's when we decided to leave," Pam added.

They spent the remainder of the weekend at my house
and, very soon after that, Pam quit her internship and
returned home to Mobile.

While the Senator may have been sorry to see her go,
it was a blessing for me finally to be rid of her.

One day the Senator began our morning meeting by
saying, "Call the doctor and ask him to send a box."

I noted this in my pad; the Senator needed a new
supply of poppers.

Then he said, "Call Jamie. Tell him I can see him on
Monday."

Jamie Wyeth was coming to town, and wanted to display the watercolor he had created for the opening of the
JFK Library. It depicted President Kennedy on his boat,
the *Victura.* Wyeth planned to present 150 signed prints
as gifts to close friends and family members.

As it happened, boats were a sore topic at the moment.
The Senator's own boat, the *Curragh,* had long been a
source of agitation. The captain was a black Bahamian
man who, for all I knew, never used his surname. What
he was known for was four longtime girlfriends stashed
in different ports. From time to time he asked us to wire
money to one or the other, and it was difficult to keep the
names and addresses straight. The captain's demands
grew increasingly insistent, and the Senator was fed up
with the entire mess. But what could he do about it? The

Bahamian, like Theresa, Rosalie, and George, knew a great deal about the Senator's private life. These matters had to be handled judiciously; the Senator could not afford merely to cut the captain loose.

Now there were more problems; I reviewed my notes and reported, "The captain says the boat needs a new radio. A 96-channel radio costs $1,295, and a 112-channel radio costs $4,478."

The Senator frowned. "Call and get more quotes," he snapped. "See if we can get something cheaper."*

"No lunch today," I dictated. "We're gonna work."

I put a staff worker to the task of searching through the Cape Cod Yellow Pages to call for price quotes on marine radios.

That afternoon pollster Lou Harris called. Harris had been close to both Jack and Bobby Kennedy, and he clearly wanted the Senator to jump into the 1980 presidential race. His latest set of figures showed growing resentment toward President Carter, and growing support for the Senator. The feeling in our office was that if Carter was handed the nomination again, it would hand the Republicans the White House. It had already reached the point where Carter simply couldn't deal with Congress effectively. For example, some time earlier, the Supreme Court had ruled that it was unconstitutional to confine someone to a mental institution against his will if he was not considered a danger to himself or others. That was the basic decision that threw thousands of disturbed, homeless people onto the streets. The Senator was very concerned about the issue and sponsored legislation to set up halfway houses throughout the country. Rosalynn

*Eventually, in consultation with the Park Agency, the Senator was able to sell his boat to a company that agreed to keep the captain. From time to time, the Senator then leased the boat. The captain remained happy, and quiet.

Carter was concerned, too, and lent her support to the bill. It passed, but Carter was unable to persuade Congress to fund it.

Privately, the Senator bristled at Carter's administrative style; the President insisted on involving himself in the minutiae of government. The Senator's view was that a President's job was to set the direction and leave the details to his staff. Beyond specific issues, the Senator was concerned about a general lowering of morale within the country.

We were all getting fed up.

"Carter is presiding over the destruction of the Democratic party," Harris moaned. According to the pollster, Kennedy scored well as a man who was truly interested and caring about people; he was an inspiring leader, and probably the only one with a chance to take on a Republican challenger and defeat him. One of Harris's key points was that the aging scandal of Chappaquiddick no longer seemed strong enough to dissuade voters. This was especially important since the controversy had never been truly explained other than what everyone knew— the Kennedy party line. The independent investigations only raised more questions than they answered. It had been a millstone around the Senator's neck since it had happened, but now it seemed it was finally being pulled off him.

In politics, coalitions are forged on a you-scratch-my-back-I'll-scratch-yours basis. The summer of 1978 was payback time for the Senator, as he crisscrossed the country, delivering campaign speeches in support of various colleagues. The schedule was exhausting. We headed to the Midwest, including a flight to South Dakota for a speech in support of a congressional candidate who had once worked for Bobby Kennedy; then it was on to California for a weekend during which the Senator managed to spend some time with John Tunney at the Bel Air home of Carroll Rosenbloom, owner of the Los Angeles Rams and a longtime friend of all the Kennedy brothers. In fact, Rosenbloom was a man with many powerful friends in Washington and Hollywood.

The weekend was a combination of business and pleasure. On the pleasure side, the Senator partied with Tunney, whose life had changed dramatically since he had lost his Senate seat in the 1976 election. He had divorced, and, in April 1977, remarried. His new wife, Kathinka, was a very pretty, dark-haired Olympic skier from Switzerland.

The business pressing on the Senator's mind was an invitation to present the keynote address at that September's meeting of the World Health Organization, to be held in Alma-Ata, capital of the Soviet Socialist Republic of Kazakhstan, in the south-central portion of the USSR, not far from the Chinese border. Soviet Premier Leonid Brezhnev had further suggested that the Senator might wish to take this opportunity to study the Soviet health-care system. The Senator had accepted the invitation eagerly, for the Soviet medical system was ballyhooed as the most modern and universal in the world. Its concept of free care for everyone was intriguing to the Senator, who had been working for years to bring better health care to the American people.

On his own, however, the Senator added a silent item to the agenda; during the trip, he determined to set up a clandestine meeting with Soviet refuseniks—citizens, mainly Jewish, who had applied for permission to emigrate but had been denied.

Now, he used this opportunity to huddle with Tunney, picking his brain concerning the Soviet Union. Tunney was practicing law as a partner in the Los Angeles firm of Manatt, Phelps, Rothenberg & Tunney, but he was also involved in several potential business deals with the

Russians. One of his associates in these ventures was the expatriate American industrialist David Karr, who was involved in a project to build a plush new hotel to serve the 1980 Moscow Olympics. Tunney and Karr had developed a helpful contact in the person of a certain Andrei, a Politburo functionary. Tunney described Andrei as a pleasant man in his late thirties or early forties, who could be trusted, insofar as any Soviet official could be. Tunney's eyes gleamed as he told the Senator about Natasha, a blond Russian woman who was Andrei's aide. She was very pro-Western and, Tunney hinted, quite sexy. Tunney mentioned that he had spent some time with Natasha on Karr's yacht in the Mediterranean and suggested that Natasha might be a point of contact with Brezhnev regarding the refuseniks.

On Monday we headed into Los Angeles for two fund-raisers—one for a black assemblywoman who was a friend of Tunney's and another for a Hispanic political group.

We arrived back in Washington about 6:00 A.M. on Wednesday. I had just set about the business of the day when I received a call from a certain Sergeant Udell of the Capitol Police, reporting that a man who had issued threats against both President Carter and Senator Kennedy was en route from Buffalo to Washington, reportedly carrying shotguns in his car. Both the FBI and the Secret Service were investigating.

I grabbed a batch of paperwork and walked over to the Senate chamber. In the cloakroom, I asked a page to call the Senator off the floor. Kennedy came out, looking sleepy, and began idly signing the routine paperwork. I said, gently, "We got a call from the Secret Service. Some lunatic up in Buffalo has been screaming about you. He's headed this way."

The Senator listened carefully but gave no overt reaction. You could almost hear him sigh, for here was the cloud of violence threatening to break out over his head once again. Unless he totally isolated himself from the public—which would greatly hinder his effectiveness as a lawmaker who prided himself in being in touch with the people—what could he do? Once in a while, as we were driving, a car would backfire and my heart would skip a beat. I'd glance casually at him, trying not to show my concern, but his eyes would mirror my thoughts, as if to say, *Yes, I know . . . it's just part of my heritage.* The only way to live with it was to acknowledge it. Usually we took the threats in stride. This one, on the face of it, was more serious than usual, simply because the federal law-enforcement agencies had chosen to become involved. Finally the Senator said, "Keep in touch with the Secret Service and the FBI and tell me what happens."

Agents intercepted the man's car on an interstate and detained him. "Nothing happened," I reported to the Senator.

And yet, I thought, *everything happens.*

13 Nineteen seventy-eight was an extraordinarily busy summer. One of the many things on the agenda during this time was the annual Celebrity Tennis Tournament at Forest Hills, to benefit the Robert F. Kennedy Foundation. Singer Andy Williams, White House Chief of Staff Hamilton Jordan, and a number of other celebrities were coming into town, and the Senator presented me with a particularly extensive guest list. Kitty, Cindy, and Barbara would all be there, along with a woman named Michelle, whom I did not know. The situation was typically delicate, as these things were when it came to dealing with the Senator's women. I managed to arrange seats for everybody in the celebrity boxes, but I had to make sure that Michelle was prudently distanced from the other women. The Senator was officially staying at Pat Lawford's house, but I made sure there were booked suites at the Plaza and another hotel. Both suites were in my name, but I knew that the Senator would use them extensively.

Throughout the tournament I found myself running from one celebrity box to another, making sure that the Senator's playmates kept a discreet distance from one another. I felt like a ball runner down on the courts.

One evening I decided to blow off steam by taking some of our staffers to Studio 54. Barbara wanted to come along, and Cindy said she would join us there, too. It was, at the moment, New York's most exclusive night spot. Housed in a former opera house, it held three thousand people, from Wall Street executives to drag queens. People stood outside on the street for hours, hoping to catch a glimpse of the celebrities inside. Co-owner Steve Rubell was famous for stationing himself at the doorway and playing God. He'd survey the crowd and decide who could enter and who could not. I didn't want to leave anything to chance, so I asked my assistant, Connie, to call ahead and ask for reservations. They didn't do that sort of thing, but someone promised to leave my name at the door.

I was in a car with the Senator, taking him to Jean and Steve Smith's house for dinner, when I mentioned where I was going. His eyes brightened and he jokingly and somewhat wistfully invited himself along. He longed to see the place. It was like the ultimate all-night party, and tales of the more decadent aspects of the club—like the subterranean VIP room and the coed bathrooms where *anything* went—had certainly made the rounds in Washington. But we both knew he simply couldn't go to a place where he might be publicly compromised. He sank down in the car seat, resigned to sit this one out. Our driver dropped off the Senator at his sister's house, and then I directed him to take me to Studio 54.

When we arrived I instructed the driver, "Don't go two inches away, because if I don't get into this place, I'm not going to hang around."

A mob of people blocked my way from the street to the door as I elbowed forward. Several tall, broad-shouldered bouncers manned the entrance, fending off the crowd. Steve Rubell was at the door, doing his thumbs-down routine. I gave Rubell my name and announced, "I'm on the list."

Rubell's eyes said: I've heard that one before. He glanced halfheartedly at a sheet of paper and replied, "I can't find your name." Suddenly his eyes shot to the back of the crowd and he forgot about me. "Make way over there!" he shouted. The crowd parted, and Cindy moved toward the door. Studio 54 always had room for one more gorgeous woman.

"Oh, hi, Rick," she said.

Rubell let us in immediately.

The large, open dance floor, terraced to provide several levels of action, was jammed with beautiful people, men and women of various sexual persuasion. You saw everything from women dressed in leather outfits with no tops to boys in pseudomilitary uniforms, and other boys in debutante gowns and girls in tuxedos, their jewelry sparkling in the reflected glow of frenetic, multicolored strobe lights. The bartenders were all muscular and barechested, and, from the looks of things, just as available as the drinks.

At the tables, many of the patrons openly smoked pot, while the aroma of poppers and ethyl chloride, a skin refrigerant that was becoming another popular "rush" inhalant, drifted off the dance floor. There were some people openly snorting coke, completely unconcerned about security, and, in the very darkest recesses, you could see a few couples discreetly but openly engaging in the early stages of sexual fulfillment. Boys with girls. Girls with girls. Boys with boys. And girls with boys and girls.

Yes, the Senator would have loved to have seen it, had he come.

And so would the press.

As Cindy and I took the dance floor, taking a generous whiff of some poppers ourselves, the irony of what I was doing hit me at the same time as the rush from the amyl nitrite did—in the span of just three years I'd evolved from an "archbishop" to a hedonist, living it to the fullest. The feeling was totally overwhelming. It took me back to something I'd done earlier in the summer.

On a Saturday afternoon, I had stood at the open door of a small airplane looking down at the vista of the Maryland countryside. A half dozen others had jumped before me, and I was the only one left, save for the instructor. *You don't have to think of a thing,* I reminded myself. *Your chute will open automatically. Just do it.*

I gulped in air, flexed my legs slightly, and stepped out of the plane. My body fell freely in the cool air, but there was no time to be scared. Within moments I felt the sweet pain of the harness straps biting into my shoulders. Above me, the chute opened, and I hung suspended in time and space. I thought, *I want to do this a hundred million times.*

Later that week, at the end of the tennis tournament, Steve Ross, the flamboyant chairman of Warner Communications, provided his corporate helicopter to take Jean and Steve Smith out to the Hamptons. The Senator and Cindy planned to fly to the Cape to head off on a boat trip. When Barbara learned that the Senator was going to the Cape, she tried to invite herself along, but the Senator didn't want her company at the moment. And yet he certainly didn't want to be the one to do the dirty work.

"Uh, you'll have to, you know, think of something to get rid of her, Ricky."

I wanted to roll my eyes, but instead said, "Okay," and then had to conjure a quick excuse to keep her away. *This is really beginning to get crazy, I thought.*

As often as I felt like a fire extinguisher for the Senator, I knew all too well that he was not alone among the

Kennedys in needing other people to help out with problems, no matter how minor they were. It was often said that people *paid* to work for the Kennedys, not the other way around, but sometimes you'd really have to wonder why.

One weekend that summer we were at Squaw Island. The Senator and Cindy were off somewhere with the kids, and I sat outside, chatting with Carol, the governess.

Sometime that afternoon, Carol decided to check in with her sister, who was with Ethel's family at the Kennedy compound. While she was on the phone, Carol started laughing hysterically. Unable to speak, she handed me the receiver.

"Hey, Grouch!" I said. "How's it going?"

"Oh, fine," Grouch replied. "It's just a typical day here. I'm looking out the window watching Ethel swat the pants off Rory and Doug."

"Why?" I asked.

"They poured gasoline on the driveway and lit it," she replied in a matter-of-fact tone. "They wanted to see how it would look. The fire department is here right now."

I laughed along with Carol and Grouch. She and Ethel certainly had their hands full in dealing with the children, even though the oldest sons were now pretty much out of the house.

Periodically the Senator's children would be as much a point of consternation for him as Ethel's were to her, but this wasn't often, and a great deal of credit went to the Senator himself. As flagrant as he could be about parading the women in his life in front of them, from the moment I had met him that day at Holy Trinity Church in 1971 I had considered the Senator to be a wonderful father. He had his faults—to be sure—but he also made what I considered to be a Herculean effort to spend time with his children. This was even more evident now that

Joan was living full-time in Boston. He often planned weekend camping excursions in New England with the kids, including a stopover to visit their mother.

Patrick, the baby of the family, was easier to deal with, at least for now, than his older siblings. Earlier in the summer, the Senator had set me to the clandestine task of researching the best available deal on a Boston Whaler, a small boat with an outboard motor, ideal for skimming along the waters off Squaw Island. The Senator surprised Patrick with the gift on his July 14 birthday and, on many subsequent weekends at the Cape, father and son went fishing together. I was somewhat amazed that the Senator could sit still for so long, but I realized that, when it came to his children, he would do anything.

His latest quest was to teach them scuba diving, one of his occasional vacation pastimes. He hired an instructor and instituted lessons in his backyard pool. I was at McLean one day, watching the kids dip in and out of the water, when I mentioned that I had gone scuba diving before, with my brother-in-law. The Senator grinned and asked, "Have you ever been diving when the sharks came around?"

"No," I said, looking a bit worried.

He laughed at my apprehension, and contended that sharks weren't dangerous unless they happened to be in the midst of a feeding frenzy. He enjoyed the activity more when it was tinged with a hint of peril. Shortly after that I set up a weekend dive down in Bermuda, and sure enough the sharks came around. It was frightening at first, like taking the plunge out of the airplane, but once I realized they weren't, thank God, in a feeding frenzy, it heightened the excitement of the dive all the more. The Senator had been right.

That same tendency to flirt with danger seemed to infuse all facets of his life, and, as hard as he tried to be a good father, his love of danger sometimes hindered his efforts to relate to the children. Kara, for example, went through a period where she was using pot with increasing frequency, which worried him. But, when the Senator again attempted to lecture Kara, she said, *"You're* gonna tell *me* not to do this? So why don't you stop using drugs yourself?"

He knew she had a point. At the same time, while the Senator didn't see his children in the same vulnerable state as Ethel's, he knew that they shared both Joan's tendency toward dependency and his own penchant for experimentation. Recently Teddy and Kara had discovered a hangout, a new Georgetown bar. The manager of the bar was a distant relative of the Kennedys, and always made them feel welcome. What worried me was, on a few occasions when I was in the bar with them, I saw a bar employee draw certain patrons off to the rest room to offer them hits of cocaine.

The Senator knew that if his children were not already involved with the drug, they would surely face temptation. He wrestled with his soul on this issue. It presented a personal predicament for him because he loved coke, but these were his children and responsibility implored him to address the matter. As a disciplinarian, the Senator was not a screamer. In the past, if a foot had to be put down on the kids' behavior, it had been Theresa's; now it was Carol's or mine, and the Senator merely indicated his support. But when he finally decided to face the issue of cocaine with them, he did so in his own style.

He chose the moment carefully. Patrick was in Boston with his mom. Kara had some of her friends over and they, along with Teddy, were in the back rooms of the house.

Cindy, who was also in the house with the Senator, told me what happened next. "Somebody had brought some coke, one of Kara's friends, I think. Ted and I knew what they were doing—he'd suspected they'd been doing it for a long time. But he didn't know what to do, how to handle it. I told him just to confront them.

"He waited until Kara's friends had left. Kara and Teddy were still in the back room when he finally decided to say something. But instead, he ended up doing some lines of coke with them."

Later the Senator told Cindy, "I guess I shouldn't have done it," which she thought was putting it mildly. And she told him so. He explained to her that he was trying to show them that Dad was their friend, and he used the opportunity to tell them his concern that substance-abuse problems might run in the family—on Joan's side. He told Cindy he wanted to teach them that if they were going to do cocaine, they should at least do it in moderation.

As Cindy finished telling me this, she grimaced, saying, "And so they all did a few lines. Dad, the teacher. Dad, the friend."

I sat there, listening to this, thinking he had finally gone off into "The Twilight Zone."

"What?" I sputtered, still not believing what I'd just heard. "This is crazy." His action was like an open endorsement of cocaine, but far worse was where it might lead. The mother of these children was an acknowledged victim of substance abuse—she had at least admitted as much and was trying to change. But the father made no such admission. To the contrary, his actions made it clear that he condoned the recreational use of drugs.

Cindy agreed. "I couldn't believe it, either. I was totally flabbergasted when he told me. It's sad, Rick. If this is Ted's idea of bonding with the kids, Jesus. . . ."

But as much as we were appalled by the example he'd just set for his kids, we certainly couldn't throw stones. As adults, we were just as irresponsible as he was with drugs, both of us using cocaine with increasing frequency, alone and with the Senator.

Joan, however, seemed to be finally getting control of her drinking. Since she had been sober for most of the summer, the Senator felt as if it was really time to squash all the speculation in the press about her alcoholism and just face it head-on. In the office we had discussions back and forth about this.

Some felt it was simply going to bring more negative publicity to a family already overwhelmed with negative publicity. Others in the office, myself included, felt it was simply better to face Joan's problem and quit trying to cover up for her.

So that summer she granted two interviews. One was to *McCall's* magazine and the other to *People*.

Before they came out, the inner office was abuzz with nervous anticipation. Since we weren't present at the interviews and even though Joan had felt they'd gone well—and told the Senator so—neither he nor we were convinced of it. Joan was a wonderful woman in many ways, struggling to overcome perhaps the hardest problem of all, but there were times when we were terrified of what she would blurt out.

As it turned out, our worries were just that.

The interviews were good—candid and sympathetic. Both issues garnered cover attention and marked a milestone for Joan, finally enabling her to talk publicly about her drinking, which was more unusual for the country then than it is now. The *McCall's* cover featured both Joan and the Senator on it, and she was interviewed by Joan Braden, the wife of television commentator Tom Braden. The Senator really preferred for her to do the cover shot alone, and privately mentioned that the whole episode made him decidedly uncomfortable. But it was to help Joan get stronger, so he did what he had to. Still, the picture on the cover looked forced, almost as if two separate shots had been spliced together.

The *People* cover had Joan solo, much to the Senator's

relief, and in this shot she was decidedly more relaxed. Although she still seemed a little puffy, and those of us in the office inwardly groaned at the amount of makeup she was still using, we didn't say a word. One step at a time, was how we had to take it.

Shortly after both magazines came out, the office was inundated with letters, most of them highly supportive of Joan. But surprisingly there were some fellow Alcoholics Anonymous members who were distressed that Joan had, in their eyes, violated one of the main tenets of AA: anonymity.

Reading a few, I sighed. They had a point, but, as I'd seen in politics, you couldn't keep everyone happy all the time.

Coverage in the press about the interviews was supportive of Joan, but several journalists cynically speculated about her motives, wondering if this wasn't all some grand scheme to set up a 1980 presidential run. From the many talks we had had about Joan, that consideration was certainly never stated, but one would have to be naïve to think it hadn't entered the Senator's mind.

After all, as we sweltered through the heat and humidity, the positive input from Lou Harris's national polls was augmented by an increasing number of calls from state party officials who reported a ground swell of support for the Senator to launch a presidential campaign. A group of Democrats in Minnesota wanted to organize a "Draft Kennedy" committee. In Iowa they were raising money for a campaign. My line to the various local callers was the standard, "The Senator is not running; whatever you do, you do on your own."

This fooled no one.

As a number of people in the office had predicted, Ken Feinberg did not work out as the Senator's AA. Increasingly, the staff came to me with issues and problems that were properly Feinberg's domain. The Senator knew that there was a problem, but he *hated* confrontation. Several times he told me in a frustrated tone that I was going to have to do something about Ken.

"I can't do that," I said finally. I pointed out that the AA was his chief of staff. In a normal organization, he would be considered my boss; in this office, we were more or less peers with different domains. "But how can I fire the chief of staff?" I asked.

"I don't know. Uh, we'll just have to figure it out."

The situation deteriorated rapidly, and the tension interfered with the Senator's efforts to concentrate on important work. He was promoting legislation to control wiretapping; he was pushing gun-control laws; he was hard at work forging an alliance with Senator Eastland and his fellow conservative Senator McClellan in his continuing effort to recodify federal criminal laws to strengthen law and order—and, in fact, this was Feinberg's particular area of interest.

The last straw came when Feinberg crossed swords with key workers in the Senator's Boston office. Finally, less than a year after Feinberg took the job, the Senator faced the distasteful task of letting him go as AA, but, instead of firing him, he transferred him to the Judiciary Committee staff as counsel.

The Senator called Eddy Martin, who had taken a post as Boston Regional Director of HUD, to ask for his recommendation on a new AA. "Just name Rick," Eddy said.

From his law office, Paul Kirk advised, "Rick is the perfect person to do the job, even if he is young."

Some time passed as the Senator mulled over the advice. Then, finally, he drew me aside and said, "I'd like you to be AA." He had decided, as I had suggested earlier, to consolidate my position. I would continue to do everything I had been doing—and more. How I was going to do it all, I didn't know, but at that point it really didn't matter.

Suddenly I was administrative assistant to Senator Edward M. Kennedy. At the age of twenty-five, I was the youngest AA in the Senate, so elevated in the hierarchy that I was required to file an annual financial-disclosure statement.

It was now my job to manage every aspect of the Senator's personal, legislative, and political agenda. Wherever he was, I was at his side. I woke him in the morning, drew his bath in the afternoon, and tucked him in at night.

He made no comment on my shaggy hair, but he suggested, "Grow a mustache. You gotta look older."

I started growing one immediately.

During the congressional elections that year, the Senator broke with a long-standing Kennedy tradition of live-and-let-live with Republican senators from Massachusetts. He backed the Democratic candidate Paul Tsongas over the incumbent, Edward Brooke. Some observers believed that this was an early signal of a Kennedy presidential run in 1980. When Tsongas won, he was in a position to look after Kennedy's interests in Massachusetts, as the Senator turned his gaze to the nation and the world.

Yet another signal came when the Senator brought in Carl Wagner as special assistant to take over Paul Kirk's old role. At age thirty-four, the Iowan was a former political operative for the American Federation of State, County and Municipal Employees; he was considered one of the best political organizers in the country. He was a dark, strikingly handsome, muscular man with one unfortunate drawback: He gave off a distinctive odor. Before Wagner walked into a room, his presence was announced by a strong smell of some alien spice. None of us wanted to broach the subject with Wagner, but his presence was extremely difficult to ignore. Before long, whenever Wagner wanted a meeting with the Senator, I was always called into the room. It was my job to position myself between the two men, as a screen.

After one such meeting, the Senator said to me, "You've *got* to talk to that man."

"What am I supposed to do," I asked, "go up to him and say, 'You stink'?"

"It's not—" the Senator stammered. "Go smell his coat. See if it's just his clothes."

One night Wagner invited me and several other staff members to his home for dinner. When the Senator heard of the invitation, he drew me aside and suggested that I take the opportunity to tactfully mention the odor to Carl.

However, the moment I entered the home, the mystery was solved. Wagner's wife was a beautiful Asian woman who routinely cooked her ethnic dishes with generous doses of curry. The odor permeated the house. I realized that there really was not very much Carl could do about the situation.

Wagner's professional aura was quite different. He was well known as a campaign strategist and his appearance on our staff was a signal to the press that the Senator was gearing up for a run at the presidency. Speculation mounted.

The Senator was used to being hounded by the press, but he seemed to be growing more sensitive about some of the more sensational personal innuendos. *The National Enquirer,* in true tabloid fashion, routinely devoted racy headlines to any Kennedy family tidbit, the more outrageous the better. It was Steve Smith who worked out the pragmatic compromise with the *Enquirer*'s management. Through Smith, the Senator agreed to provide the tabloid with factual information and comments on any legitimate Kennedy family story, so long as the paper backed away from the more lurid speculation. I was now assigned as the contact man. Once a week, I received a call from an "inquiring" reporter to see if there was any family news to report.

It was one of the more unusual assignments as the Senator's administrative assistant but certainly not the only one. With growing frequency, I was also becoming the emotional counselor for several of his friends, most of whom were women. I began to worry where all this would end.

One Monday morning I dropped a leading comment: "I hear you had a wild weekend."

The Senator responded with a laugh.

"You know, we've got a problem," I counseled. "Kitty is ready to rip out Cindy's hair." Kitty, his friend from Rhode Island, was a frequent partner in his escapades with Cindy.

"Deal with it, Ricky," he commanded.

This became a constant worry. By now, Cindy and I spoke on a daily basis, and I grew concerned that, as much as she loved the Senator, she might crack under the strain of this bizarre relationship.

"He tells me things, about his brothers, about feelings he has toward various members of his family," Cindy disclosed to me. She said that this was especially true when he was high. A loosened tongue is a well-known effect of cocaine. Cindy said that the Senator confided that he had loved and respected his brothers, but that he had always felt in competition with them and, after they were killed, he was tortured by guilt. Cindy would listen with sympathy, often high on coke herself, which magnified the emotions she experienced hearing the Senator's psychological floodgates open. But she wasn't a therapist, only a lover, and often moaned, "I don't know how to respond to all that. I just listen. Sometimes I feel that I should say something, but I don't know what."

I said, "Look, I can understand how difficult it is. You're having to deal with his pent-up emotions at the same time you're dealing with your relationship and this thing with Kitty, but you've got to try and stop him from doing so much coke and from drinking too much. He really needs to ease up on the accelerator, you know what I mean?"

Cindy surprised me when she responded to this advice with a warning of her own, "Rick, you seem tired, you know. You've got to slow down, too."

I dismissed her words; I didn't have time to think about myself. And besides, I thought somewhat smugly, I didn't have a problem with coke or booze.

Not long after that, when Cindy called one night, ostensibly to talk over a few details concerning the Senator's schedule, I realized that she was the one who sounded tired, so I asked a leading question: "How are things going?"

She mentioned a few minor frustrations and anxieties, running down them slowly, like reading off a laundry list. Finally she said, "I'm really worried, Rick. I think I'm pregnant." She paused and added, "I have to take care of it."

"Are you sure?" I asked.

"Yes."

"Is he aware of it?"

"No, I don't want to bother him."

We spoke for about forty-five minutes. In part, she believed that a pregnancy would force the Senator to divorce Joan and marry her. But I advised her, just as I had others, "If you think that there is any possibility of him leaving Joan—I don't think it's practical."

"Oh, I know, Rick," Cindy said. "But, you know, there's always a chance."

She was being naïve. "Cindy, as long as there's the presidency to consider, I wouldn't count on it."

The pragmatic part of Cindy knew that a divorce from Joan followed by marriage to a pregnant lover would dash any hopes that the Senator could ever mount a viable campaign for the presidency. I tried to be gentle and understanding; my heart was breaking for her. But she also had to be realistic. The writing had been on the wall a long time: His career came first.

She finally said, "You know the guy and I know the guy. As long as there's a chance or goal of being President of the United States, he's not going to divorce her. There's no way." She added, "But I just don't know what to do."

I didn't feel that it was my place to point out what was probably the only viable option.

She indicated she knew anyway. "No, I know what I have to do." She thanked me for listening, and dropped the subject. A few days later, Cindy left on a quick trip to California. After she returned, I heard nothing more about the pregnancy.

14

For a time I dated Sheila, the former girlfriend of my housemate, Jack Leslie. At first I was cheered by a relationship unblotted by the Senator's shadow. I was careful to shield her from the darker aspects of my life. She saw me as a hardworking and rather straitlaced government servant—and, though our friendship ran hot and cold, I thought that it was perhaps time to settle down.

I was in this frame of mind when I chanced to walk by a spectacular brick house at 3730 W Street, NW, in the Glover Park area of the city, just north of Georgetown. It was the builder's house on the old Archibald Glover estate, a large five-story structure, set on a hill, totally surrounded by trees so that it appeared to be an oasis in the midst of the city. On either side of the house, brick archways stood sentinel, leading to doors at the side. It was my dream house, at least from the outside, and the best part of the dream was the FOR SALE sign that stood in front.

I had recently sold a ski house in Vermont and netted a good profit, so I was in a position to buy. When a few people at the office agreed to come into the deal as non-residential investors, I had enough leverage to make the purchase. We bought the house and I asked Sandra Kirk, a decorator, to supervise the necessary renovations. Several of the rooms needed to be gutted entirely, but, as soon as the bedroom was ready, I ordered a six-line phone system and moved in.

The phones, naturally, started ringing right away. I was asleep in my new bedroom when I was awakened at 3:00 A.M. by a call from a wire service reporter who asked, "Did you hear that the Pope died?"

"No," I replied sleepily.

"We'd like a statement from the Senator."

I knew that the reporter was working on a story for the morning news, and if we waited until business hours to provide a statement, we would lose the opportunity; he would quote someone else. So I simply mumbled, "The Senator says he is deeply moved and personally saddened by the loss. Pope Paul the Sixth has done great things for the world and was a great humanitarian."

The reporter thanked me and hung up. Later, near dawn, a White House staffer called with a request: President Carter wanted the Senator to be part of the official U.S. delegation to the August 12 funeral. "We can't reach the Senator," the voice said. "Can you tell me where he is?" I gave out the Boston number.

That morning brought a flurry of details. Perhaps the biggest question was whether or not Joan would accompany the Senator to Rome. I spoke with Dr. Hawthorne and he advised against it. Even after the *McCall's* and *People* cover stories, Joan was walking the thin line of recovery, and the feeling was that the last thing she needed was further scrutiny by the press, especially at such a visible event. I told the Senator this and he seemed relieved she wasn't going. The rest of the day was taken up with the details of rearranging the Senator's schedule.

The delegation was headed by First Lady Rosalynn Carter and, in addition to the Senator, included New

York governor Hugh Carey, Representative Robert
Giaimo of Connecticut, David Walters, the President's
representative to the Vatican, and Lionel Castillo, Com-
missioner of Immigration and Naturalization. The White
House protocol office cleared the way quickly. Mrs.
Carter planned to arrive in Rome three days prior to the
funeral, but the Senator didn't want to spend that much
time away from the office—nor did he wish to socialize
with Mrs. Carter. From the outset of the Carter presidency there had been a tension between the two men.
More pointedly, President and Mrs. Carter did not include the Senator in an abundance of White House functions—a major faux pas in the President's already-
strained relationship with the Hill—and the Senator saw
no need to make himself available for this occasion.

On a more personal level he felt the Carters were complete bores, too uptight, and not at all sophisticated. He
thought the President's family, especially his potbellied,
beer-guzzling brother, Billy, was an embarrassment to
the country, and Lillian, the President's mother, was simply gaga. He loathed it when the press compared Mrs.
Lillian to Rose Kennedy.

He utilized the reasonable excuse that his schedule was
too tight, saying that he would have to link up with the
party in Rome. In the meantime, he designated me as his
agent, to fly to Italy on *Air Force One* and prepare the
way for his visit.

In Rome, I checked into the Excelsior Hotel and began
to arrange things for the Senator's arrival. It was a tense
time, since Italy had been the target of recent terrorist
attacks. About six months earlier, Italy's prime minister,
Aldo Moro, had been kidnapped and executed. Now, in
nervous anticipation of a city full of dignitaries, troops
armed with machine guns were visible on the street. Others guarded the hallways of our hotel. It occurred to me
that the best way for the Senator to ingratiate himself

with the Italian people was to show empathy for their current concerns. When I learned that the Moro assassination site had become a sort of national shrine—Italians still visited it daily to lay flowers there—I decided that it would be a great public relations gesture for the Senator to pay his respects.

Robert Hunter, who had been on the Senator's staff in the early seventies and now worked for the National Security Agency, offered to help me coordinate the Senator's schedule. He was with me at the U.S. Embassy when I said, "We're going to need a special car to pick up the Senator at the airport, and then we'd like to go to the spot where Moro was assassinated."

"No, you can't do that," an embassy official snapped.

Hunter took me aside and counseled, "Absolutely no way, Rick. Remember, I was the Senator's foreign policy adviser. It would be a big mistake to do this, a diplomatic faux pas."

Hunter is a nice guy, but I thought he was a bit too pompous. I remembered that he worked for Carter now, not for Kennedy. So I ignored his warning and placed a call to Washington to see how the Senator would react to my idea. I said, "I think it would be great for you to go and get you picture taken laying flowers at the site. Moro's a national hero here, just like your brother is in the U.S."

The Senator said he would discuss my idea with others and get back to me.

A few hours later he called back and said, "We'll go with what you say, Rick. Oh, God, let's hope, uh, you're right."

We had a motorcade waiting when the Senator arrived, and we drove straight from the airport to the Moro assassination site. Eager Italian press photographers took memorable shots of the Senator paying his respects.

The next morning, the front pages of all the Italian

newspapers featured photos and glowing stories of the Senator's visit. In one step, the Senator had taken the lead with the American presence in Italy. The White House, we heard, was understandably livid. But who cared? From that moment on, wherever the Senator went in Rome, he was met with open affection. In her story wired back to *The Washington Star,* Mary McGrory wrote that the success of the Moro gesture was an example of the "flawless staff work that is expected" of the Senator's "tribe."

That day, Terence Cardinal Cooke gave the delegation an official tour of the Vatican. Mrs. Carter was at the front of the entourage alongside Cooke, as the Senator and I lingered near the back of the group, a bit bored. There was a hint of familiarity in the Senator's eyes; in fact, we had both seen the Vatican before.*

The delegation members expressed their disappointment when the Cardinal informed us that we could not view the Sistine Chapel or the papal apartments; both areas were in the process of restoration and, in addition, workers were preparing the Sistine Chapel for the closed-door sessions of the College of Cardinals, who would soon meet to elect a new Pope. The Sistine Chapel and the papal apartments were sealed off and protected by Swiss guards.

As we reached the end of a long hallway, Cardinal Cooke ushered the group off to the right. On a whim, the Senator nudged me and whispered, "Let's go to the left."

The two of us wandered off by ourselves and were soon

---

*The Kennedy family had been very close to Cardinal Pacelli, who was elected in 1939 as Pope Pius XII. The Kennedys journeyed to the Vatican for the coronation; in a private audience with the family, the new Pope drew seven-year-old Ted onto his lap, patted his head, and told him he was a smart little fellow. Then Pius XII administered First Communion to Ted, the first time a Pope had done such a thing in more than two hundred years.

lost. We spotted one of the Swiss guards, and I tried out my limited French vocabulary. He seemed not to understand and the Senator, laughing, took over; he spoke French well. "How can we get to the Sistine Chapel?" he asked.

The guard's face showed instant recognition of the famous visitor. Placing his ornamental spear to one side, he beckoned for us to follow him. He led us directly to the Captain of the Guard, who obliged us with a private tour of the Sistine Chapel and the papal apartments.

The chapel buzzed with workmen. "This is where the cardinals will meet," the captain pointed out. In a reverential voice he added, "The votes will be taken and put on the table here." He launched into a lengthy, detailed explanation of how the cardinals would celebrate the Mass each morning and then go about their solemn business.

More than a half hour passed before the Senator and I found our way outside, to discover that the rest of the delegation was waiting impatiently for us. Mrs. Carter was seated in her car, fuming with indignation.

"Sorry, sorry," the Senator apologized, half-seriously. "We just finished a tour of the Sistine Chapel."

Hearing this, Mrs. Carter's eyes narrowed on the Senator, and her face turned about four shades of red, but she didn't say a word.

Later, the Senator and I were sharing a drink at the bar of the Hotel Excelsior when Governor Carey spotted us. He reported with a grin, "My God, Rosalynn was absolutely furious. She kept berating the cardinal, 'Why could *he* go into the Sistine Chapel and I couldn't go in there?' I thought she was gonna have a heart attack, she was so upset."

The Senator just laughed and tossed back a drink.

That afternoon we met secretly with Cardinal Casaroli, the Vatican's Secretary of State, to discuss tactics for helping refuseniks get out of the Soviet Union; Casaroli was an expert in dealing with Communist bloc countries, and we wanted his input.

In the evening Mary McGrory and Jimmy Breslin, who was also covering the trip, joined us at the home of Gianni Agnelli, the jet-setting owner of the Fiat Corporation. His apartment was located directly above a police station, which provided great security. This official protection was augmented by an army of private guards. Agnelli was such an obvious target for terrorists that he changed his schedule more than a dozen times a day, just to keep his pursuers off guard.

That man who was considered to be one of the wealthiest and most powerful persons in Europe greeted us in the company of two of the most beautiful and elegant women I have ever seen. And the two men at his side were, perhaps, even more elegant and beautiful than the women. Throughout the evening, the five Italians hung all over one another.

An English butler served us cocktails on the patio, which offered a spectacular view of Rome. The Senator set up a tennis game for the morning; Agnelli could not play, because he was suffering from a back injury, but three of his gorgeous companions agreed to a match.

On the ride back to the hotel that night, the Senator said to me, "I wonder if Agnelli's gay. . . . Do you think he's gay? Those guys were so good-looking, it's beyond belief. Every one looked like a movie star, or a model. Christ. And they seemed to be awfully touchy-feely."

"That's just the Italian in them," I offered. "You know how Europeans are. They're just sort of, you know, more physical with everyone than Americans. It doesn't mean he's gay."

"Hmmmmm . . ." he said, clearly thinking about it.

After the tennis match the next morning, the Senator returned to Agnelli's apartment for breakfast and a

The three brothers: Jack, Bobby, and Ted. *(Nelson Tiffany/ Gamma Liaison)*

The Senator with Joan, Kara, and Ted—a happy moment at home. *(Schaefer & Seawell/Black Star)*

A somber EMK and Joan leaving Hyannis for Mary Jo Kopechne's funeral. *(UPI/Bettmann)*

Escorting Teddy, Jr., to a waiting car after leaving the hospital. *(UPI/Bettmann)*

Waiting for the Senator as he heads to a Judiciary Committee hearing. *(Dennis Brack/Black Star)*

Mrs. Onassis and the Senator at the RFK Memorial Tennis Tournament. This was Jackie's first public appearance after the death of Aristotle Onassis. *(David Burnett/Liaison)*

Greeting the crowds during the 1979 visit of the Pope to the Boston Common. Author is first on left. *(Gilles Peress/Magnum)*

Warren Beatty, long active in the Democratic Party, played host to a private visit by the Senator at Beatty's Los Angeles home during the 1980 presidential campaign. Jack Nicholson was also in attendance. *(Beatty: AP/Wide World; Nicholson: Donaldson/Liaison)*

In New York during the campaign. Joan is just behind the Senator.
(Alex Webb/Magnum)

Joe Kennedy, Jr., and the Senator. *(Peter Southwick/Liaison)*

During the 1980 Democratic Convention, there were long nights of strategy at the Waldorf. Here, Ron Brown, current Secretary of Commerce, the Senator, and Susan Estrich discuss platform issues as Joan listens in. *(AP/Wide World)*

The next day, the author, the Senator, and Joan leaving NBC studios after doing the "Today Show." *(AP/Wide World)*

The Senator testifying at the trial of his nephew, William Kennedy Smith. *(J. K. Owen/Black Star)*

The Senator and Clarence Thomas during Thomas's confirmation hearings for his seat on the Supreme Court. *(UPI/Bettmann)*

Giving what has become known as the "mea culpa" speech dealing with his personal and political life, the Senator spoke at Harvard in the fall of 1991. *(UPI/Bettmann)*

relaxing session in his hot tub. "We had a ball," he told me when he arrived back at the hotel.

At 11:00 A.M. on the day of the funeral, the delegation went for a private viewing of the Pope's body. When the motorcade reached the Vatican gate, we found mobs of people filling the streets, screaming, "Kennedy! Kennedy! Kennedy!"

I could just imagine what Rosalynn Carter was thinking about that.

Prior to the funeral, the Senator wanted to view the crypt of Pope Pius XII, and then we were led up to St. Peter's Basilica, where Pope Paul lay in state. A pair of brilliantly liveried Swiss guards stood sentry duty. A few priests prayed quietly over the body. A sick-sweet smell of incense filled the air.

The official state funeral was at 6:00 P.M. It was a formal, white-tie affair. Staffers were not permitted to be with the official delegation for the funeral ceremony, but as Swiss guards attempted to separate us, the Senator tugged at my arm and pulled me along with him.

"Senator, he can't come," one of the Italian security men said.

With a wave of his hand, the Senator dismissed the interruption. "He's a relative," he explained.

And so I stood up in front for the funeral, along with the First Lady, two senators, a governor, a mayor, and several congressmen. Other aides fumed in indignation.

White House personnel failed to provide French air traffic controllers with the required twenty-four-hour notice, so *Air Force One* was prohibited from flying over French airspace. The pilot had to take us home via an alternate route over Germany, and the detour necessitated a refueling stop in Shannon.

During the brief layover, Mrs. Carter decided to visit the duty-free shop. People recognized her, and a crowd formed, eyed by wary Secret Service agents.

At the edge of the crowd, a bystander asked, "Who is it? Who is it?"

An airport security guard replied, "It's the wife of the President of the United States."

The incredulous bystander asked in amazement, "Mrs. Kennedy?"

After we were back in Washington, the Senator, on August 22, instructed me to withdraw $4,200 in cash from his personal account. He did not tell me what it was for, but I knew that he was buying cocaine regularly now, using Cindy and Barbara as intermediaries. I knew some of his other sources as well.

But I was surprised to realize he had yet another source. One day a slim, cylindrical mailing tube arrived at the office via regular mail. It was marked PERSONAL, addressed to the Senator, ATTENTION: RICK. I opened the brown paper wrapping and slipped the contents out of the tube, to find a note card and a packet of white powder. Quickly I rewrapped the package and left it on the Senator's desk; he did not say anything to me about it.

Later that night, I said to Cindy, "I think I opened something I probably shouldn't have." I described the contents of the package.

Cindy laughed and said in an offhand manner, "Oh yeah, that guy provides good stuff."

This issue grew a bit sticky when the source's girlfriend called to invite the Senator to a party at her Washington apartment. When I checked with the Senator, he protested that his schedule was too tight, and he suggested, "Why don't you just go, Rick. There's something from my friend that I want you to pick up."

At the reception, the girlfriend found a moment to draw me off to the privacy of the bedroom. She handed me a mailing tube, similar to the one that had arrived at the office some time earlier. "This is for Ted," she announced. Capriciously she added, "Let's open it up. I'm always wondering what's going on between those two."

"No, no," I cautioned. "I don't think we should open it. It's personal." I considered this woman to be a saint. She probably had no idea what her boyfriend was shipping to the Senator, and, if she found out, would most certainly be appalled.

But she was very curious. She teased, "Oh, come on, Rick. We can open it up." Her fingernails ripped at the paper.

"Really, I feel very uncomfortable," I warned. "If the Senator sees that this has been opened—"

"Okay," she agreed quickly.

It was about this time that press rumors surfaced concerning Hamilton Jordan, Carter's chief of staff. A girlfriend, perhaps disgruntled, charged that one night when she and Jordan were at Studio 54, co-owner Steve Rubell had invited them to a private room, where they snorted cocaine. When the Senator and I discussed the scandal, I realized that the alleged incident had occurred during the Celebrity Tennis Tournament. I smacked my head and said, "Gee, I was in Studio Fifty-four at just about the same time."

Jordan denied the rumor, and an investigation later cleared him. But the claim that the White House chief of staff had snorted cocaine was quickly turning into a scandal. On the one hand, the Senator and I thought that the press made too much of the story. But, the Senator mused, "We're talking about somebody who may influence the President to press the button."

I vowed to myself: If and when we ever get to the White House, we will clean up our act.

After all, I knew that I could stop doing coke anytime I wanted.

Barbara called me on Sunday afternoon, very upset, from her home in Florida. I knew that the Senator was in Florida for the weekend, and I wondered what he had done now. Barbara explained that she and the Senator had driven out to see Lori, who was staying at her boy-friend's house, a huge home with a pool and tennis court. Lori's boyfriend was not there at the time. For a while, Barbara and the Senator watched Lori and two of her girlfriends play tennis.

When Lori and her friends finished their tennis game, they headed for the shower room. The Senator was very drunk and, as Barbara put it, "feeling his oats." He wandered off, and the next thing Barbara knew, she heard Lori screaming, "Get out of here!" Barbara ran for the house and discovered that the Senator had stripped and calmly stepped into the shower with Lori and her girlfriends.

This lead to a screaming fight between Barbara and Lori. "Lori thinks I'm an idiot for seeing him," Barbara said to me. She was also concerned that Lori might tell others about the incident.

I tried to act as an intermediary. I phoned Lori and calmed her down as best I could. "The guy was drunk," I reasoned.

"I don't give a shit. He's a pig, Rick."

We talked for a few more minutes, and then hung up. That was the last I ever heard from Lori.

Just as that fire had been put out, there was another one to worry about.

Los Angeles Rams owner Carroll Rosenbloom drowned. The Senator was very supportive of his widow, Georgia, who had now inherited the Rams, and kept in touch with her. One day, through the FBI, we learned that Rosenbloom, who had always been quite concerned with security precautions, had long ago installed an elab-orate taping system in his home and had amassed a vast library of tapes documenting conversations inside the house. Now we learned that the FBI had custody of the tapes. The newspapers speculated about the revelations contained on those tapes concerning the diverse guests whom Rosenbloom had entertained over the years. Apparently, in addition to politicians, businessmen, entertainers, and sports celebrities, Rosenbloom had counted various mobsters as his friends.

"Oh, shit . . ." the Senator said to me in private, "I wonder what they have on those tapes. Jesus, I can't remember everything I've, uh, you know, done there. But I know some of the things I've done there . . . I wonder how long those tapes have been going on. You know, my brothers stayed at that house, too."

As soon as he could, the Senator turned this touchy issue over to Steve Smith to investigate. Smith checked with some of his FBI connections but was unable to gain any meaningful information. We could only conjecture that, if there was information on those tapes incriminating to the Senator and his family, the stories would probably surface if and when the Senator ran for President.

And so, we'd just have to wait it out.

Meanwhile there were other things the Senator was worried about. I remember getting a call late on a Saturday night not long after that.

"Uh, you know there's this foam stuff all over," the Senator complained, clearly a little tanked up.

I was tired, and found myself supremely exasperated by the phone call. I asked sarcastically, "What do you want me to do, come over and clean your hot tub for you?"

"Yeah, I know it's a bad time," he acknowledged. "But I can't get rid of this foam and I don't know what it is."

I sat on the edge of my bed, putting my hand to my head, thinking this was really beyond the pale. . . . *Just go the fuck away,* I fumed, about one step from saying it. Instead, I sighed and promised, "Look, Monday morning, I'll call the hot-tub guy. It probably just needs more chlorine, or something like that."

The Senator grew petulant. I could hear him sniffing on the phone. "You know, Ricky, we're trying to use the hot tub here, and there's all this foam . . . what the hell am I supposed to do?"

"I'll take care of it on Monday," I said firmly, and hung up. I was tempted to take the phone off the hook, but the Senator knew I had six lines at home, and a busy signal wouldn't fool him.

Thankfully he didn't call back. He probably just moved the party inside.

As it turned out, foam was not the worst problem concerning the hot tub. An undeveloped piece of property sat adjacent and above the backyard area of the Senator's home in McLean; what concerned him most was that it offered an unrestricted view of the hot tub.

Some time earlier, an agent for the property had called me to announce the land was for sale. The Senator asked Joe Hakim to come down from the New York office to evaluate the land; Hakim concluded that the asking price was far too high, and the Senator decided not to make an offer. I warned him, "If you're unwilling to pay the price, you're going to have to deal with the consequences."

Now the consequences loomed. The Senator panicked when he learned that someone had purchased the lot and planned to build a home on it.

We consulted with a landscape architect, who told us that a row of trees, planted in a strategic location, would screen the view.

"I gotta get those trees in," the Senator said repeatedly.

For a time, it appeared to be the most important issue in his life.

And then opportunity knocked, redirecting his attention to the Senate.

Senator Eastland announced his retirement, and this presented a shot for Kennedy to become chairman of the Senate Judiciary Committee. It was a rare chance at building a unique power base.

The Senator qualified for the Judiciary chair in terms of seniority, but he had to win over certain key votes, both on the Judiciary Committee and the Rules Committee. We spent considerable time in negotiations on this issue, and I was once more fascinated to see him interact deftly with conservative colleagues. Gaining Eastland's endorsement was the key task, and the Senator was savvy enough to show the proper amount of deference, allowing Eastland to adopt a fatherly attitude. Senators Thurmond and Hatch were key allies also. They all seemed genuinely fond of Kennedy, even if they crossed swords on issues.

I thought, *The Senator can charm the pants off anybody.*

Once the new post became a reality, we faced the task of expanding our staff from 35 people to 150, in the space of a few months.

We labored to organize the pending move from our offices in the relatively old Russell Building to Eastland's former office in the relatively new Dirksen Building. Across the hall were the offices of the Judiciary Committee. The Senator wanted to move not only the furniture, the files, and the people, but he wanted to move the *atmosphere,* and this was somewhat difficult, because the ceilings in the Dirksen Building were lower and contributed to a cramped feeling. I supervised the repainting of Eastland's former suite of offices and drew out floor plans for the alignment of the desks, trying to utilize the space as best as possible.

In terms of staff, we concentrated our attention on the key spots, and labored to persuade top-notch people to join forces with us. The Senator hired David Boies, one of the nation's most respected litigators, away from the law firm of Cravath, Swaine, Moore to be the committee's new chief counsel. Boies proved to be a brilliant, issues-oriented attorney. He wore suits that appeared to be straight off the rack from Sears, but he liked to drive fast cars, which the Senator could certainly appreciate.

We were just getting settled when a new family problem emerged. At about 5:30 P.M. on September 5, David Kennedy, now twenty-four years old, was robbed of thirty dollars and beaten up in the lobby of the dilapidated Shelton Plaza Hotel in Harlem. He told police that he had been driving in the area when his BMW sports coupe was waved down by two men, who then forced him into the hotel, where a third assailant appeared. They took his money at knife point.

Our office issued a quick statement blandly explaining that David was on a leave of absence from Harvard and was simply in New York to visit friends. But there was much more to the story, and the press soon ferreted out some of the details. For one thing, the hotel in question was a seedy dive known for narcotics traffic. Police reports indicated that twenty-five glassine envelopes containing heroin had been found in one of the hotel stairwells. Not exactly a Hilton.

I got pulled into the aftermath, coordinating discussions with the family to set up treatment for David. I worked with Steve Smith; Dave Haskell, the head of the RFK memorial; Larry Horowitz of our Health Subcommittee; and several physicians and counselors in Massachusetts, including the renowned Dr. Robert Coles, Harvard's resident authority on child psychology. Ethel frequently called upon Coles for help with her children, although it appeared she had given up on David some time ago. One suggestion was that we find David a "sponsor," someone who could pal around with him and serve as a combination friend/confidant/policeman. In essence, a guardian to protect David from himself.

Along with David's older brother Joe, I planned the details of an "intervention" wherein David's family confronted him with his problem. Working together, the family persuaded him to seek help and we placed David in a drug rehab program at McLean Hospital, outside of Boston. The official word was that he was hospitalized for treatment of bacterial endocarditis—a condition often caused by heroin abuse. Steve Smith's spin on it to the press was that he was suffering from "an ailment similar to drug addiction," which was an understatement at best. The Senator asked Jack's old friend Lem Billings to assume the role of sponsor, which was unfortunate since Lem himself was also using drugs. We arranged for David to be able to take a final test in one of his Harvard courses.

And then we held our breath.

It seemed as if we had just finished dealing with David's addiction when the question of Joan's came up again.

The Senator had visited the Soviet Union several years earlier, and was anxious to return. Joan shared this interest, and we hoped that she could come along on the September trip, but Dr. Hawthorne advised us that she was not up to it. While Joan was still working very hard on maintaining her sobriety, the doctor felt the pressure of such a highly visible trip might trigger a relapse. Nobody wanted to risk it, and so the decision was made that she not go.

We decided not to invite either Tunney or David Karr, although they had helped greatly with our planning. The Senator did not want to publicize his association with Karr, who was rumored to have some "funny" connections (including the mob, the CIA, and Israeli intelligence). Nor did he want to leave the impression that he was using his own clout to open business doors for Tunney in the Soviet Union.

There were hundreds of details to consider. One of our most critical concerns was whether or not the Senator could gain an audience with Soviet premier Leonid Brezhnev. This meeting would receive good press coverage in the U.S. and elevate the Senator to the status of an international statesman—an area where President Carter was beginning to look weak. U.S.–Soviet relations were at low ebb and we calculated that Carter's deteriorating relationship with Brezhnev favored our chances for a meeting; perhaps the premier might wish to deal Carter a symbolic slap in the face by meeting with his chief party rival. There was a humanitarian reason for the meeting as well as a political one. The Senator wanted Brezhnev to commit to freeing Soviet refuseniks.

We spoke frequently with Andrei, our contact on the Politburo staff, but our inquiries produced evasive answers regarding the premier's availability. Unofficially, we heard that Brezhnev was seriously ill; perhaps he had cancer; perhaps he was dying. We finally resigned ourselves to the fact that the issue of a Brezhnev-Kennedy meeting would not be resolved until we were actually in Moscow.

Nevertheless, we had to consider the delicate protocol question: What gift should a U.S. senator take to a Soviet premier? The Senator came up with the novel idea of gathering foodstuffs from the regions we visited and presenting the premier with a variety of specialty items drawn from the corners of his very own country.

There were more clandestine tasks, too. We knew that whatever Brezhnev might or might not say to the Senator regarding the refuseniks, Soviet officials would be alert to the possibility that we might attempt to contact the group on our own. It seemed obvious that the officials would do their best to prevent it. The Senator wanted to go ahead with such plans, but he did not wish to anger Soviet officials to the point where they refused to release anyone. Our foreign-policy adviser, Jan Kalicki, finally advised us that certain U.S. Embassy personnel could help us set up a rendezvous, but warned us to confine our planning sessions to the special secure room at the embassy building.

At the last moment an international incident threatened the entire trip. An American businessman was arrested after he attempted to buy something in Moscow, offering illegal dollars instead of rubles. This was considered a major crime, and the Soviets proclaimed their intent to deal harshly with the offender. The Senator considered calling off the trip in protest, but he was unsure what to do, so we proceeded with our planning.

Even with all the more unusual tasks I was expected to execute on the Senator's behalf, there were also moments of great reward. I was surprised and delighted when, only days before departure, the Senator asked me to journey to Moscow as his advance man, and then to accompany him about the Soviet Union. This decision launched a flurry of activity. I raced about Washington to get my papers in order.

15 After a seventeen-hour trip, including a layover in Frankfurt, I arrived in Moscow in late afternoon. The moment my plane arrived at the terminal, a Soviet guide stepped aboard accompanied by KGB security agents and a representative from Andrei's office at the Politburo. The guide strode directly toward me, introduced himself as Peter, and announced in perfect English that he would accompany me everywhere I went as long as I was in the Soviet Union.

Andrei awaited me at the hotel—an old, ornate palace, reserved for diplomats and special visitors—and explained that he would arrange anything that I and the Senator wanted.

The next morning I was scheduled to meet with the chargé d'affaires at the U.S. Embassy. At the appointed hour, Peter was nowhere in sight, so I simply walked out onto the Moscow streets and flagged a cab. I showed the driver the address of the embassy, which I had scrawled onto a piece of paper.

The chargé d'affaires ushered me into the secure room, a large conference area with lead-lined, padded walls. We sat at a table large enough to hold twenty people, then he pressed a button and a plastic bubble descended over our heads. In private, he offered the welcome news that the Soviets had released the American businessman, paving a diplomatic path for the Senator's arrival. We had only just begun our discussions when the telephone buzzed and someone informed us that police cars had surrounded the embassy. We left the secure room to investigate.

Peter stood outside, ashen-faced, searching for me. "Please don't do that," he implored. "If you want me to stay out of trouble, don't ever leave me again."

I was sympathetic but firm. "I needed to come to the embassy," I said. "I have to do what I have to do."

The chargé d'affaires and I returned to our station under the bubble in the secure room. I had many questions. Would Brezhnev be available for a meeting with the Senator? Would we be able to arrange a rendezvous with the refuseniks?

I spent the rest of the day touring Moscow with Peter. That night, Andrei took me to Natasha's apartment, and I had a chance to meet the blonde whom Tunney found so mysterious and appealing. By Soviet standards she certainly was a stunner, and so was her apartment, which was small, but appointed with Danish Modern furniture. I couldn't imagine that she was anything other than a KGB agent. When the Senator saw her, there could be *trouble*.

The Senator arrived the following day, accompanied by Larry Horowitz, Jan Kalicki, and Ken Regan, our photographer. Along with Andrei, Peter, and the by-now-familiar contingent of security personnel, I met them at the airport. The moment he stepped off the plane, the Senator grabbed me by the lapel, and, laughing, said, "Ricky, Ricky, I gotta tell you what happened." We were whisked off to the VIP lounge for a chance to talk.

The Senator was still laughing. "We were sitting in the

plane, working away," he detailed, "and Larry gets up and goes to the bathroom. Ah, a half hour goes by, maybe thirty-five minutes. All of a sudden we, uh, see the pilot coming down the aisle, with tools, going to the back of the plane. We're all looking back to see what's happening. Then we see the pilot walking back toward the cockpit and Larry's coming behind him, sheepishly." Horowitz had locked himself in the bathroom. "They had to take the hinges off the door to get him out," the Senator said, holding his sides, laughing.

Within minutes we were taken directly to the personal airplane of Leonid Brezhnev. The aircraft was appointed in a similar manner as *Air Force One,* but the decor was drab and the electronics not as up to date. First on our agenda was an extended flight to Tashkent, the capital of the Soviet Socialist Republic of Uzbekistan. The schedule called for us to spend the night there, then fly only a few hundred miles east to the UN conference in Alma-Ata. Finally we would return to Moscow for a few days that would include, we hoped, a face-to-face meeting with Brezhnev.

We had been airborne for about a half hour when I noticed the Senator squirming uncomfortably in his seat. "Ricky, my back is itching," he complained. "I don't know, it must be a mosquito bite or something like that."

"Take your shirt off," I suggested.

He did so, and I examined the skin of his back, which was covered with dark pink lumps.

I asked suspiciously, "What did you do last weekend?"

"I was just on the Cape with the kids."

"Who else? Was Cindy there?"

"Yeah, you know Cindy was there."

"Did you guys go sailing?" I asked.

He nodded, now scratching his back furiously.

I thought, *Oh, boy.* "Ummm, did you by chance do anything on the beach?"

"Yeah," he groaned, now in agony and clearly frustrated. "We, er, uh . . ."

"I betcha that's poison ivy."

"Oh, my God . . ." he responded. "You must be right."

"Let's get Larry," I suggested. Horowitz was along in twin roles, as adviser on health issues and as the Senator's personal physician.

"Don't tell Larry what you think it is—or how I got it," the Senator ordered. "You know how full of himself he gets."

Horowitz examined the Senator's back and muttered uncertainly. "This is probably an allergic reaction to something you ate yesterday."

"What about poison ivy?" I asked.

"I'm not sure," Horowitz said. "When we land, we'll ask for a doctor." Horowitz spoke with the pilot, who arranged for a Soviet physician to meet us in Tashkent.

Several swigs of vodka seemed to ease the Senator's discomfort, and before long he felt well enough to roam about. Along with Kalicki, Horowitz, and Regan, he moved toward the back of the aircraft. I settled back in my seat, thinking, *Well, at least we're not on our way to Alaska.* Back in the late sixties, the Senator had been involved in a celebrated incident. He'd been in Alaska for three days with the Subcommittee on Indian Education, which was holding field hearings. He'd begun drinking on the flight (out of RFK's old silver flask), stumbling up and down the aisles, yelling, "Es-ki-mo Power!" and saying, "They're going to shoot my ass off the way they shot Bobby's." Just as soon as someone would coax him back to his seat, he'd be up again, rambling on, mostly incoherently, about Jack and Bobby, throwing pillows at a stewardess and dinner rolls at reporters. It was not one of his finer moments.

Soon I heard laughter emanating from the back, disrupting my thoughts, and briefly, I thought, *Oh, no. . . .*

Some minutes later the Senator's voice called out, "Ricky, Ricky, come here."

As I approached, he announced, waving his hand in the general direction of the Soviets, "They say that Russians can drink more than Americans, and we told them there's no way. America is number one." I was about to ask why he was interjecting me into the midst of this international debate when he added, "We volunteered you to prove it to them."

Everyone else in the group already appeared glassy-eyed. Andrei, with a giggle, pointed toward a young KGB officer, just about my age, who was assigned to uphold the honor of the Soviet Union.

Still suffering from jet lag, I thought, *What have I gotten myself into?*

Someone produced two large ten-ounce glasses. Andrei filled them to the brim with clear, undiluted vodka. "You gotta be kidding me," I demurred.

"You can't fail us, Rick," the Senator coached, his breath blowing out whiffs of alcohol. "You can't fail us."

The Soviet lad gulped down the contents of his vodka glass and stared a challenge at me.

"You'll be out on the floor in two seconds," Horowitz muttered.

I lifted my glass and followed the Soviet boy's lead. Cheers from the American side greeted me as I displayed the empty vessel.

Undaunted, Andrei refilled our glasses, this time with scotch. My opponent and I each drained our glasses once more, to the accompaniment of laughter and applause.

Once more Andrei refilled the glasses, returning to vodka. Once more we drank.

Suddenly, just as Andrei tried to hand him another glassful of scotch, the Soviet lad hit the floor. He lay there in the aisle of Brezhnev's airplane, motionless. American cheers greeted my ears, and the Senator slapped me on the back, congratulating me.

"Excuse me," I mumbled, suddenly feeling ill. I turned and stumbled back toward the front of the plane, steadying myself against the seat backs. In the background, I could hear the Senator saying loudly, "I told you he could do it. That's Ricky."

Somehow I managed to make it to the bathroom at the front of the plane, where I collapsed onto the floor. I hung my head over the toilet and disgorged as much of the alcohol as I could. Then I tottered back to my seat and sank into a comalike sleep.

I was still very drunk when, late that evening, we arrived in Tashkent, but the Senator pushed me forward, forcing me to function. Once on the tarmac, we encountered a reception line of sorts, headed by a rough-looking man in a tribal headdress. The Senator forced me in front of him, steadying me so that I would not fall. He whispered in my ear, teasing, "Oh, Ricky, you're swaying. What, you're not feeling well? You gonna be able to stand up? C'mon, c'mon, you gotta stay on your feet."

I elbowed him, and he responded with a boozy chuckle.

Someone introduced the mayor of Tashkent, and I pumped his hand. Then I shook the hand of the man in the tribal headdress. I heard Andrei introduce him as the president of the republic. He flashed a toothless grin at me as the Senator whispered in my ear, "Oh, brother. You gotta be kidding." Only with great difficulty did I stifle my laughter.

I realized that I had the hiccups. Then I thought I was going to be sick. I experienced a fleeting, horrible vision of vomiting all over the president of the Republic of Uzbekistan, and hoped that Regan would not memorialize the moment on photographic film. He had a perverse knack for catching us in some of our worst moments.

Somehow I managed to control myself. In a haze, I watched the Senator enter a car along with Kalicki and the president of the republic. Horowitz, Regan, and I were ushered into a second car, and Andrei joined us, explaining that we were driving to a special dacha, reserved for important guests.

"I can't believe how drunk I am," I moaned to Horowitz, who rolled his eyes unsympathetically.

It was late night before we arrived at the dacha. A Soviet doctor appeared to examine the rash on the Senator's back and confirmed the diagnosis—poison ivy.

By now I was aching for sleep, but we had to share another round of drinks with the president of the republic. I was thankful when he left after a single drink. *Now I can get some sleep,* I thought.

But the moment we were left alone, the Senator called for a review of tomorrow's agenda. We had to start early in the morning to complete the schedule of a very full day.

The Senator and I were still awake, going over the details, long after the others had gone to bed. Then the Senator, too, decided that he had had enough. "Wake me up at five-thirty," he requested, before leaving me alone. In the quiet of the night, with my head pounding, I asked myself, *Why the hell am I the one staying up?* And I answered, *You're the one who has to get everything ready for tomorrow. It's your job.*

After a mere two hours' sleep, my portable alarm clock blared in my ear. I crawled out of the sack, groaning, my head feeling as if it were going to split wide open. Dutifully, I woke the Senator.

He was a bit shaky also, so he prescribed his personal hangover potion for both of us—a Bloody Mary. It helped. The Senator dressed and went outside to run laps around the dacha.

Afterward, he took a bath, and I applied the cream potion prescribed to counteract his poison ivy. My head was still splitting and I could barely see straight. But after his first bath, he wanted another one, just to clean off the potion. So I drew that one as well.

Before attending to the major business of the day, we asked Andrei to take us to a local market so that the Senator could make his initial purchase for the food basket he was preparing for Brezhnev.

After that, Andrei took us on a tour of a Tashkent hospital, a surprisingly outdated facility. At the end of the tour we were ushered to a conference room for a panel discussion with several Soviet physicians. The Senator took his seat and, glancing to one side, noticed that the chair labeled DR. HOROWITZ was empty. He beckoned me over and asked, "Where is Larry?"

I shook my head in ignorance. This was a major gaffe. Horowitz was staff chief of the Health Subcommittee of the U.S. Senate. The Soviet doctors wanted to hear what he had to say.

Several minutes passed, but Horowitz did not show, so the panel discussion began without him. The Senator shot quizzical glances at me, but I could respond only with shrugs.

Another forty minutes passed, and the Senator's face grew ever more flushed. Suddenly, Horowitz entered the room. Trying not to make a scene, he slipped quietly into his chair at the speakers' table. I immediately moved toward him to find out what happened, and the Senator, ignoring the protocol of the meeting, rose from his chair and came over also.

"Where the hell were you?" the Senator hissed.

"I don't want to talk about it now," Horowitz snapped in return. "I'm not gonna talk about it."

Supremely miffed, the Senator returned to his seat.

Immediately after the meeting, the Senator and I both cornered Horowitz. Peter and Andrei were there, too. "Where were you?" the Senator demanded, nearly apoplectic. "You were forty minutes late. You just disappeared."

Horowitz's face turned beet red, but he did not answer.

Half in jest, the Senator asked, "Did you get locked in the bathroom again?"

Hearing that, Horowitz appeared as if he would be ill.

"Larry, what happened?" I asked.

"I don't want to get into it," he huffed.

We probed until we got the story. He had decided to slip off on his own to investigate those areas of the hospital that the Soviets had chosen not to let us see. He had made his way to a lower floor and entered a laboratory. The door slammed shut behind him and locked him in.

"Oh, Larry, I can't believe it," the Senator said, exasperated. Horowitz had a tight, mortified expression on his face, which the Senator immediately mimicked. We all burst into laughter.

Andrei reminded us of our schedule, so he piled us into a caravan of cars for a trip to a rural health clinic, outside Tashkent. Along the way, our driver encountered an unfamiliar fork in the dirt road and took a wrong turn.

The Senator realized immediately that here was a chance for us to see a locale that Andrei had not prepared. "Let's stop here and take a look," he suggested, hopping out of the car. The rest of us joined him.

"What? What?" Peter asked nervously. But he and Andrei could only follow.

To my surprise, the simple folk of the countryside recognized the Senator immediately. Their Asiatic faces broke into broad grins. Toothless old men rushed up to pump the Senator's hand. Suddenly, one woman grabbed the Senator by the arm and cackled excitedly, tugging at him.

"Let's look and see what she wants," he suggested.

The woman drew us toward her hut. She took us inside and pointed to a picture on the wall. After our eyes adjusted to the gloom, we saw a magazine photograph, clipped and framed, of President John F. Kennedy.

The Senator beamed, and so did Andrei.

We returned to the cars and headed for our planned destination. A banquet awaited us at the rural health-care center, but first we had to meet the community leaders in a reception tent. Our hosts passed around a bowl.

"This is the local custom," Andrei said. "Everybody has to take a drink, or they will be offended."

Someone handed it to the Senator, but he pushed it toward me, asking, "What is it?"

I glanced inside and saw a whitish liquid. "I don't know," I replied.

"Well, you taste it first."

"I'm not gonna taste it first."

Horowitz chimed in: "Rick, you gotta taste it."

Thanks, Larry. Everyone in the tent stared at me. I took a tentative sip and found it to be warm and sour, like curdled cream. I gagged on it. The wretched liquid slid to my stomach and settled onto vodka and scotch.

"Don't throw up," Horowitz ordered under his breath.

"It's mare's milk," Andrei finally explained.

Somehow I summoned a smile, and feigned another sip. This seemed to satisfy everyone, and both the Senator and Horowitz were spared the ordeal.

By the next day we were in Alma-Ata for the United Nations Conference on Primary Health Care. The Senator presented the keynote address, stressing that the subject of health care was an area in which people of the world could and should cooperate, sharing information and technology. His statesmanlike words brought a standing ovation.

In Moscow, we were taken to a dacha, located high on a hill overlooking the city, where we waited to see if the audience with Brezhnev had been arranged. Word came the next afternoon at the American Embassy, where we received a message that the Brezhnev meeting was on for that very day.

We piled into our cars and the caravan sped through Moscow, using a special VIP lane. We drove under a huge archway and then around the back of the Kremlin.

The Senator, Andrei, and Peter strode ahead of us toward Brezhnev's office, as Horowitz and I struggled with the crate of food from Tashkent and Alma-Alta. We ended up in an anteroom, where the Senator already waited.

Finally we were ushered into Brezhnev's main office. Our host was not there, and we waited for several more minutes before the aging Soviet premier shuffled into the room, accompanied by a bevy of personal attendants, grim-faced men in dark rumpled suits, who seemed prepared to catch Brezhnev if he should fall.

The premier beamed his thanks when the Senator presented him with a leather-bound copy of *JFK: Words Jack Loved,* and his grin grew wider when the Senator gestured and Horowitz and I stumbled forward with our crate of food.

We sat at a long table, the Soviets on one side and us on the other. Brezhnev was phasing in and out of conversation; sometimes he was coherent, but it was apparent, even through the interpreters, that at other times he lost the thread of discussion.

In the midst of the meeting, I excused myself politely, for I had to make some phone calls to the embassy to coordinate our travel plans. By the time I returned, the meeting was breaking up. Aides ushered the premier out of the room on wobbly legs.

We headed back toward the embassy and the security of the bubble. In the car, the Senator gave me a general briefing on what I had missed, including Brezhnev's reaction to the topic of the refuseniks. He had presented Brezhnev with a list of names, and asked the premier to consider allowing them to emigrate. The premier responded simply by saying that he would "look into" the matter.

Back inside the bubble, we reviewed our plans. We did not wish to offend Brezhnev unduly, nor did we wish to bring any serious consequences upon Andrei or Peter. Could we pull off a meeting with the refuseniks without creating an international incident?

Our embassy contact thought that we could. The Soviets viewed Kennedy not merely as a U.S. senator but as a potential President, and they would be careful. Hearing this, the Senator decided to forge ahead. The meeting was set for very late on this, our last night in the Soviet Union.

To keep up appearances, we had to follow our schedule, which meant a reception at Natasha's apartment. She had insisted on the opportunity to throw a good-bye party for us.

The Senator expressed his amazement at the elegance of Natasha's home, and we were both impressed by the array of food, set out in buffet style. Even more striking were Natasha's designer clothes and lavish jewelry. It seemed obvious that she was a plant, and that her party was a planned diversion to keep us busy on our last night in Moscow. This was made somewhat more evident by the arrival of several of Natasha's "friends," all comely, all handsomely dressed, all, somehow, signaling their availability with coy conversations in impeccable English. "KGB," I whispered to the Senator. "This is a setup."

He nodded his agreement and approached the evening with a wary twinkle in his eye. I breathed a silent prayer of relief, knowing that he would be on his best behavior. About ten-thirty he remarked politely that we had to leave, for we had an early flight the next morning. Natasha and her friends pouted.

By 11:00 P.M. we were back at the dacha. We informed the Soviet security personnel that we expected a phone call from the embassy, but, as far as they were concerned, we were ensconced for the night. Our man finally phoned about 12:30 A.M. Over the open line, he said that he was coming over to discuss our travel plans for the morning.

He arrived a short time later. The sentries, expecting him, allowed him inside the dacha.

"The way we gotta do this—" he explained, "—we just go out, get into the car, drive to the gate, and leave. If anything happens, if they try to stop us, I'll deal with it."

We stepped outside. The embassy man slid into the driver's seat, and the Senator took the passenger seat in front. Horowitz, Kalicki, and I crawled in the back.

The embassy man drove to the iron gate and found it closed. Peter and the head of the KGB detachment came over. "You can't go out," the KGB man said sternly.

The Senator turned to me and commanded, "Get out and tell him we are going."

I climbed out of the backseat and faced the KGB man. A guard emerged from the sentry box and stood next to him, his machine gun pointed casually.

Swallowing my anxiety, I warned, "You are going to have an incident. We have an appointment. We are going out."

"Well, where are you going?" the KGB man asked.

"We're going to visit some people in Moscow."

"You're not supposed to go out."

In measured words, I asked, "Are you going to prevent Senator Kennedy from going out?"

"It's my job to protect him. And I can't protect him if I don't know where he's going."

We were at an impasse. I slid back into the car and reported the conversation. The Senator suggested, "Tell him that we're going to this apartment building, and we will permit them to follow behind us. But they are not to interrupt us."

Once more I emerged from the car. I repeated the Senator's words to the KGB man, and repeated, "You better understand that there could be a major incident here if you don't permit us to go."

"One moment, please," he responded. He disappeared into the guardhouse, made a quick phone call, and returned with instructions to open the gate.

We drove off into the night, with a KGB contingent on our tail. By the time we arrived at our destination, only about fifteen minutes later, other KGB units had already stationed themselves around the perimeter of the designated apartment building, but they allowed us inside.

The elevator was broken, so we had to walk up about seven floors. We knocked at the designated apartment and an elderly woman opened the door a crack. She stared out at the sight of a young man, dressed in a business suit, pounding on her door in the middle of the night, and her eyes filled with terror. I realized suddenly that the group of desperate people inside had been alerted we would try to come, but they had no way of knowing with certainty whether it would be Americans or Soviets who would actually show up.

"Kennedy, Kennedy," I whispered.

The old woman did not move or otherwise signal recognition until I felt the Senator slide up behind me. Then a trace of a smile crossed her face. She let out a deep sigh and opened the door to us.

There were a dozen people here. Only a handful of them were refuseniks, but all were dissidents, brave enough to openly criticize their government. The group included Andrei Sakharov. The Senator introduced everyone, drawing nods of approval when he noted that Larry Horowitz's grandfather hailed from Kiev and that Jan Kalicki, too, was of Russian ancestry. The fact that both men were Jewish was also pleasing to this group.

It was a warm, wonderful several hours. Before we left, the refuseniks gave each of us a warm hug.

Later, after only a few precious hours of sleep, we left our dacha for the airport. The Senator had me check in with the embassy at the last moment to see if Brezhnev had yet issued any word concerning the refuseniks. He had not.

We flew an Aeroflot plane to Frankfurt, where, by transatlantic phone, we checked with our office and received apparent confirmation that Brezhnev would release the refuseniks on our list.*

In a celebrating mood, the Senator rushed off to the duty-free shop to buy Cuban cigars. A staffer warned, "You can't buy those!" It was illegal to bring Cuban tobacco into the United States.

"Rick, can I get them?" the Senator pleaded. "Is it okay if I get them?"

I shrugged and asked, "Do you think they will check your bags?"

"No," he replied, "they never stop us for anything."

Ah, the privileges of being a senator. With that, he bought the contraband cigars.

---

*When we returned to Washington, the Senator announced the releases at a press conference. The Soviets, apparently feeling that he had spoken too soon, held back on allowing the refuseniks to leave. However, later that year two of the families on the list were allowed to emigrate.

16 The phone woke me in the middle of the night.

I was sound asleep, dreaming something or other about the office. The caller identified himself as an AP reporter. "I need a statement from the Senator," he said. "The Pope died."

I found this supremely confusing. Rubbing my eyes, I said, "The Pope died two months ago."

"No," the reporter said. "The new Pope died. Heart attack."

I suggested, "Well, why don't you just hunt up the statement we released two months ago and use it again?"

"Fine," he agreed.

I hung up the phone, rolled over, and went back to sleep. I was utterly and totally exhausted. The time following the trip to Russia had been especially busy.

We had been traveling the country for Democratic Senate and congressional candidates. We had visited Iowa, Arkansas, Missouri, Michigan, and Illinois, but we weren't through yet. As part of the payback for Senator Cannon's support on the Cannon/Kennedy airline deregulation bill, Kennedy had agreed to appear this Tuesday in Nevada in support of Cannon's reelection campaign. But we faced a problem, for that was the very day President Carter was scheduled to sign the deregulation bill. Both Cannon and Kennedy, as cosponsors, needed to be there. We had informed Cannon that we could not make it to Nevada for the speech unless he arranged special transportation, and he did so.

So, on Monday night, we flew from Chicago to Washington, arrived at Dulles Airport about 6:00 A.M., rushed home to freshen up, and appeared at the White House for the Cabinet Room signing ceremony that put deregulation into law. Then, Cannon, Kennedy, and I jumped onto a White House helicopter and flew to Andrews Air Force Base, where we boarded a military flight to Las Vegas. That night, the Senator presented an effective speech in favor of Cannon's candidacy. He mingled with the crowd for a few moments before we raced back to the military plane for an appearance in New York.

Once, during the late-night flight, as the Senator and I plodded through paperwork, exhaustion overtook me. I reminisced about the "good old days" a year or so ago, when the Senator had routinely left for home in the evening with a single briefcaseful of work. These days, it was almost always two full briefcases.

The Senator looked at me for a moment, thinking about what I'd just said, and then reminded me of what he had said after the untimely death of Mary Murtaugh: "You gotta live it to the fullest."

The Senator and I labored equally hard when we were in the office, running from one appointment to the next. Besides the very long days at the office, there were very long nights with and without the Senator. With slowly building frequency I, too, was escalating my use of alcohol and coke as a way to loosen up after a particularly grueling day. The Senator believed, and it rubbed off on me, that working hard meant rewarding yourself by playing hard.

And he was certainly doing that.

The wild weekends in McLean were growing more frequent now. More than once, seeking out the Senator at his home to discuss some pressing point of business, I found him in the hot tub, naked, with a variety of others. It was clear they weren't simply there for the drinks and company. Bullets of coke lay conveniently nearby. Sometimes he said, "Come on, Rick, why don't you join us?"

If I was there in the evening, I could tell how things were going to get cranked up, and always politely declined. On infrequent occasions, always in the daytime, I did join him and Cindy in the tub. The water was therapeutic, and I knew it gave him a great deal of relief for his back, but once the drinks started being gulped down, the coke being snorted, and the Senator and Cindy started necking, I always got decidedly uncomfortable and would leave.

I was glad to be close enough to the Senator to know him perhaps better than anyone except Cindy, but there were limits.

Besides, at this point, I wasn't even sure how well I knew myself. Or how well I *wanted* to know myself.

On weekends I could usually count on a portion of free time, on Friday or Saturday night, to head for the Georgetown bars with my Washington buddies, to pick up women and to get blasted. Just as I'm sure sex, alcohol, and coke helped the Senator shield himself from the more painful recesses of his soul, all three worked as an anesthesia for me, numbing me to the more demanding pressures and stresses of my life.

The pressures of my schedule forced me to distance myself from my family and friends back home in Connecticut. Occasionally one of my old high school buddies would call and mention that he was hearing great things about me and suggest that we get together. Usually I was too busy. If I did set up a dinner engagement at a restaurant, I often had to cancel at the last moment. If I scheduled a dinner party at home, I might have to leave my friends to entertain themselves while I spoke on the phone for an hour.

All too often I had to defer a planned visit with Mom and Dad in Hartford. I knew that I was always welcome at home, but, after a time, the invitations subsided.

Guilt haunted me. But there wasn't even time to think about it beyond a moment of regret and a resolve to correct the situation . . . later.

My master's degree fell by the wayside. I finished my first round of classes, but I knew that I would never get around to composing a thesis. It didn't matter at that point. I couldn't envision myself anywhere but at the Senator's side.

Others, however, realized that you could get only so close to the Senator, and anything else was delusional.

One old girlfriend, for example, had long since given up her fantasies of a lasting romance with the Senator, but she still remained friendly with both him and me. About this time, she arrived in town for several days, bringing her current boyfriend with her. They spent some time at the Senator's house, and then she brought him over to meet me. She introduced him merely as Josh.

During the course of that weekend, as others dropped by, I was surprised to hear her introduce him by various other names.

"What's going on?" I asked her. "Who is this guy?"

She giggled that "Josh" was using aliases because he was a fugitive; there was a warrant out for his arrest in Florida on a charge of cocaine smuggling. She said that the Colombian drug cartel was also looking for him because he had stolen some money from them. The reason they had come to Washington was to speak with a lawyer about enrolling him in the Federal Witness Protection Program.

I stared at her in utter disbelief. This was too much. I

was furious. "I can't believe you took him to the Senator's house!" I raged. "Get him the fuck out of here."

As she was leaving she said to me, "Gee, Rick, I never knew you and the Senator cared so much. . . ."

Life went on.

Time magazine commented, "At this point, Kennedy seems to be emerging as the Democratic alternative to Carter if the president's trouble increases in the months ahead."

At the Democratic midterm convention in Memphis in December 1978, the Senator was scheduled to give a speech on the subject of national health insurance, but he seized the opportunity to attack President Carter's emphasis on military spending at the expense of social programs. It was a clear attempt to define his differences with Carter and offer the left wing of the Democratic party an alternative. And it worked, at least for the moment, bringing the delegates to their feet.

In actuality, many of the differences between the President and the Senator were largely a matter of slightly different approaches to the same problems. In fact, Senate voting records revealed that Kennedy supported Carter's legislative proposals 84 percent of the time—the fourth-highest score among one hundred senators.

The most obvious difference between the two men, as perceived by the general public, was in the intangible area of "leadership." If the Senator was going to challenge Carter for the presidency in 1980—and this was a mighty big "if"—it would have to be a battle of style, rather than substance.

In this arena, the President appeared highly vulnerable. Carter's own pollster, Patrick Caddell, conceded that the President was perceived as "an individual who often flip-flops on issues and positions." He warned that "American society . . . needs some kind of direction."

Kennedy had a firm vision, a feeling of where the

country should be going. He truly cared about people, and he believed—in his gut—that his presence in the White House could make a difference, could make things better for all. In a decade and a half in the Senate, he had accomplished as much or more than any of his colleagues, and he was the unquestioned standard-bearer of the liberal philosophy.

Above all, he was effective. He had developed into a master of the political compromise, able to forge the most unlikely of voting coalitions. As a result, the list of his legislative accomplishments was staggering.

More and more, his speeches carried a presidential aura and the legislation that he backed reflected his vision.

Lou Harris called constantly to update me on the latest figures reflecting a steady decline in Carter's popularity. He reported that in a theoretical race between Carter and the likely Republican nominee, Ronald Reagan, Carter would lose. Yet at the same time, Harris's polls showed that Kennedy could whip Reagan. Harris argued that Carter was creating a leadership vacuum in the Democratic party that only the Senator could fill. Here was a clear opportunity to rally the party, unite the Democrats, and win the presidency. It was an opportunity he had to take now.

Draft Kennedy movements sprung up in more states. It looked increasingly as if there was a chance at another Kennedy presidency.

Surveying the political landscape, I realized there was no one else who *could* be as great a President.

But occasionally I felt that he was spinning out of control, far worse than Jack had ever done. And so was I.

"I want you to handle this—and no one else," the Senator said to me in late spring. "I think we've got to do a meeting to talk about where we're going with Joan." He handed me a scrap of paper with two names and phone numbers. "Talk to Hawthorne," he said. "He'll give you some other names."

On the phone, Dr. Hawthorne and I produced a list of some of the most renowned psychiatrists in the nation—specialists in the treatment of substance-abuse problems. Joan's celebration of sobriety, with the cover stories in *People* and *McCall's,* had ended shortly before Christmas of 1978, when she had started drinking again. Depressed, she didn't even attend the holiday vacation with the family in Aspen, let alone McLean, but opted to spend Christmas alone with her demons in Boston. After that, she struggled, shakily at times, to remain sober. During the spring of 1979, Joan reentered the treatment program at McLean Hospital near Boston, and, after spending a period of time there, moved to a small halfway house on the grounds of the hospital.

After considerable effort I was able to arrange a time when several of the doctors could meet in Washington with Dr. Hawthorne and members of the family, including the Senator and Joan, Kara, Teddy, and Patrick, the Senator's sisters Eunice and Jean, and sister-in-law Ethel.

"We need a completely neutral location," Dr. Hawthorne advised. It took me a month to arrange the details. I booked suites at a hotel in Crystal City, Virginia, convenient to National Airport. Dr. Hawthorne and three of the specialists—one from Yale, one from the Mayo Clinic, and another from California—began their meeting on a Thursday afternoon. They reviewed Joan's case history and, in strictest privacy, discussed her case and her unique position in American life.

That evening, Joan flew in from Boston. She spent the night with the Senator and their children in McLean.

By Friday morning, the physicians were ready for their first round of meetings with us. We assembled in one of the suites: the Senator, Eunice, Ethel, Jean, and I. The doctors presented their collective findings. Joan's was a classic case, they agreed. She was a lifetime alcoholic whose problems were exacerbated by the circumstances of her life but not caused by them. One doctor declared, "There is nothing we can prescribe that will cure her. If she wants to get better, she'll get better, but she's got to do it herself. She's got to have the support of the people who love her."

Joan and the children joined us for the afternoon session. At first, Joan appeared a bit defensive at all the attention, and I wondered if Dr. Hawthorne had briefed her adequately.

Nevertheless, we pushed ahead. Dr. Hawthorne moderated the discussion, looking, in turn, to each person seated in the living room–style suite, drawing from us our feelings about how Joan would react to a possible presidential campaign.

Eunice was outspoken, and clearly rallying to Joan's side. She wondered openly whether a presidential campaign was in Joan's best interest.

Ethel and Jean were relatively quiet, but their feelings were clear: If the Senator wanted to run, they would support him, and help Joan all they could. It was Ethel, wide-eyed, who whispered, "It could be dangerous."

Kara, home from her first year at Trinity College in Hartford, decreed that she would support her father's candidacy only if her mother agreed.

"Dad could be a great President," Teddy said. "He has a lot to offer the country."

Fourteen-year-old Patrick, obviously shy in the face of this inquisition, sided with Kara. I was impressed with how all three children responded to this very adult meeting. They seemed to be maturing—Kara especially—into responsible, levelheaded individuals.

When his turn came, the Senator declared, "I want to

be President." He thought the timing was right. But he made it clear that he would defer to his family on this vital point.

I was surprised when Dr. Hawthorne turned to me, including me as a member of the family. He pointed out to the others that I was the one who had most closely monitored Joan's treatment, serving as the intermediary between himself and the Senator. I said simply, "Whatever the decision, I'll be here to help."

Finally it was Joan's turn to speak. After listening to her family, she had warmed up. She knew that the people in the room loved her, even if that love was flawed. "I want Ted to be President," she declared firmly. "And I think I'm strong enough. But I need more time."

"Fine," Dr. Hawthorne counseled. "This is the beginning of a process. We don't need an immediate decision."

The encounter session adjourned. Joan and the Senator went to McLean to spend the weekend with their children.

On Monday morning the Senator said to me, "Uh, I thought it worked out real well. Now, I, uh, want you to call Paul Kirk, to plan a series of meetings, to consider the issues involved in creating and well, you know, staffing a campaign organization." He suggested, "But, Ricky, let's do it somewhere where no one will see me."

Joan seemed to have resolved many things. She was searching for her own identity, and appeared to hold on to the concept of defining herself as Mrs. Kennedy; I believed that at times she was terrified by the thought of losing that label. Beyond that, she really wanted to live in the White House. With this clear goal in mind she was making tentative progress in overcoming her alcoholism. It was obvious that she was assuming more control of the details of her life, and this boded well for a presidential campaign.

Joan made plans to spend more time at McLean, and

when she was around nothing was left to chance. Both her schedule and the Senator's were programmed very carefully so that they could attend the kids' school functions, participate in campaign strategy meetings, make personal appearances, and, in general, take care of business while spending little time together, particularly alone in the house. We were creating the illusion of a marriage.

There was another consideration. Once, when Joan was due in for a full week, Larry Horowitz cautioned me, "Just make sure the Senator is cooling it with the liquor, okay?"

"We lock up the liquor cabinet when Joan is around," I told him. "But I'll remind the Senator to do that."

It turned out to be a simple precaution, but, in truth, Joan was doing well.

As it was, the tentative steps toward a presidential race were being made. The Senator was beefing up his speaking schedule.

We were flying from Boston to Cleveland in a small plane with three seats arranged in a file, one behind the other. The pilot sat up front, the Senator in the middle, and I was in the rear seat. During the first portion of the trip, the Senator craned his neck and I leaned forward so that we could discuss the details of the speech he was scheduled to give in Ohio. But as we neared our destination, we encountered an unexpected storm. Lightning swirled in the skies all around us and the plane bounced on heavy winds. We settled into our seats to ride out the turbulence.

Suddenly the plane's engine made a sputtering sound and the pilot's hands flew to various controls. The Senator turned and shouted to me over the noise, "I feel just like I did in 1964 when I went down in the plane crash."

The light aircraft began to bounce more heavily within the storm. I gripped the sides of my seat and clenched my teeth, saying silent prayers to Mother Mary. The nose of the craft plunged earthward in a frightening dive, but the pilot recovered quickly. The Senator repeated, "It feels just like it."

Then he leaned forward, with his chin over the pilot's shoulder. "Your altimeter is going down," he warned. "Check your flaps."

The pilot followed the Senator's advice and the plane steadied. Within minutes the engine regained its full power. We rode out the remainder of the storm and found calmer weather.

I asked the Senator, "How did you know what you were doing?"

"I know how to fly a plane," he responded. He explained that when he was western coordinator for his brother's 1960 presidential campaign, he had had to cover such vast distances that he took pilot training.

"Great," I said. "Tell me when you're going to go up; I'll be in another state."

He laughed.

In fact, one of the hidden snags of a possible presidential campaign was the Senator's chronic back pain, the legacy of the old plane crash. Prior to the campaign, that pain grew worse, and the Senator consulted with doctors in Massachusetts, who concluded that some of the vertebrae in his back were fusing; bone was eating into muscle tissue. They advised that they could correct the condition surgically, but he would then have to spend six months flat on his back. The Senator knew that his schedule simply would not permit this, so he determined to live with the pain.

That summer of 1979, he spent as much time as possible at the Cape, lying low.

Late one night when he was out of town, the police called me from McLean, reporting that the burglar alarm at 636 Chain Bridge Road had activated. A patrol car was on its way.

I hopped from bed, dressed, and sped to the Senator's house. By the time I arrived, officers had controlled the situation. They had found a disoriented and rambling woman roaming about on the lower floor of the otherwise-empty house, and were questioning her. They took her away for observation and later released her.

But she was back only a few nights later. The police and I went through the same routine, only this time the courts decided that she was stalking the Senator, and that was reason enough to commit her to an institution.

The incident was a reminder of how vulnerable the Senator was, and it was perhaps the most serious argument against a presidential campaign. Whenever he even vaguely considered the possibility of a run for the presidency, the Senator had to face the reality that someone might take a shot at him. Hickory Hill, with Ethel and her eleven fatherless children, was a stark reminder of the price of being a candidate. In nearby Arlington National Cemetery, where the flame on Jack's grave burned day and night, Ted Kennedy was also reminded of the price of being a President.

As we moved further into the preelection year of 1979, it became increasingly apparent that the Carter/Kennedy relationship was strained. Many Americans worried that the nation was in danger of losing its position of world leadership. A continuing energy crisis loomed. The economy appeared shaky. Carter returned to Washington on July 1 from an international economic summit in Japan, to learn that his approval rating had slipped to a dismal 25 percent.

Carter sequestered himself at Camp David for more than a week, conducting private conversations with the nation's intellectual, economic, and political gurus. Then, on July 15, he presented an emphatic televised address to the nation. He spoke bluntly about the "crisis of confidence . . . that strikes at the very heart, soul and spirit of our national will." He warned that the country was suffering from "malaise."

Many in the country were appalled by the speech, even furious. If there was a malaise, they felt, it was one generated by Carter himself.

The press and the polls got worse. Someone asked Carter what would happen if Kennedy declared his candidacy. The President snapped, "If Kennedy runs, I'll whip his ass." He was quite willing to repeat the remark, to make sure that he was not misunderstood.

When the Senator heard of this, he chuckled. "I always knew the White House would stand behind me, but I didn't realize how close they would be," he said.

17 As the torchbearer of liberalism in America, a
role he proudly cherished, there were, nevertheless,
a few areas where even the Senator wasn't sure of his
ground. The Senator had long struggled to find the proper
stance on the burgeoning issue of gay rights. He knew
that, as a leading liberal, he should be in favor of equal
treatment for everybody, but he, and others in the office,
seemed to have a hang-up on the subject.

It was Eddy Martin who, over the years, had consist-
ently warned, "If you come out for gay rights, the steelworkers in Boston are not going to vote for you."

"They'll go bananas," the Senator agreed with considerable chagrin. "What am I going to do?"

The question went unanswered for a while. Eddy went
on to work for HUD, and gay activists were turning up
the heat for a response. So I argued for a more pragmatic
approach. "Look, the steelworkers in Boston believe
you're the most liberal senator in America, so they assume you support gay rights. You think it makes any
difference to them as long as you don't waver on being
pro-union? That's all they care about. As long as you
don't abandon that, what are you worried about?"

Still the Senator wavered. Eventually his colleague

Paul Tsongas, the new junior senator from Massachusetts, beat him to the punch, declaring that he was in favor of equal-rights legislation for gays.

On the personal front, Cindy was turning to me more and more for the solace of conversation. She had become a lonely person, living with constant intrigue and a schedule pretty much dictated by the Senator's availability. In a weird way, it was a mirror of my own existence with the Senator.

At times I felt the three of us were almost in a bizarre ménage à trois, she taking care of his sexual and emotional life while I took care of his political and personal life, and the Senator, in his own way, took care of us. Cindy and I both saw and heard things that we could tell no one else—so we shared them with one another. We still spoke by phone daily, two and three times a day, and often at night, as well.

Now, on this weekend, we had a few quiet hours alone together. We were out at the Squaw Island house and everyone else was gone for the day. The afternoon was sunny and clear, but a strong sea breeze whipped the air. We sat on lawn chairs, with blankets wrapped around our legs. Cindy should have been in a good mood, but this afternoon she seemed particularly troubled.

After a time, she mentioned that she and the Senator had done coke the night before. We talked for a bit about his tendency for overdoing liquor and drugs. I said, "You know, we could probably do him a favor and try to get him to put the breaks on."

Cindy's response surprised me. "On one level, I agree with you, Rick. But you know what? On another level, I think it has this therapeutic effect on him."

We both knew that cocaine has the ability to relax inhibitions. Cindy was with him more than anyone else when he was high, which meant she was also privy to witness him at his most unguarded moments.

As if reading my thoughts, she unconsciously hugged herself for reassurance and said, "You know, there's so much he's buried. I just wish he had someone, you know, professional, to talk to. It might help him cut down on the partying."

I could be his adviser, his drinking buddy, his chief of staff, but I couldn't be his psychiatrist. Besides, I just didn't know how to assimilate it all. I was the right-hand man to the person who would be, perhaps, the next President of the United States. We had a campaign looming, and I wanted to devote my energies to that, not psychoanalyzing Edward Moore Kennedy.

We had ended the week on a pensive note, and I was glad to plunge into work Monday. Besides, there were other issues in my life to worry about. My girlfiend Sheila and I talked about getting married. But I knew I wasn't ready. Worse, I hadn't been totally honest with Sheila, who knew nothing about the secret agenda of my days and nights. She knew that my time was monopolized by the Senator, but she had no idea either that he was considering a run for the presidency—something I couldn't tell her—or that we spent some of our nights carousing. It wasn't fair to her, I know, but I was too selfish to give it more than a fleeting thought. I knew that if I looked at my life too hard, I might not like what I found. And so I didn't think about it at all.

One afternoon around this time, Joan Baez called on the Senator's private line and asked me to relay the message that she was coming to Washington for a concert and press conference on behalf of the boat people. As chairman of the Refugee Subcommittee, the Senator had a strong interest in the issue. Apparently he had befriended Joan Baez in the past. Now, she asked, did the Senator want to "get together" while she was in town?

"Yeah, have her come out Wednesday night," he said

when I told him. "Why don't you go pick her up and bring her out?"

She brought a female friend with her. I picked them up at the Madison Hotel at ten that evening, and drove the two women out to McLean. The famed folksinger was friendly, intelligent, and interesting.

"C'mon in for a drink, Ricky," the Senator invited.

The four of us sat around for a time, drinking and talking, until the others decided to continue the party in the Senator's hot tub. The Senator grabbed a bottle of wine and several glasses and said, "C'mon, Ricky, let's go."

"No, I'm tired," I said, truly exhausted by the end of the week. "I'm going home."

He looked disappointed, but he didn't push the issue.

At home, the renovations on my house were nearly done. Dad had a business appointment in Washington and Mom came along especially to visit me. I didn't invite them to stay at my home because I knew Dad wouldn't. He was one of those men who really didn't want to impose himself, and a hotel gave him the freedom he liked.

But, of course, Mom wanted to see the house. They came over and were supposed to find themselves greeted by Sheila. Typically, I had been called away on urgent business. While they were there, Cindy dropped over, too, and Barbara called. Earlier, Sandra had come and gone, concerned with a final decorating detail. My parents watched these very attractive women darting in and out, the phones ringing, and probably wondered if I was running an illicit business.

I maneuvered my schedule so I could see them for dinner at The Foundry. Our table—in the best location— was waiting when we walked in. The waiters were obsequious. Various patrons called out greetings and, throughout dinner, acquaintances from the Hill and from the press walked over to say hello. Mom was obviously impressed, but Dad appeared thoughtful and suspicious.

Mom had a lot of questions about Capitol Hill, and about everything that the Senator was accomplishing. She was a devoted Kennedy fan and at home often kept a number of television sets tuned to different channels so she wouldn't miss a beat. Most of all this night, she wanted to hear the gossip concerning the Senator's possible presidential campaign.

In the middle of dinner, I excused myself to make a call, and, as I was walking to the phone, I thought, rather guiltily, *What are they doing here? I've got a million things to do and all they want is chitchat.*

For the first time in my life, I didn't want to bother with my parents. What was I becoming?

I knew I was burning the candle at both ends, but it didn't seem to catch up to me until one Sunday morning when my housekeeper fixed me a mushroom omelet. I devoured it and then settled back to peruse the thick *Washington Post.*

Suddenly the letters began to dance in front of me. I rubbed my eyes and tried to read the comics, but the multicolored characters seemed to jump off the paper and hop into my lap.

I must be coming down with something, I thought. Either that or I'm really stressed-out.

Casting aside the newspaper, I turned on the television set and found "Meet the Press." Before I knew it, the panelists and the guests were in the living room with me, chatting away as if I were on the show with them.

Am I going crazy? I wondered, now seriously worried . . . and scared.

I told my housekeeper to take the rest of the day off.

Then I stumbled into my bedroom to sleep off whatever strange affliction had hold of me. But the black walls of my bedroom closed in. I felt as if I were in a cave. My heartbeat accelerated and I gasped for breath. *Is this a panic attack? Or a heart attack?*

The phone rang and I lunged for it.

"Hi," Cindy said cheerily. "How ya doing?" She was calling from McLean.

"I don't know what's happening," I complained. "I feel sick. I feel strange."

Cindy suggested that it must have been something I ate. "What have you had?" she asked.

"Just a mushroom omelet."

"Uh-oh," Cindy said. I heard her whisper something to the Senator, who was obviously at her side. I heard him laugh. Then Cindy explained. "When Kitty and I were over at your house yesterday, we put some mushrooms in the refrigerator. We forgot to take them with us and we forgot to tell you about them."

"Mushrooms?" I asked, confused.

"Mexican mushrooms," she said. "They're psychedelic."

"Oooh . . . God," I moaned, my mind spinning along with the room.

The last sounds I heard were she and the Senator in hysterics at the other end of the phone.

Not long after that, Cindy came to my house on a Saturday afternoon and joined me outside at the pool. We planned to go to dinner that night, then meet several of our friends at a club.

"We got some Quaaludes," she announced. "Do you want to try one?"

Quaaludes were the latest fad drug. They were downers, heavy-duty relaxants that were reported to make the user feel especially sensual. "Sure," I replied.

She offered me one of the clear capsules and I washed it down with a beer.

For a time I felt nothing, and I was disappointed. This was supposed to be the big new drug? It was a total letdown. But later, as we sat down at a table at the club, I felt sleep overtaking me, and then a wave of nausea. *How could anyone have sex on these?* I wondered.

But the next time the Senator sent me to his private desk, I checked his cigar box. There, in with the cocaine and rice, was a supply of clear capsules.

Network reporter Cassie Mackin, with whom the Senator had been drinking during his famous visit to Alaska during the late 1960s, was preparing a feature on the Senator. She and a tape crew followed him around Capitol Hill, taking footage of him in the Senate chamber, at hearings, and in the halls. Mackin wanted to run some tape of a normal day in the office, but we had some reservations. To conduct our business, we needed the freedom to speak and act naturally, without concern for cameras and microphones.

We worked out a compromise. We would allow the cameras in, to tape the background footage, but the sound equipment was to be turned off.

On a Wednesday, the crew set up in the Senator's office. Attempting to ignore their presence, we dove into the early-afternoon routine, which always included numerous phone calls. One of those was to Representative Edward J. Markey, the Democratic congressman from Massachusetts's Seventh District. He was a young, energetic liberal, a solid Kennedy colleague, a man whom we all knew well.

"Is Congressman Markey there?" I asked over the phone. "Senator Kennedy would like to speak with him."

When Markey took the phone, I said, "Congressman, please hold for the Senator."

I passed the phone over. The Senator glanced up from a pile of paperwork, looking suddenly puzzled. He clamped his hand over the mouthpiece and whispered in panic, "Ricky, what's his name? What's his name?"

"Markey," I reminded him.

"No, no, no. What's his first name?"

"Ed!"

The Senator nodded, removed his hand from the mouthpiece, and said in a syrupy tone, "Oh, Ed, how are you?"

To our chagrin, that exchange, in its entirety and *with sound,* ran on the evening news the following night, Thursday.

On Friday, the Senator took a morning flight to Boston. I was to join him later. As I boarded my afternoon flight, I suddenly heard the familiar voice of Ed Markey, calling out a greeting: "Oh, hi . . . uh, what's your name?"

"Ed, I'm really sorry," I apologized. "You know how it goes. Sometimes you have a block."

"Yeah, yeah," he said, disgruntled.

The television piece served only to further speculation about a Kennedy run for the nomination.

Conveniently, my new house featured a basement apartment with a separate entrance, perfect for a clandestine campaign office. Various committees met here, away from the inquiring eyes of the press.

We lined up a capable, high-powered staff. Steve Smith agreed to serve as campaign manager, a post that he had held for Bobby Kennedy in 1968.

Paul Kirk arranged a leave of absence from his law firm so that he could rejoin us for the great adventure.

Phil Bakes came on board as deputy campaign manager for administration. An aggressive Harvard graduate, only half a decade older than I, he was a former employee of the Anti-Trust Subcommittee who had worked with the Senator on deregulation issues.

The Senator's distant cousin Robert ("Bobby Fitz") Fitzgerald took charge of fund-raising. From the outset, he and the Senator had their own agenda; Fitz was one of the few who could get to the Senator without passing through me. Once a fund-raising decision was made, Fitz ran with it.

Rick Stearns, a state prosecutor in Massachusetts, agreed to come on board as our chief delegate counter.

Larry Horowitz and Stu Shapiro of the Health Subcommittee would alternate the duty as our traveling physician and health-issues adviser.

Carey Parker and Bob Shrum would handle the speech writing and serve as our "issues" people, ready to research and expound on any concerns that arose during the course of the campaign. Parker had been with the Senator longer than any of the rest of us, and he had a fine grasp of the Senator's ideas, as well as his manner of articulating them; Shrum, a heavyset, absentminded professor type, was a former legislative assistant to Senator McGovern, and was one of the better political writers in the business. When Shrum first joined us, we had to be careful that Parker's nose did not get out of joint, but they soon became good friends.

As a legal consultant, we hired Stephen Breyer, a Harvard Law School professor and consultant to the Judiciary Committee's Administrative Practice and Procedures Subcommittee.

An old friend, Dick Drayne, signed on as press secretary for our Washington office. Our traveling press secretary was Tom Southwick, a former reporter for *Congressional Quarterly.* He was only thirty years old, and some thought that was too young for such an important job. I bristled at that, for I was only twenty-six myself.

Carey Parker drafted a "book" for us, a briefing paper

to prepare the Senator for the inevitable questions concerning Chappaquiddick. Bob Shrum, Carl Wagner, and Tom Southwick offered suggestions and refinements. When it was ready, I placed it in the Senator's briefcase.

The tenth anniversary of the tragedy was upon us, and still its legacy would not go away. What more could the Senator say? The briefing book advised a straight, consistent, repentant line: There is no new information about Chappaquiddick. All questions have been answered. My actions were wrong and indefensible. I accept full responsibility.

Whatever the facts were in 1969, we still had to deal with the public perception a decade later.

Upon our advice, the Senator agreed to place a phone call to the parents of the victim, Mary Jo Kopechne.

"How do you think they'll react?" he asked.

I shrugged.

"Oooh, brother." He sighed, clearly not wanting to do it. He ordered the call put through, and I saw him shudder. That night would never, ever escape him.

When the Kopechnes were on the line, he apologized for the renewed attention caused by the anniversary of the tragedy, and by the speculation concerning his candidacy. The Kopechnes said they understood, and thanked him for the call.

"Thank God, that's over with," he said, after hanging up. After that, we decided that Chappaquiddick was a "manageable problem."

The election reform laws that the Senator had helped to pass in the aftermath of Watergate impacted on our plans. It was now illegal for an individual to contribute more than one thousand dollars to any one candidate. Thus, to be eligible for the new federal matching funds, the Senator was going to have to raise money from a far wider base than ever before.

Much of my time was spent in administrative details.

Numerous Senate staffers planned to join the campaign team, and I had to make sure they were officially transferred from the Senate payroll to the campaign payroll.

I would take a heavy pay cut, from my $48,000 salary as administrative assistant to $20,000.

All of this was necessary, but premature, for the Senator had still not made a final decision. He had a cookout at his home on Squaw Island, where he invited numerous friends and extended family members. As he grilled the hamburgers, he moderated the discussion. The question of the moment was: Should he run?

The consensus was yes.

I found a location in Washington, a former Cadillac dealership on K Street near Dupont Circle, central to the city's business district and offering plenty of space. Quietly I negotiated favorable rental terms, and apprised the Senator of my choice for a presidential campaign headquarters.

Late one night we drove over together so that he could approve my decision. He agreed to lease the building, but still he wavered on his decision.

Nevertheless, if he was going to run, we wanted to make sure he looked presidential. His half-moon glasses gave him a "granny" image that didn't fit with the "Kennedy youth" look, so we switched him to full-lens glasses with wire frames. We outfitted him with new tailored suits, but faced considerable problems with his weight, which tended to swing up and down.

I chided him about the bulging waistline. He liked to lace his coffee with cream and sugar; I forced him to switch to nondairy creamer and Sweet'n Low.

Once a month, regular as clockwork, a sweet little old lady named Gertrude sent the Senator a box of chocolate chip cookies from Boston. They were his favorite. Now, whenever the box arrived, I tried to hide it, but he sniffed it out. "Oh," he exclaimed, "Gertrude sent the cookies again. Where are they?'' When I tried to stonewall, he grew genuinely furious with me. "Ricky, I want those cookies!"

For lunches in his private office, I dictated healthier entrees, such as fish or a chef's salad. He grimaced, picking at the food, moaning about wanting a hamburger, but he knew that my motives were good.

One Monday morning he informed me that he had tasted a creamy French salad dressing over the weekend and had loved it; he wanted me to order a supply.

"It must have fifteen million calories in it," I warned.

"Never mind," he countered. "I want it for lunch today. Call the mailroom and send somebody out for a bottle."

I tried to ration him. At lunch, with a healthy salad in front of him, he prepared to load it with creamy French dressing. I grabbed the bottle and doled out a single teaspoonful.

"I want more! I want more!" he demanded, pounding his fists on the table in mock revolt.

I returned the bottle of salad dressing to the small refrigerator. The Senator jumped to his feet, ran to the refrigerator, grabbed the bottle, and smothered his salad. Grinning sheepishly, he said, "Ricky, I'm the boss."

For a time, he went through every fad diet, usually suggested to him by Eunice or Larry Horowitz. I came to expect an announcement on Monday morning: "All I can eat is . . ."

He even tried the Scarsdale diet.

And he started jogging more, further fueling speculation.

During the Senate races that summer, a series of CBS "Evening News" reports in late August concluded that Carter faced an all but unstoppable obstacle to renomination if the Senator decided to challenge him.

Toward the end of August, I called Hamilton Jordan

at the White House. "The Senator has something personal he wishes to discuss with the President," I said. Jordan suggested lunch. We consulted our respective calendars and set a date early in September.

The day before, someone called me from the White House kitchen, asking me what the Senator would like to eat. I recommended a chef's salad with low-calorie dressing.

I accompanied the Senator to the White House so that I could record his thoughts immediately afterward, during the drive back to the office. As he went upstairs for lunch, I waited in the Map Room, talking things over with Jordan. After a time, Jordan excused himself and left me alone. I delved into my briefcase and studied reports for the next hour and fifteen minutes.

Upstairs in the residential quarters, on an outdoor terrace overlooking the Rose Garden, Mrs. Carter joined the President and Senator for a brief time, and the atmosphere remained cordial.

The First Lady left and, over their luncheon, the two national leaders discussed various current issues and the conversation remained civilized. The Senator spoke about his feeling that the country was adrift and needed stronger leadership. He quietly announced that for the sake of the Democratic party, and the country, he was going to make an effort to attain the presidency. Unstated was the hope that the President would gracefully bow out, leaving the Senator with an open field.

But it was not going to be that easy. President Carter demurred politely. He agreed that the country was beset by problems, but declared his belief that *he* was dealing with these problems effectively.

They finished their discussion over coffee, and then the President and the Senator returned to the Map Room, along with Jordan. Jordan introduced me to the Presi-

dent, who greeted me warmly. To my astonishment, he
then left the Senator with Jordan and took me on a tour
of the Map Room, taking his time, commenting, "This is
where President Roosevelt and Churchill met." He
pulled out various maps to show them to me, seemingly
unhurried. I said to myself, *No wonder this guy won in '76.
He has the ability to make you feel like you're the most
important person in the world.*

Finally the President and Jordan walked us out to the
Rose Garden, to our car, where driver Jay Morgan
waited. The President shook hands with us both and
wished us a good day.

Afterward, as we rode back to the Senate, I commented, "God, the President was so nice to me. It was
incredible."

The Senator was livid. He snapped, "That's just because he wanted to irritate me. He did that on purpose.
He knew I was waiting. He wanted me to get the impression that he was unfazed by what I said."

On the drive back, as he detailed what had transpired
during lunch, the Senator could not resist an imitation of
Carter's southern drawl. He grinned at me and purred,
"Meester Prez-e-dent."

We both laughed.

We had reason to be glib, for the polls—and the press
coverage—were universally positive. On September 6 we
leaked a story to the press, indicating that neither Rose
nor Joan would oppose the Senator's candidacy.

The following day, CBS's Bruce Morton cited a poll
showing the Senator with a 53–16 lead over Carter and
reported, "The consensus among political professionals
here is that Edward Kennedy can have the Democratic
presidential nomination anytime he wants it."

Leslie Stahl quoted House Speaker Tip O'Neill as saying of the Senator: "I don't think he can be denied the nomination if he runs."*

However, Carter pulled a masterstroke of partisan politics in order to negate any influence that might be wielded by the powerful Speaker of the House. The president invited O'Neill to be his guest at the seventh game of the World Series between the Pittsburgh Pirates and the Baltimore Orioles. During the game, Carter asked O'Neill to serve as chairman of the 1980 Democratic National Convention. From the moment O'Neill accepted, he was neutralized. As convention chairman, he would have to remain officially uncommitted to any candidate.

Not long after that, on an overcast, threatening morning, we flew to Boston to meet Pope John Paul II. At Logan Airport, the Senator stood in front of the receiving line, along with First Lady Rosalynn Carter and Tip O'Neill. Farther down the line, I waited with Joan, Kara, Teddy, and Patrick.

Later we went to Boston Common, where tens of thousands of people had assembled to see the Pope celebrate the Mass. An altar was set up at one end of the Common. We located the VIP area and made our way to a special seating section of folding chairs, arranged near the altar. The heavens opened, soaking us. Patrick and I shared an umbrella, but the rain did not spoil the magic of the hour.

Afterward, as the Senator and his family went to their apartment, I headed for the Ritz, checked into a suite, and informed the desk that I was expecting a visitor: Kitty Brewer.

---

*Later, in his book *Man of the House,* O'Neill disclosed that he warned the Senator against running. "Forget the polls," he advised. "You can't beat an incumbent president." He added, "Besides, you've got the morality issue." He called Chappaquiddick a "millstone . . . that just won't go away."

She arrived early in the evening and the Senator appeared shortly thereafter. "We're having food sent up," he said. "I'll be out of here by eleven." He was just leaving when I returned at about that time.

Late summer turned into fall and on October 18, Milton Gwirtzman, a Washington attorney and sometime speech writer, who considered himself much closer to the Senator than he really was, called to inform me: "Rick, I'm sending over a memo that is for the Senator's eyes only."

"Okay," I replied with a sigh. I knew that the Senator would want me to read it first anyway. He always rolled his eyes when something came in from "Miltie."

Gwirtzman's "top secret" missive was a two-page, single-spaced typewritten letter, addressed to the Senator. Gwirtzman said he wrote at the suggestion of Steve Smith. Gwirtzman's letter prompted the Senator, as a potential candidate, to consider how he would deal with the womanizing issue. He pointed out that Hamilton Jordan's alleged sniff of cocaine brought six minutes of coverage as the lead on the national news and predicted allegations of womanizing—whether true or not—would get even more coverage.

He suggested the Senator ask himself six tough questions:

1. Had he violated the law (underage girls, illegal drugs)?
2. Was he involved with women who had links to unfriendly governments?
3. Were any liaisons arranged by persons seeking legislative favors?
4. Were any of the women famous?
5. Had he fathered any illegitimate children?
6. Did anyone have any pictures?

Steve Smith, Gwirtzman said, wanted to help the Senator prepare a response.

Gwirtzman then offered this piece of advice: "Whatever you do, tell the truth."

He suggested that the Senator respond that, during his wife's illness, he did see other women, "but this part of my life is behind me."

After reading Miltie's "top secret" questions, we knew we could not give six "No" answers. It was just like our little secret. Poor Miltie never knew just how accurate some of his concerns were.

But I did—and I decided to set up strict ground rules for his conduct during a campaign. "There are certain things you cannot do," I lectured. "The personal staff is off limits. Stay away from any women on the advance staff. It will get out. The press is going to be all over the place, and there is no way you'll be able to keep secrets from them." I told him that we could arrange meetings with Cindy or Kitty or Barbara by bringing them into my hotel room. "But the staff is off limits," I repeated.

"I agree," he responded. "I'm not stupid."

18 October 20 was a brisk autumn day, what one observer described as "political weather." This day, the dedication of the John F. Kennedy Presidential Library would provide an opportunity for the unannounced candidate to contrast his speaking style with that of the President of the United States. Both Carter and Kennedy were scheduled to present speeches, and we hoped that Carter would flub his opportunity.

After a by-now normal hectic morning of preparing and organizing the family, we arrived at I. M. Pei's impressive black-and-white, concrete-and-glass creation. The President arrived, and took some time making his way to the podium. He stopped to shake the hands of the assembled Kennedy cronies, some from Jack's Camelot days, some from Bobby's Impossible Dream era, and some from the enemy camp that would now challenge him for his job. He surprised everyone, most especially Jackie Onassis, by kissing her on the cheek. Carter had never met Mrs. Onassis before. The former First Lady recoiled as if bitten by a snake. My eyes met the Senator's. I heard someone behind me whisper, "I can't believe he just did that."

Young Joe Kennedy presented a volatile speech. He

had been miffed to learn that the library's biographical presentation included a forty-five-minute film about his Uncle Jack and only a fifteen-minute film on his father. His irritation had grown when it was decided to cut five minutes from each film—this making the difference even more disproportionate. He had staged a tantrum, refusing to deliver his dedication speech, until the Senator had cajoled him into it. Now, his demeanor was stern, and he directed his anger at Carter. The words were unduly harsh and brought a grimace from the Senator, but the assembled cousins loved it.

The Senator took the podium, glanced toward the ocean, and remarked of his brother Jack, "His passion for the sea would have made him a great explorer. He might have sailed with Magellan, navigating beyond the charts to the new and better world he sought."

Unfortunately, for our purposes, the President presented a fine speech, using witty quotations from Jack Kennedy to mock the Senator's current presidential ambitions.

It was then that we realized that if the Senator was going to announce formally, he had to do it soon. California governor Jerry Brown (who was also outdistancing Carter in the polls, albeit by a considerably lesser margin) seemed ready to enter the race. We made plans for a formal press conference on Wednesday, November 7, in Boston's Faneuil Hall.

Everyone *knew* that the Senator was going to run, but until he announced it formally he had to remain coy on the subject. During this interim period he was beset with interview requests.

"Barbara Walters called me again last night," Eunice Shriver reported to me on the phone. "Would you please talk Eddie into giving her an interview."

I sighed, but I promised to relay the message.

"It would be a good piece," Eunice promised. "We can check out the questions in advance."

When I had a moment with the Senator, I reported the call. Once more Barbara Walters was requesting an interview, through the conduit of her friend Eunice.

"Forget it!" the Senator snapped. "Can you imagine Barbara asking me, 'Whom did you sleep with last night?'"

A more palatable request came from CBS newsman Roger Mudd. The Kennedy/Mudd relationship went back many years. We had even done a personal favor for Mudd by hiring his son as a summer intern. To all of us, this seemed to be a great opportunity to launch the pre-campaign publicity, although we were very wary about any attempts Mudd might make to get the Senator to throw his hat into the ring prematurely. Nevertheless, the Senator was sure that Mudd would provide a friendly forum, and he agreed.

A taping crew visited the office and recorded a lengthy interview. Mudd's questions were pointed, and the Senator's answers were somewhat evasive. We were not ecstatic with the results, but the Senator was certain that Mudd and his editors would treat him kindly.

Then Mudd upped the ante, suggesting that CBS bring its cameras to Squaw Island to record footage of a typical Kennedy family weekend. Mudd was persistent, pestering the Senator with phone calls. He blithely assumed acquiescence and badgered the Senator for a date. The Senator debated the pros and cons with our group of advisers. The consensus was that no harm could be done by allowing the taping.

"What do you want?" I asked the Senator as the appointed weekend approached. "Do you want Tom and me to be up there with you?" Press secretary Southwick and I were scheduled to travel to the Cape to sit in on the session.

But the Senator knew that we had been working very hard, and he suggested, "Why don't you just stay in Washington and take the weekend off? I can handle this. It's just going to be pictures of the family, and there's a town meeting in the morning that they can film." He added with a shrug, "It's just Roger."

At the appointed time, Mudd and his crew arrived at Squaw Island and were greeted by a chaotic array of Kennedy offspring and pets. Phones rang, dogs yelped, and children popped in and out. The taping crew hovered amid the turmoil, recording it. Finally Mudd said to the Senator, "Can I get two more minutes with you?"

The Senator demurred. "Well," he said, "I thought we already did that."

"Oh, come on, Senator," Mudd insisted. "We're all set up here."

Reluctantly, the Senator agreed. The two men settled on captain's chairs overlooking the Atlantic. The cameras rolled.

As soon as Mudd and his crew departed, the Senator called me in a rage. "That son of a bitch ambushed me. Cornered me with the worst questions! I should've known it, damn it!"

We spent the next several days concentrating on damage control. We considered calling a special press conference so that the Senator could announce his candidacy sooner than planned. This would put CBS in a bind, for the equal-time provision of the nation's basic broadcasting law would force them to provide valuable airtime for all the declared Republican and Democratic candidates.

But in the end, we did not wish to be rushed. The Senator wanted to make his announcement at the scheduled time, in Boston, and we thought we could weather the storm.

Meanwhile, an October issue of *Time* magazine appeared, with a cover story about the Senator. Accompanied by photos of him strolling on the beach with his mother, playing touch football with his niece, pressing the flesh in Philadelphia, relaxing at the helm of his fifty-five-foot sloop, and brainstorming in his book-lined library in McLean, the text spoke of his newly subdued life-style, contending that, according to "intimates," he was troubled by his problems with Joan "and his lingering sense of guilt over . . . Chappaquiddick." The magazine indicated that it was only after he experienced marital difficulties that he turned to "dalliances" with women such as socialites Amanda Burden, Paige Lee Hufty, skier Suzie Chaffee, and Margaret Trudeau, "among others." *Time* noted that for the past year "there has been no report of an affair," and quoted the Senator's proclamation: "It doesn't happen." The piece also quoted *Washington Star* gossip columnist Betty Beale: "He never frequents parties and he never goes out."

The same issue of the magazine quoted a Carter spokesman as wondering whether the Senator had "the stomach" to handle the rigors of a campaign. Another Carter aide warned, "He's going to get clawed. He's going to bleed. . . ."

Well, the bleeding began on November 3, when "Saturday Night Live" opened with a scene of a crowd eagerly awaiting the Senator's press conference announcing that he was a presidential candidate. The role of the Senator was played by comedian Bill Murray, who arrived late, dripping wet, covered with seaweed, and unable to explain what had happened to him.

But that brief, if biting, skit was a minor scratch compared to the damage inflicted the following evening, during the hour-long special "CBS Reports: Teddy." Early in the report, as the screen depicted Roger Mudd and Ted Kennedy relaxing in the idyllic environment of Squaw Island, Mudd asked how fair the press had been to the Kennedys, and to what degree should the press separate the issues of a politician's public and private life?

The Senator responded, "Well, I think there's a natural inquisitiveness of people about all aspects of—of people's lives. I—I mean, I sort of understand that."

Thus encouraged, Mudd inquired, "What is the present state of your marriage, Senator?"

Caught off guard, the Senator, who was not a good spontaneous speaker at the best of times, stumbled. He replied, "Well, I think it's a—we've had some difficult times, but I think we'll have—we've—I think been able to make some very good progress and it's—I would say it's—it's—it's—I'm delighted that we're able to share the time and relationship that we—that we do share."

"Are you separated or are you just . . . what?" Mudd probed.

The Senator scrambled for an explanation: "Well, I don't know whether there's a single word that should—have a description for it. Joan's involved in a continuing program to deal with the problems of—of alcoholism, and—and she's going magnificently well, and I'm immensely proud of the fact that she's faced up to it and made the progress that she's made. And I'm—but that progress continues, and that—it's the type of disease that one has to continue to—to work."

After a commercial break, the show resumed. Unfortunately it was dealing very dramatically with Chappaquiddick. Roger Mudd and a camera crew had gone over to the island, and Mudd had driven repeatedly over the same route and under the same conditions that the Senator had taken on that fateful night. Even worse, the CBS crew had placed a camera on the car's front fender, with the lights of the car being the only illumination, moving smoothly at first down the paved road, and then turning, and bouncing up and down along the rough

25¢

path, until the camera abruptly stopped wher͟ had gone off the bridge.

It was chilling, even for me, his closest aide. It ͟ ͟ ͟ed like an amazingly realistic re-creation.

The Senator's off-camera voice declared, concerning Chappaquiddick: "I'd respond to any particular question that you'd have. I'll answer any question that—that you have to that you have right now—I'll answer any question you want to ask me, and I'll answer any question that is asked me during the course of a—a campaign—I'm glad to answer any question that you have right now on any aspects of any of it."

Mudd editorialized, noting that the Senator "still does not seem at ease" with the subject. He suggested that the Senator might wish to "say something more."

The Senator, very ill-at-ease, mumbled, "Oh, there's—the problem is—from that night—I found the conduct, the er, ah, the behavior almost beyond belief myself. I mean that's why it has been—but I think that's—that's—that's the way it was. Now I find it as I have stated that I have that the conduct that—that evening in—in this as a result of the impact of the accident of the—and the sense of loss, the sense of hope and the sense of tragedy and the whole set of—circumstances, that the, er, ah, behavior was inexplicable."

Mercifully, the network cut to a commercial. When the telecast resumed, the scene switched to the Senator's office, where Mudd had interviewed him three weeks earlier. Mudd asked the Senator why he wanted to be President.

The interview was going downhill fast.

He stammered, "Well, I'm—were I to—make the—announcement . . . is because I have a great belief in this country, that it is—has more natural resources than any nation in the world, has the greatest educated population in the world, the greatest capacity for innovation in the world, and the greatest political system in the world. . . . And the energies and the resourcefulness of this nation, I think, should be focused on these problems in a way that brings a sense of restoration in this country by its people to . . . And I would basically feel that—that it's imperative for this country to either move forward, that it can't stand still, or otherwise it moves back."

The good news was that, this same night, ABC ran the first network showing of *Jaws,* which devoured 57 percent of the viewing audience. The bad news was that those who did watch the Mudd interview included the nation's most influential political writers, campaign officials, and opinionmakers.

The reviews were universally bad, even from reporters whom we considered friends. Unlike the Senator, these observers did not believe that CBS had sandbagged us.

The worst news, from both a patriotic and political standpoint, came next. Militant students in the new Islamic Republic of Iran had seized the U.S. Embassy in Teheran and held American citizens hostage, demanding the return of the exiled Shah Mohammed Reza Pahlevi. Suddenly and unexpectedly, Americans were united in their anger and fear. Partisan considerations took a backseat. It was time to rally 'round the flag.

Just as suddenly, Secret Service agents were assigned to guard the Senator. This came directly from President Carter, who was smart enough to know that one thing he never wanted to be accused of was letting the third brother get shot. Wherever the Senator went now, it would be by bulletproof limousine, led and trailed by a long motorcade of black sedans and station wagons, their red lights stuck on their hoods and flashing behind their grilles, filled with agents packing Uzis.

Joan moved back home so she could appear with him at every opportunity. With Joan and the children gearing up for the campaign trail, a governess was no longer necessary. Carol resigned and accepted a job in our campaign organization.

The morning of November 7 found us in Boston, tingling with anticipation. There were a thousand details to handle.

It was important to create the media image of one big happy family. We could afford to let no one know that, on the previous night, Joan had slept alone in the bedroom of the Boston apartment as the Senator tossed and turned on the sofa.

Joan's secretary, Marcia Chellis, spent the morning attending to Joan's appearance, as others rehearsed her for her moment in the sun. Eddy Martin (working unofficially for us as a campaign adviser) had arranged for Joan to answer a special question. While Joan practiced her answer and the Senator studied his notes, I made sure the beds were made, so that a nosy reporter could not determine last night's sleeping arrangements.

Later that morning, in Faneuil Hall, the Senator addressed the voters. Secret Service agents eyed the spectators warily—this was their first public test, guarding a man whose candidacy clearly troubled them more than any other politician's. Campaign workers hovered. The press was everywhere.

Speaking from a prepared text, the Senator was decisive and coherent:

> Today I speak to all the citizens of America, but I wanted to speak to you from home, here in Boston. For many months we have been sinking into crisis. Yet we hear no clear summons from the center of power. Aims are not set. The means of realizing them are neglected. Conflicts in directions confuse our purpose. Government falters. Fear spreads that our leaders have resigned themselves to retreat.

The Senator pressed on. He announced that, despite the fact that a Democrat was in the White House, eligible for reelection, he was a candidate for President of the United States. One of his reasons was to prevent other Democrats—senators, congressmen, governors, and mayors—from losing their own offices due to an ineffective President.

He concluded his televised speech with a rallying cry:

> Let us carry forward the golden promise that is America. And if we succeed at that, then someday we can look back and say that this hall was rightly chosen for this day by renewing the promise of our forebears. We will have earned our place on this platform.

Following the speech, the Senator took questions. He answered the first few and then pointed to Eddy Martin's cronies, planted in the audience. The man asked, "Senator, is Joan in favor of your running for President?"

The Senator paused slightly. Then, as if on impulse, he turned to his wife and said, "Well, let Joan answer that."

Joan came to his side, glanced warmly at her husband, and responded by saying how much she loved him and her family. She declared that she was really looking forward to living in the White House.

For better or worse, the campaign was under way. We made arrangements to lease a Boeing 727 from United Airlines, which they promised to outfit lavishly, turning it into a flying office.

The aircraft was not ready yet, so we leased three planes—one for us and two for the press—for our first major swing through New Hampshire, Maine, Illinois, Colorado, and California. The question was, Who should come along?

A consensus emerged in early strategy sessions that, at least during this initial stage, Joan's presence might hinder rather than help. The press, seeing her at the Senator's side, might be more likely to raise the "character" issue. But making the decision to exclude Joan was simpler than implementing it. A healthier Joan was a feistier Joan; she was looking forward to the trip and probably already had her bags packed.

It was my job to explain our political reasoning to Dr. Hawthorne, by phone, and I was quick to add that we considered this decision to be in Joan's best interest.

"That's good," he agreed. "It's less stress for Joan."

Dr. Hawthorne took the responsibility, explaining to Joan that *he* thought it best for her to stay home.

Joan accepted this opinion with grace, and, with that settled, we set off.

Unfortunately, the Senator's great moment was upstaged by continuing coverage of the Iranian hostage crisis, which seemed to be growing more serious by the moment. The Senator's announcement was drowned out on television and buried in the newspapers.

Our efforts to minimize Joan's presence failed to defuse the "character" issue. Whereas precampaign polls had indicated that Chappaquiddick would not be a major issue, the press now jumped on it.

Columnist William Safire coined the term *Waterquiddick*.

The New York Times picked up on that theme, warning that if it was ever proven that the Senator "used his enormous influence to protect himself and his career by leading a cover-up of misconduct . . . there will hang over him not just a cloud of tragedy, but one of corruption, of the Watergate kind."

Political cartoonist Oliphant produced a caricature of former President Nixon eyeing the Senator and musing, "So once upon a time he went on TV and lied to the people; so what's wrong with that?"

And then there were other things to consider. . . .

On Wednesday, November 28, thirty-eight-year-old Suzanne Osgood of Boston entered our offices shortly before 10:00 A.M., armed with a five-inch hunting knife, screaming incoherently. Secret Service agent Joseph Meusburger wrestled the knife away from her, suffering a small cut on his left wrist. Upon investigation, we learned that the assailant had a history of mental problems. In addition, reporters learned that she was a member of the 1963 class at Wheaton College in Norton, Massachusetts, and was a classmate of Esther Newberg, one of the women who had attended the Chappaquiddick party in 1969 with the Senator and Mary Jo Kopechne.

It was eerie to say the least. From that moment on, the Senator and I developed a particular affinity for Meusburger.

The evening of December 2, we found ourselves in a San Francisco hotel suite, trying to recover from fourteen hours of nonstop campaigning. In the bedroom of the suite, the Senator was giving an interview to Rollin Post, a longtime Bay Area political analyst for KRON-TV. Kara, Pat Lawford, and Tom Southwick had collapsed, the three of them lying across one of the beds, out of camera range. Larry Horowitz and I were in the next room, propped against a wall, idly listening to the course of the question-and-answer session. The Senator himself was exhausted and off guard.

When Post asked how the Senator felt about Carter's decision to allow the deposed Shah of Iran to enter the United States, we heard the Senator say that the deposed Shah had presided over "one of the most violent regimes in the history of mankind. How—how do we justify, in the—the United States on the one hand accepting that individual because he would like to come here and stay here with his umpteen billion dollars that he's stolen from Iran, and at the same time say to the Hispanics who are here legally that they have to wait nine years to bring their wife and their children into this country?"

Horowitz and I both cringed. "Did he say what I think he said?" I asked. Horowitz nodded.

It was a huge gaffe. In America, at the moment, a politician dared not attack the Shah. The Ayatollah was the devil that had taken Americans hostage, and, by comparison, the Shah was the good guy. Yet here was the Senator, agreeing with Khomeini's assertion that the Shah was a criminal.

The moment the interview ended, Horowitz and I grabbed Southwick and asked, "Tom, did the Senator say what we think he said?" We posed the same question to the Senator, who responded, "Yeah, I did. I believe it." He pointed out that he had geared his comments to the large Hispanic community in California.

For once, the Senator was the lead item on every evening news show, but this was not the coverage we wanted. As Horowitz and I had feared, the stories generally presented only the first portion of the statement and did not include the Senator's comments regarding Hispanic immigrants, which helped put the issue in perspective.

Reporter Leslie Stahl declared that Carter's advisers were convinced that the Senator had blundered "and decided to draw attention to it." Indeed, Carter jumped on the "unpatriotic" comment and used it to attack us.

But the most harmful response came from the streets of Teheran, where mobs of Iranians took to the streets, cheering for Senator Kennedy. This was not an endorsement we craved.

We were in Reno the following day and the press followed up unmercifully, dogging the Senator to expand on his comments about the Shah. By then, we had managed to throw together an official explanation: The Senator simply wanted to make clear that his support for the freedom of the hostages did not mean that he had gone soft on dictators.

The explanation did not wash well, either publicly or privately, and we discovered this when we headed to Southern California later that month for a whirlwind visit with various celebrities, arranged by producers Ted Ashley and George Stevens. Our goal was to enlist them as volunteer performers in a series of fund-raising events. Our first stop was the Malibu home of Neil Diamond. The singer was supportive of the Senator's campaign but expressed dismay over what he perceived to be the damaging comments about the Shah. The Senator attempted to explain that the press reports were incomplete and misleading, but Diamond remained dubious and we were unable to convince him to actively join our cause.

Our next stop was at Barbra Streisand's sprawling ranch in one of the canyons near Malibu. We spent several hours with Streisand and her companion, Jon Peters, discussing issues, most particularly the situation in Israel. When we asked Streisand if she would perform at a fund-raising concert, she was supportive but reluctant. She said that she had not done a political benefit since she sang for the McGovern campaign in 1972 and, although she agreed with the Senator's position on the issues, she disliked performing before large crowds of people.

"But I'll think about it," Streisand promised, clearly not making a commitment.

Finally we headed for the Hollywood Hills home of Warren Beatty. As we walked through the gate toward the front of the house, we heard a pack of menacing guard dogs signaling our approach. Flanked by the Senator, backed by an army of wary Secret Service agents, I rang the doorbell.

After a few moments, the door opened, revealing Warren Beatty, clad only in a pair of wet undershorts. He smiled and invited us in. One of the Secret Service agents accompanied us inside.

The house was centered upon a glass-enclosed atrium,

where a beautiful young bikini-clad woman languished in a hot tub. Jack Nicholson sat at a table in one corner of the kitchen. He, too, wore only sopping undershorts as he engaged in conversation with another nubile beauty, his famous eyebrows raised, the grin looking very mischievous.

Despite this somewhat bizarre atmosphere, we engaged Beatty and Nicholson in an intelligent discussion, but they, too, were wary of the Senator's political future in the wake of the Shah comment and would not, at this time, agree to appear at a fund-raiser.

Still, politics was politics and pleasure was pleasure. Beatty was determined that the Senator go away at least happy in some respect. So he drew us over to the woman in his hot tub.

"Hi," the Senator said with enthusiasm.

"Hello," she responded with a giggle.

We tried to make small talk, but it seemed very awkward. The Senator and I were in business suits and Beatty stood next to us in his shorts, while the woman's bathing suit covered little of her. The Senator seemed to be enjoying himself.

Concerned with our schedule, I tried to move things along. Beatty had agreed to let the Senator use his home to freshen up for yet another appointment this evening, so I suggested, "I'll start a bath for you."

"Why take a bath?" Beatty interjected. "Just get into the hot tub."

The Senator liked that idea, and he sent me out to the Secret Service car to get his fresh change of clothes.

Outside, as I leaned into the trunk of the car, I heard another vehicle drive up. Beatty's guard dogs announced the new arrival. I turned around and was surprised to see a familiar face. "Barbara!" I exclaimed, suddenly remembering that she was a friend of Beatty's. "What are you doing here?"

The effervescent Florida blonde flashed a smile and said, "The Senator called and said he was going to be here. He told me to come by."

I followed her into the house.

"Hi, Warren!" she squealed, planting a kiss on Beatty's lips. "Hi, Jack!" She kissed Nicholson also. "I see you finally met Rick."

Beatty appeared confused.

"You know Rick," Barbara implored, as if Beatty were dim-witted. "You've called his house looking for me—remember?"

In fact, Beatty called every time Barbara stayed with me.

Nicholson and his girlfriend trotted off to another section of the house. Beatty's friend emerged from the hot tub, toweled off, and relaxed in a chair. Barbara greeted the Senator with a "My baby!" and a bear hug and disappeared with him into Beatty's guest room. They reemerged minutes later, both wrapped in towels. With a practiced air, they headed for the hot tub, dropped their towels, and—stark naked—eased into the water.

I chatted uncomfortably with the Secret Service agent, the silent witness to this entire episode.

After about fifteen minutes the Senator and Barbara stepped out of the water and dried themselves off. Then they disappeared into the guest room.

Less than half an hour later, the Senator and Barbara came out. She wore a sundress. He was attired in a fresh starched shirt and a pressed suit. He had a bounce in his step and a twinkle in his eye. He flashed a wide smile at me and said, loudly enough for everyone to hear, "She's a wild one!"

I muttered, "I'm glad we're all refreshed."

As volumes of criticism fed back to us concerning the Shah comment, the Senator took out his frustrations on

Tom Southwick. His press secretary had been in the room at the time, and the Senator argued that he should have cut off the interview when he saw that the Senator was heading for trouble. Larry Horowitz gained the Senator's ear and repeated his concerns that Southwick was too young for the job; his opinion was seconded by others back in our Washington office.

Night after night, Iran dogged us: The hostage crisis dominated the news and relegated our fledgling campaign to little, if any, coverage. A very small group of us, including the Senator, decided that the only way we could get the hostages out of the headlines was to find some way to free them. It would also be, we all knew, a major embarrassment to Carter, if *we* got them released.

Someone suggested that we enlist the aid of James Abourezk, the former senator from South Dakota who had retired the previous year after only a single term in order to found the American Arab Anti-Discrimination Committee. We determined that a private effort to intervene would be legal so long as Abourezk did not portray himself as an official representative of the U.S. government.

At the Senator's request, Abourezk traveled to Iran in December and spoke with various officials. But he returned with a report that the government of the Islamic Republic of Iran was too disorganized to coordinate any substantive discussions.

The Senator asked Abourezk to continue his efforts, quietly, which he did for several months to no avail. We also used other sources in Europe, but again with no success. In fact, the effort threatened to backfire on us. At one point, as we were flying between campaign stops, Steve Smith reached us on the airplane phone. The Senator was busy, so I took the call. Smith said, "Just tell Ted that the news shows are all covering a demonstration in Teheran. All the Iranians are shouting 'Hooray for Senator Kennedy.' " Smith added sarcastically, "Your little mission over there has done a great deal for us."

As if this wasn't bad enough, *The Washington Monthly*'s December issue headlined an article by Suzannah Lessard entitled, "Kennedy's Woman Problem: Women's Kennedy Problem." Lessard did not cite the names of any of the Senator's girlfriends, or reveal her sources, but she detailed his longtime pattern of sexual affairs with a fair degree of accuracy. She described how an aide or friend would invite a woman to lunch with the Senator, followed by a casual "dalliance," and suggested that the pattern indicated "a severe case of arrested development, a kind of narcissistic intemperance, a large, babyish ego that must constantly be fed."

In its comment on this latest controversy, *Time* noted that, whether true or false, the story had Washington tongues wagging. It quoted writer Henry Fairlie's comment regarding a dinner party where "for a full hour and a half, fourteen talented and interesting men and women talked of nothing but the sexual activities of Edward Kennedy."

At the same time, my youngest sister, Peg, having just graduated from Boston College, came to Washington to work as a campaign volunteer. In general, she was taken aback by the glitz and glamour of Washington, upset by the frenetic pace—and in particular how everyone was out for himself.

As the holidays neared and we contemplated the rigors of the coming months, I decided to throw a gala Christmas bash, with the objective of boosting the morale of the campaign staff. Peg agreed to act as hostess. The guest list numbered about 250.

The day of the party, Peg drew me aside and announced that she was quitting the campaign. She was going to catch a plane home, today. With effort, I persuaded her to stay for the party.

I was decidedly more nervous this evening than usual, even though it was supposed to be a celebration. One reason was that Cindy was there. When the Senator arrived, he went over to talk to her despite the fact that Joan, and the children—and the press corps—were all watching. Cindy and the Senator then proceeded to engage in an intimate, physically close conversation. It was a blatant indiscretion—just what I feared.

"I can't believe this," Peg moaned to me. "And Joan was right there! With the kids!"

Cindy stayed late, and we had a chance to chat seriously. A couple of times we even headed off into the bathroom together to do a few hits of coke. Cindy was in a mood to face reality. She spelled out what she had long ago realized—the Senator was not about to file for divorce. Making matters worse was the fact that he was also involved with a number of other women. There was no hope. In the small hours of the party, Cindy decided that it was time for her to get out of Washington. If she found it necessary to leave Washington, and her job, I told her I would help her find a campaign position in one of the key primary states. That would tide her over for a time, at least.

As we talked, she had tears in her eyes and I realized just how much this beautiful, wonderful woman truly loved Edward Kennedy.

Frustrated and miserable, Peg returned home to Connecticut shortly after the party. Her comments to my parents must have reinforced my father's concerns, because, the next time I was home, he asked, "Rick, are you happy?"

"Yes," I answered with less conviction than I had in the past.

His eyes said, *I don't believe you—and I hate the way you're living.* But at the time I was unwilling to change and totally absorbed with the Senator's demands.

With Joan home, the Senator desperately needed a place to meet women. Before the holidays, he found it at my home. All we had to do was schedule a staff meeting in my basement or a simple visit. Prior to the Senator's arrival, the Secret Service swept the house; then they waited outside and left us alone. Agents provided us with a supply of buttons emblazoned with the word STAFF. Security-coded colors were changed periodically. If the Senator brought a companion along with him, as long as she was wearing the appropriate button, she appeared to be just another participant at the meeting. After business was concluded, the Senator utilized my bedroom upstairs.

The pattern was established early in the campaign, and continued throughout its duration.

The Secret Service agents seemed to view it as a game, and I suppose it was. I smiled and shook my head, partly in amusement, partly in frustration, when I read the Senator's Christmas card from his Palm Beach girlfriend, Helga Wagner. It included a black-and-white photograph of the winsome blonde, wearing a soft peasant blouse.

The Secret Service, while enjoying the game of "not seeing" the Senator's exploits, nevertheless raised a far more sensitive issue. They provided the Senator with two versions of a bulletproof vest. One was built into a trench coat and was reasonably comfortable; this would come in handy on rainy days. But the fair-weather version, made to be worn under a shirt and suit jacket, was heavy and cumbersome. The Senator tried it on and expressed his irritation. The weight caused pains to shoot up his back.

I was able to talk the Secret Service into providing a lighter version, but the Senator still did not want to wear it, and I could see that we were headed for confrontations on the issue.

And then there were appearances to consider.

It was my lot to try to persuade him to wear makeup

for television appearances. The macho side of him rebelled. "You've got to," I persisted. I reminded him of the stakes. This was a presidential campaign, and the image that he presented on television was of critical importance. He finally agreed, but only if I would apply the makeup personally.

The Senator's customary New Year's resolution was to cut back on his drinking. He often remained on the wagon throughout Lent, perhaps as a means of convincing himself that he could stop drinking anytime he wished. This year, I realized, cutting down on his alcohol intake would have a salutary effect on his weight.

"And you've got to stay away from Gertrude's chocolate chip cookies," I lectured.

Paul Kirk, Tom Southwick, the Senator, and I sat around one day discussing Joan's appearance. Someone declared, "She's got to get a new wardrobe."

Someone else said, "Joan just doesn't—her clothes are a mess."

The four of us—men—decided that Joan's taste in clothes, which ran to bright colors and bold plaids, was gauche. "And she wears way too much makeup," the Senator added. He said to me, "Rick, let's call and see if we can get somebody to straighten out her wardrobe."

I phoned Dr. Hawthorne, explained the wisdom of our reasoning, and suggested, "If you could sort of raise the issue . . ."

"Oh, God," he said. Then he asked, "What are you guys looking for?"

"Basic, conservative women's suits. For television, they like blue. And tone down the makeup. Maybe she could go to one of those, you know, colorologists?"

Dr. Hawthorne, a relatively young man, seemed fascinated by this high-powered world, but was only now beginning to realize its demands. He said he would talk to Joan, but he repeated, "Oh God . . ."

Throughout this period, I devoted considerable effort to coordinating the campaign schedules of the immediate and extended family.

Unable to avoid the "character" issue, we now decided to counter by fostering a "family man" image. Therefore, Joan was to be at the Senator's side as much as possible. Kara, Teddy, and Patrick would all take time off from school to contribute to the effort.

We would utilize the nephews and nieces as much as possible. Maria Shriver arranged for a leave of absence from her job as hostess of "PM Magazine." Sydney Lawford, Bobby Shriver, and Joe Kennedy also made themselves available.

But we decided not to impose too heavily on Ethel's time, reasoning that she had her hands full with her own family.

We had at our disposal perhaps the most visible and intriguing cast of characters ever assembled for a single campaign, and our Washington office established a "family desk" to act as the clan's master scheduling arm. The Senator and I frequently discussed the proper utilization of the resources. "I want Eunice with me in Iowa as much as possible," he said.

"Why?" I asked.

"She'll help with the anti-abortionists," he explained.

Jean Smith and Teddy were to be used to promote concerns of the handicapped.

We knew that Jackie, Caroline, and John, Jr., would be available for only a handful of occasions, so we determined to play these trump cards when the stakes were high. Jackie, in particular, could be our greatest draw at important fund-raisers.

We arranged for a Learjet to bring in Rose for a quick stop in Iowa; beyond that, we would limit her appearances to Florida. But the rest of the family worked hard.

19 Increasingly we began to realize how much we had been hurt by the Mudd interview. It depicted the Senator as what one observer called a "stumblebum" and set the tenor for press coverage of the campaign.

Throughout the early campaigning, the Senator produced one memorable gem after another:

"We should expedite the synfuels program through the process of expediting."

"We must face the problems we are facing as we have always faced the problems we have faced."

In disbelief, I often watched these debacles together with speechwriters Carey Parker and Bob Shrum and press secretary Tom Southwick. We shared pained glances with one another, shook our heads, and muttered, "What did he say?"

We could expect the Senator to return red-faced and angry at himself. Sometimes he complained, "We didn't have enough time to practice this."

But at least he had the ability to laugh once he got over the initial embarrassment. In Iowa, after he pledged to "help every fam farmily," I caught him backstage and mimicked, "fam farmily!"

"Oh, my gosh," he said. He dissolved into laughter and complained paradoxically, "This isn't fun."

The gaffes promoted a disastrous slip in the polls, and prompted comments such as the one from *The Boston Globe*'s Ellen Goodman, who said that the Senator did not appear to want to win the presidency.

One critic wrote: "The front half and back half of his sentences match up less frequently than most politicians."

We thought, perhaps, that a TelePrompTer would help him whenever he presented a major address. The speech was typed on a special machine, presented in large capital letters, and reflected up on mirrors. The device was still in a primitive stage, manually operated. Someone had to sit in a cubbyhole at the base of the machine and scroll the speech by hand. On one occasion the TelePrompTer paper broke and the Senator, having lost his place in his manuscript, had to ad-lib the last portion of his speech. In a rage afterward, he vowed, "I'm never using one of those things again."

In desperation, Steve Smith persuaded Norman Lear to join us as a volunteer consultant. The veteran TV producer helped a great deal, but this was a move we should have made much earlier.

Over a holiday break in the campaigning, a group of us descended on Palm Beach—where the Senator and his family were vacationing with Rose—to continue the fight to smooth the Senator's presentation. Paul Kirk and Eddy Martin flew in for the first few days.

Steve Smith hurled the challenge: How can we turn around the faltering campaign?

Parker and Shrum took the lead in suggesting that we scrap the "leadership" theme, pointing out that it was not working. They suggested that it was time for the Senator to come out forcefully on the issues, casting himself, accurately, as the leader of the liberal wing of the

Democratic party, in direct opposition to the more conservative President.

After some heated argument, the Senator sided with his speechwriters. From now on, he declared, he would say what he really thought. He pounded a desk and vowed, "If I'm going down, I'm going to go down fighting for the things I believe in."

In order to impress the media with this major turnaround, we knew that we had to debut it in a highly visible arena. Phone calls flew back and forth for days before we finalized the location—my alma mater of Georgetown University—and the date, January 28. That was after the Iowa caucuses, where we now trailed badly in the polls, but it was the best we could do.

For the remainder of the week in Palm Beach, we allowed the Senator a little rest.

On December 27, 1979, the Soviet army invaded Afghanistan. President Carter called it "a steppingstone to their possible control over much of the world's oil supplies," and pronounced the invasion "the most serious threat to world peace since the Second World War."

Afghanistan, like Iran, kept Carter in the headlines. Worse, for our purposes, the twin crises provided a convenient excuse for the President to avoid confrontations with the Senator. Carter announced that, for the duration of the international dramas, he would suspend "active campaigning." He canceled a scheduled televised debate with the Senator.

The press dubbed this the Rose Garden campaign.

Meanwhile we took delivery on our leased Boeing 727 and set off on our first task—to topple Carter in the Iowa caucuses on Monday, January 21, the first of four such events to choose the state's fifty convention delegates.

Joe Kennedy was in charge of the Iowa campaign. So critical was this first test that we allotted a full seventeen days of appearances in Iowa, interspersed with quick trips to other appointments around the country.

We found ourselves in Iowa on a freezing winter night, booked into a Holiday Inn. The doors of the rooms were cut too short, and each featured a gap at the bottom that allowed icy air to stream inside. The Senator and I were booked into adjacent rooms.

"Where do you have Joan?" I asked the advance man. He told me that Joan was in a room far down the hall. "Shit," I said, "we gotta move." I knew that the reporters would pick up immediately on the separate sleeping arrangements. If we let *that* story leak out this early, it would surely dog us the rest of the way. The motel was full, so I helped to move Joan, along with her conservative new wardrobe, to my room, and I arranged to move in for the night with Sally Fitzgerald and Marcia Chellis.

The Senator was soaking his back in a hot tub when he heard the commotion of the luggage being moved around. "What's going on?" he asked.

When I explained the problem and my solution to it, he leaned back in the tub and closed his eyes. He knew that I had done the right thing, but I sensed that he was growing more and more agitated over his strange marriage. Joan was getting better, more able to assert herself and displaying ever more independence from the Senator. She had a laugh, and a twinkle in her eye, and seemed to be finally coming into her own. The Senator, however, had been through it so many times before that he couldn't even give her the courtesy of being friendly. Instead, he often pretended she wasn't even there, growing more cold and distant with each passing day. He knew that just as much as the campaign depended on his performance, Joan's was crucial too . . . and this worried him. What if she had a relapse?

I finally said, "Show some emotion toward her when you appear in public together."

He promised to try, but I knew that his heart was not in it.

That night we all slept wrapped in coats against the attacking cold.

The next day we attended a function where we were harassed by demonstrators—anti-abortionists wearing ghost costumes who chanted slogans in our faces. Some protesters wore frogman wet suits to mock Chappaquiddick.

As part of the political process, the Senator was forced to stand in endless receiving lines, shaking hands and smiling as if he enjoyed the activity. The simple act of standing erect for extended periods produced severe back pain. One of the Secret Service agents took over the duty of supporting a chair behind him so that he could lean against it and relieve some of the pressure.

On one occasion, as the line dragged slowly past him, the Senator caught my eye from across the room. I immediately brought him a glass of water. As he drank from it, the Secret Service agent at my side said, "I've never seen two people who can communicate without talking like that. No wonder you don't need to carry a walkie-talkie. How did you know he wanted water?"

"When you're with someone twenty-four hours a day, you can do it," I told him. "He just gave me a signal."

"What?"

"It was in his eyes."

"You and the Senator are just alike."

It was not the first time that observation had been made. I didn't have time to wonder how I felt about the comparison.

In Iowa, 110,000 Democrats turned out to register their opinions. This was twice the number that had participated in the 1976 caucuses, and Carter won, 59 percent to 31 percent—nearly a 2–1 margin. The Senator's first reaction was to order the writers to prepare a statement declaring his withdrawal from the race, but he soon recanted that sentiment.

Nevertheless, the press began a sort of deathwatch. On NBC's "Today" show, Tom Brokaw called Carter's win "a stunning landslide victory . . . a major blow for Senator Kennedy." On ABC's "Good Morning America," Cassie Mackin declared that "no one in the Kennedy campaign was prepared for a defeat like this one." On CBS, Roger Mudd said, "After the defeat Kennedy took here tonight, if he does not come out of Maine and New Hampshire really blazing, I think it will be all over for him."

And yet, now that at least some segments of the press seemed to be writing off the Senator, reporters in general began to treat him somewhat more kindly.

Still, it didn't help. The previous summer we had thought the presidency was his for the grabbing, and now, in just a few months' time, the Senator had snatched defeat from the jaws of victory.

Already we could see the money growing scarce. We angered officials at United Airlines by canceling the rental contract on our 727 after only the first month— and after they had conducted a costly refurbishing of its facilities. We simply could not afford the luxury, so we switched to a lumbering Fairchild, which the Senator nicknamed "Flim Flam One."

Two days after winning the Iowa caucuses, President Carter delivered his State of the Union message to a joint session of Congress. Live, on prime-time television, he took a popular, hard-line stance on the Iranian hostage crisis and the Soviet invasion of Afghanistan.

We desperately needed an effective counterpunch, and our opportunity was the Senator's January 28 speech at Georgetown University. We canceled a weekend campaign swing through New England—including a Saturday-night appearance in Rhode Island along with Jackie

Onassis—in order to concentrate on this pivotal occasion.

On Saturday the Senator received an hour-long briefing on international affairs from Deputy Secretary of State Warren Christopher. The rest of us were busy preparing for the Monday-morning speech. The advance staff lined up about two hundred hard-core Kennedy supporters to be in the audience and gave them orders to jump-start the applause at the appropriate places.

Not only did Parker and Shrum prepare a lyrical, strong, and cogent speech, but we pressured the Senator into memorizing it. We set up a podium in the basement at McLean and rehearsed him repeatedly. We arranged for a TelePrompTer in case his memory faltered. By Sunday night the Senator felt ready. His mood was upbeat.

I drove to McLean early on Monday morning and announced that it was time to apply his makeup.

"Ricky, do I have to do this?" he asked.

I reminded him that we expected major TV coverage, and he acquiesced. But he squirmed as I brushed on a bit of cover-up to hide the lines beneath his eyes. Then I touched his cheeks with pancake makeup and added a little blush.

He was pleased that the Secret Service did not insist that he wear a bulletproof vest. This was to be a captive audience, a closed, safe environment.

As we rode in a Secret Service car, the Senator reviewed the speech manuscript once more.

At Georgetown, Father Henley, the university president, greeted us cordially; he had arrived on the job during my senior year, and he remembered me.

I deposited the Senator backstage, in the custody of Parker and Shrum, who immediately began to grill him on key passages. Then I went out to the front of the auditorium to evaluate the crowd.

The room was nearly full, but stragglers were still in

the aisles, and there was a general hum of private conversation. I checked the sound system, assured myself that the TV cameras were ready to roll, then said to the advance staff, "Let's move it."

The Senator shone that morning. He spoke with force and without hesitation, invoking the memories of FDR's New Deal and Harry Truman's Fair Deal. He charged that Carter's policies had ignored the young, the old, the sick, the poor, the disadvantaged, minorities, and women—in short, all those whom he characterized as having been "left out of the American dream."

The Senator declared that he wanted to be the President "who at last closes tax loopholes and tames monopoly."

Once more the Senator charged that the admission of the Shah into the United States had triggered the hostage crisis, and he called for a UN commission to study Iranian grievances against the Shah—once the hostages were released. By now, after months of Carter's ineffective response to the Ayatollah's machinations, the public was receptive to the message.

He concluded, "Sometimes a party must sail against the wind. Now is such a time."

I watched and listened carefully from one side of the stage, in the company of several of the advance people and the head of the Secret Service detail.

At the end, the crowd rose to its feet in tribute.

Even as the applause continued, I was busy gathering feedback.

"A ten-strike . . ." said one.

"A home run . . ." boomed another.

Tom Southwick's task was to eavesdrop on the reporters, and he came to me with the comment, "It was pretty good, Rick."

I ran backstage to relay these comments to the Senator. *Thank you, Mother Mary,* I said over and over. *Maybe we can turn it around. . . .*

Indeed, the reviews were almost unanimous in their praise. House Speaker Tip O'Neill, who had been careful to remain neutral in this fight among his fellow Democrats, commented, "Anyone who discounts Ted Kennedy as a factor in this race has another thought coming." The Kennedys, he added, "don't know what defeat means."

Newspapers, columnists, and commentators heralded the comeback of Edward M. Kennedy.

The one news report that angered us was by Phil Jones of CBS, who made a point of noting that the Senator spoke with the aid of a TelePrompTer. "That was a cheap shot," the Senator muttered. Ronald Reagan used TelePrompTers all the time, and no one ever mentioned it. We were pleased when CBS replaced Jones on the Kennedy beat with Jed Duvall. The Senator did not exert any pressure on CBS to remove Jones from the beat, but I wondered whether or not Steve Smith might have called in a marker. Smith knew plenty of network bigwigs on a social basis and it was possible that he played a behind-the-scenes role in this episode. If he did, the Senator would not want to know about it, again preferring to be "officially unaware."

Following the Georgetown speech, we flew to New England. As he disembarked from a Delta Airlines plane at Boston's Logan International Airport, a high school band greeted him with a rendition of "A Little Help from My Friends." Grinning, he vowed: "We're going up to Maine and then New Hampshire and all the way through to California. Then we'll see who is going to whip whose what."

I breathed a sigh of relief. The old Kennedy style, it seemed, was finally back.

20 Style, we knew, couldn't be presented to the public without money. And we were desperate for money.

Phil Bakes presented the Senator with a memo outlining the campaign's indebtedness. We had $200,000 in cash, but we owed over $1 million, including $400,000 to Chemical Bank and $75,000 to Charles Guggenheim. We had also missed a payroll for campaign workers, but fortunately many agreed to remain.

Our next scheduled stop was Puerto Rico. When someone suggested that we expand our activities there, it jump-started an old argument. Months earlier, as we had planned our itinerary, Puerto Rico had loomed as a sore spot. It was known as a locale where Democratic candidates could raise large amounts of money, and there were also clear political reasons for a visit. In mid-March, Puerto Rico would hold its first-ever Democratic presidential primary, and the party had made it a worthwhile prize. Forty-one delegates were available; only nineteen states were to have larger delegations at the convention. Beyond that, the trip would give us good press coverage in New York City, with its heavy Puerto Rican population.

One of our staff members raised a problem. "You have to be careful," this adviser cautioned. "You can raise maybe three hundred thousand dollars, but two hundred thousand of that is going to be in *cash,* and you don't know where it comes from."

The Senator's cousin Bobby Fitzgerald, known to all as Bobby Fitz, was one of three people in charge of fund-raising. He enthusiastically promoted the idea of the trip, even if we had to limit ourselves to legitimate contributions.

Steve Smith and others bandied the issue about. Someone asked openly, "Should we take the chance? We need the money."

The stakes were particularly high for the Senator. Accepting an illegal cash contribution would look bad for any candidate, of course, but the Senator himself, in the wake of the Watergate scandal, had sponsored campaign-funding reform legislation. He had championed the idea of allowing taxpayers to designate one dollar of their annual income-tax payments to finance federal elections. He had raged against the influence peddlers who came in and bought the loyalties of politicians.

The Secret Service was not happy with the visit. The idea of heading down to Puerto Rico—a volatile environment, populated with numerous terrorist groups—worried them. A special team of sharpshooters was assigned to accompany us, and the total detail increased to three shifts of agents, with fifty-four on each shift, for a total of 162 agents covering the Senator. This was an extraordinary amount of protection, more than Carter had.

At one function in San Juan, the Senator characterized himself as an "old friend" of Puerto Rico, and charged that President Carter had forgotten about the Commonwealth: "He turned his back on the majority of families on the island who still live in poverty." The Senator pledged that, as President, he would appoint a special deputy "to restore the personal interest and attention of the United States to the issues and opportunities facing the Puerto Rican people." He sidestepped the controversial issue of statehood, but proclaimed, "It is your decision. You must make a choice."

When the Senator asked for campaign contributions, Puerto Rican businessmen began pulling one-hundred-dollar bills out of their wallets. "No, no," our staff members pleaded. "Please write checks." We were careful to keep the contributions on the record, and to limit them to the legal total of one thousand dollars per donor.

In Maine, only twenty-two convention delegates were at stake—only about one percent of the votes needed to secure the nomination. But after the loss in Iowa, we now viewed the February 10 Maine caucuses as vital. The Senator declared that he had to beat Carter in Maine and New Hampshire if he was going to be able to stay in the race, but this was a formidable challenge.

Nevertheless, the Senator looked and acted like a man who, following his triumph at Georgetown, knew that he was on a roll. He drew laughter and applause whenever he chided Carter to get out of the Rose Garden and onto the campaign trail. His call for national health-care coverage brought an enthusiastic response. He announced that Joan had decided to enroll in graduate school and, beaming, noted that this decision would force him to spend more of his own time with his children.

Teddy and nineteen-year-old John F. Kennedy, Jr., joined us for a stop at Auburn High School. The two handsome young heirs to the Kennedy heritage received an adoring welcome. JFK, Jr., listened attentively to the Senator's speech and added two or three sentences of his own. Then, in an instant, the shy young man was gone, whisked off by his own contingent of security personnel.

CBS reporter Chris Wallace filed a negative report

wherein he offered a few snide remarks about the Senator's use of crib notes at a speaking engagement. It seemed to be a very low blow. Every politician had cue cards at the ready. Who could remember everything, especially when you were called upon to present dozens of speeches every day? We couldn't believe that Wallace had chosen to zero in on such a petty criticism.

But, a few days later, at a paper mill in Maine, we watched Chris Wallace tape his segment for the evening news. On the ground in front of him, safely out of camera view, were his own crib sheets. With a mischievous glint in his eye, the Senator stepped up and chided, "Oh, gee, Chris, are those your notes on the ground there? Are you using those notes while you're talking to the audience out there?"

Wallace laughed at being caught, but the Senator's interruption was, of course, edited from the tape.

At 4:38 P.M. on Sunday, CBS declared Carter "the winner" in the Maine caucus. Too many of our potential supporters heard that and, adopting a loser's attitude, didn't bother to vote. We were livid with the press's premature call on the race, but what could we do?

One week later we organized the family into one big fund-raising machine. Jackie Onassis was our stellar attraction at a Sunday fifty-dollar-per-person reception at Regis College in Weston, Massachusetts. She was about an hour late in arriving, but none of the paying guests seemed to mind. They strained for a glimpse of the nation's most enigmatic woman. She wore a bright-red dress, trimmed in purple braid, and smiled graciously. She sipped champagne and nibbled on spinach quiche as she greeted the seemingly endless queue of patrons, signing autographs for many of them and thanking them for their support in her typically breathy, hard-to-hear voice. When it was over with, just as quickly as she had come, she was gone.

The event raised $17,500 in campaign funds.

That Thursday, on the eve of the Senator's forty-eighth birthday, we staged sixty parties throughout the state. The Senator appeared at a late-afternoon labor-sponsored fund-raiser at Boston's Parker House, then headed for a twenty-five-dollar-per-person event at Anthony's Pier 4. That same night, Ethel Kennedy appeared at events in Beacon Hill and South End, Caroline Kennedy was in Pittsfield, and John Kennedy, Jr., covered the towns of Worcester and Webster. Bobby Shriver was in North Andover and Salem, Eunice Shriver made a Boston appearance and stopped at a party in Taunton, Teddy, Jr., was in Halifax and Randolph, Kara appeared at an event on the Cape, and Joe Kennedy covered Brockton and Cambridge.

Everywhere we went that day, it seemed somebody was trying to give the Senator some birthday cake. At first he eyed the cakes longingly. Then he broke down and took a bite. Soon he was having a grand old time, shaking hands, stuffing more cake in his mouth at each stop, ignoring my admonishments.

Finally I said, "No more cake."

Wiping a piece of chocolate away from his lips, he grinned mischievously. "Oh, Ricky, come on . . . not even on my birthday?"

Despite all the welcome assistance from the family, the Senator had to assume the role of key fund-raiser, and it was a constant struggle to get him to come forward and ask for campaign contributions.

In New Hampshire we scheduled a private meeting for the Senator with a man who had the family and business connections to provide as much as fifty thousand dollars. Both Paul Kirk and Eddy Martin assured him, "All you have to do is ask him."

"Do I have to?" the Senator moaned. "I hate asking for money."

Kirk took me aside and counseled, "You be there in the room, Rick. Make sure he does it."

The meeting took place in a lovely bucolic setting in Concord, at a rustic mill that had been converted into office space. I was present during the initial stages of the meeting, but after a few pleasantries, the Senator turned to me and said, "Rick, we want to spend a few minutes alone."

I left the two men and joined Martin and Kirk outside.

"Why did you leave the room?" they scolded.

"Well, he told me to. I couldn't fight him on it," I said.

After the meeting was over, we asked the Senator if he had asked the man for a contribution. "Yeah, I asked him," he replied.

"Great," we chorused.

But later, Bobby Fitz reported that the Senator had evaded the issue, never making a direct request. The potential contributor exclaimed, "He's right on the issues. He's right about everything. He asked for my support and I said I'd support him. But he never came out and said he needed any money!"

Still, the family continued to rally around us. We arranged for various members to accompany us for a few days at a time in New Hampshire, traveling in cumbersome caravans—cars full of family, a double detail of Secret Service agents, a doctor, a nurse and two paramedics, and as many as a hundred reporters—to stump the byroads of the small state. It was my responsibility to coordinate the details, to make sure everything was in order. I was the thorn in everyone's flesh, yelling at various staffers, "Move your ass! Get in there!" When everyone and everything was in position, I was the last person to jump into the car—or be pushed in by Secret Service personnel—and yell, "Go!" The agents were so obviously concerned about the Senator's visibility and accessibility that reporters began to refer to Kennedy—out of earshot—as the moving target.

One of the stumping family members was the Senator's niece, Sydney Lawford, a down-to-earth young woman about twenty years old. She was energetic and vivacious, and a brave campaigner. One day, as our caravan screamed down a state road between campaign stops, she announced that she had to go to the bathroom.

"Hold it, hold it," the Senator commanded.

A few minutes later she said, "Uncle Teddy, I can't hold it any longer."

"Pull over to the side," I instructed our Secret Service driver.

The moment we stopped, the cars behind us halted also. A contingent of reporters jumped out of the press van to record whatever it was the candidate was going to do here on the apron of a New Hampshire highway.

The Senator pointed to a wooded area on a hilltop adjacent to the road and said to me, "You've got to take her up there."

Stepping out of the car, I turned to the reporters and announced, "Okay, guys, everybody back into the van. This is just a pit stop."

With a smirk on his face, someone asked, "The Senator's gotta go?"

"No, not the Senator. Just get back into the van."

Laughing, the reporters piled back inside their vehicle. They were beginning to have a bit of fun with the campaign.

Sydney was mortified by the attention, but she was also desperate. "I have to go s-o-o-o bad," she wailed. Hand in hand, we trudged up the hill as Secret Servicemen assumed lookout posts, guns at the ready under their coats in case somebody wanted to take a shot at the Senator's niece while she peed. The winter weather was freezing.

We reached the woods and Sydney disappeared for a few moments. I shook my head, thinking, *And now I'm the bathroom monitor, too?* Then I heard her yell, "Rick, I don't have any toilet paper!"

"Oh, you know . . ." I moaned. "Wait here." As I ran back down the hill toward the car, the Senator saw me coming and rolled down the window. "We need toilet paper," I explained.

He held his sides. "I'm laughing so hard, *I'm* gonna have to go," he said.

I raced to another car in our caravan, located some tissues, and recruited one of the women from the advance staff. "I'm not going to take toilet paper up to this woman," I said. "You do it."

Red-faced, she undertook the errand, which the press corps recorded on videotape. Naturally.

Perhaps we could have overcome the Senator's difficulty with his public presentation if we had not miscalculated so badly on the "character" issue. A *New York Times*–CBS poll reported that 24 percent of the nation's *Democrats* would not vote for the Senator under any circumstances, due to questions concerning his personal life and integrity. The ultraconservative *Reader's Digest* stepped up the attack. The February issue, timed neatly to coincide with the New Hampshire primary, included an article entitled "Chappaquiddick: The Still Unanswered Questions," which focused fresh attention on our most vulnerable point.

Lagging badly in the polls, on the weekend prior to the New Hampshire primary we gave it everything we had. An army of fifteen hundred volunteers rang doorbells and manned the phones, contacting voters, urging them to go to the polls and vote for the Senator. We unleashed new television ads: One featured Rose, noting pointedly that her son was a devoted family man; another quoted

Ethel praising the Senator's efforts as surrogate father to her children.

On the morning of the New Hampshire primary, the Senator appeared on NBC's "Today" show. Host Tom Brokaw asked if his candidacy could survive a loss in New Hampshire. "I'm very hopeful that we'll do well," the Senator replied. He attempted to shrug off the question and, instead, hammered away at the issues. He began to talk about fuel prices and inflation.

"Can you survive?" Brokaw pressed.

"Well, the Maine caucuses were closer than the polls indicated," the Senator demurred.

Brokaw tried a third time for a straight answer.

The Senator contended that he was doing "increasingly well" because of the issues that he had raised in recent weeks. He ventured the opinion that New Hampshire voters would not "rubber-stamp the policies that have not worked."

Brokaw tried from another angle, asking, "If you run second twenty-four hours from now—"

"Maybe we can talk at that time," the Senator snapped.

In the end, incumbency prevailed, even here in the Senator's backyard. It was a crushing blow. In a rare free moment I found myself sitting alone in my bedroom in some nameless motel in some nameless city, totally depressed. This was not the way it was supposed to be going. I knew the Senator was just as deflated as I was and he had so much more to lose. I took out a bullet of coke, which we both carried sporadically on the campaign trail, and took a hit. Increasingly, it was the only thing keeping us going.

Somehow the Senator managed to put a positive spin on the results. "Tonight we are proclaiming victory," he said, thrusting up his left fist in a defiant gesture. Later, he added, "We're in it to stay."

Indeed, he could hardly quit now, for the following week's primary was in his home state of Massachusetts. Unhappily, Democratic Governor Edward King had already announced his support for President Carter. What's more, the Senator's endorsement of Paul Tsongas over incumbent Edward Brooke—the only black in the U.S. Senate—two years earlier had undermined his long-standing support from the black community.

Although the Senator planned only token campaign stops in the South, conceding those states to the President, we did squeeze in a quick trip to Birmingham, Alabama. During his speech there, he was heckled with "You're a murderer!" cries from anti-abortionists.

Signs in the crowd asked: HOW CAN YOU RESCUE THE COUNTRY WHEN YOU COULDN'T RESCUE MARY JO?

I shuddered.

When the Senator proclaimed that he was in favor of gun control partly because "my family has been touched by violence," some in the crowd cheered and applauded.

My mouth hung open.

As things grew worse, the Senator began dismissing the public opinion polls. After one particularly dismal poll was published, he scrawled a note in heavy black ink on his monogrammed stationery:

To Paul, Steve, Phil, Peter Hart:

There will be no more polls taken for my campaign—They always leak and I have not benefited from them. That's it.

—your favorite candidate

After the New Hampshire debacle, his mood wavered. Some days he was up, but even on the days he was down, he still tried to put the best face on it, knowing the press was ever-prying. He started eating more, thinking, *Screw the diet.* Finally, the Senator, Steve Smith, and others met to discuss the future. Everyone agreed that we had to continue, at least through Massachusetts. But what then? The Senator was tired, and he complained, "I'm not having any fun."

21 Finally we got a break when the U.S. Ambassador to the United Nations, Donald F. McHenry, voted in favor of a UN resolution to dismantle Israeli settlements in the occupied territories of the West Bank, Gaza, and East Jerusalem.

American Jews were enraged. The Senator took the initiative in pointing out that this was a Carter administration decision. The President's response, which we thought was typically weak, was that he claimed not to have read the resolution.

We were delighted.

The Senator, like the seasoned politician he was, knew he could put Carter on the defensive. A television ad had the Senator blasting Carter: "*Never again* should America cast its vote in the United Nations against the security of Israel. *Never again* should the President have to give the excuse that he didn't know what was happening and that the Secretary of State didn't know what he was doing."

And now, after all the negative articles, it seemed that the press fell in love with the Senator. Maybe it was because they knew he was going down with a good fight, or maybe it was something else . . . that spark of admiration so many of us had when we witnessed the Kennedy style at its best. For some in the press, this was their third Kennedy presidential campaign.

As Carter remained in the White House, hauling volumes of Iranian history to the Oval Office for late-night reading—as if that were going to do him any good—the Senator stormed his home state. On Sunday night, two days before the primary, he warned an audience of labor leaders gathered at the Boston Park Plaza Hotel, "We are facing the most serious economic crisis since the time of the Depression." At dawn on Monday, he went to the General Electric plant in Lynn, Massachusetts, to shake hands with the working men and women of his state. Later, speaking at St. Patrick's Church, he scorched Carter for failing "to make good on our promise of justice in America." He finished off the day with appearances in Worcester. Finally, late at night, he flew to Hyannis to await the results of Tuesday's balloting.

We won the Democratic primary in Massachusetts on March 4, gathering an impressive 67 percent of the vote. When a reporter asked if this was a turnaround in the campaign, the Senator responded with a wordless smile.

Conceding the South to Carter, we turned our attention to Illinois and New York.

We arrived in Chicago on a campaign stop and, as part of our accelerating cost-cutting measures, checked into a waterfront hotel offering less-than-first-class accommodations. I booked a two-room suite in my name, to share with the Senator. Secret Service agents came in to familiarize themselves with the layout, but did not disturb the privacy of the Senator's bedroom. The Senator was feeling especially good tonight, and I knew that his mood had nothing to do with the campaign.

Cindy was in town.

The Senator was busy for the evening, so Cindy met me for an early dinner. Later, as I accompanied her into the suite to rendezvous with the Senator, I was exasperated. "What am I gonna do? Am I supposed to sit here while you guys are in the next room?"

They laughed, holding each other. She squealed. The Senator said, "Well, Ricky, if you leave, uh, the Secret Service is going to know, ah, that Cindy is in here alone with me. There might be some press out there who would pick up on it. So you have to stay. I mean, ah, what can we do?"

I didn't say a word as they traipsed off to the bedroom, already tugging at each other's clothes.

Irritated, I did a quick hit from a bullet—Cindy had brought a new supply for the Senator—and tried to busy myself in the parlor. I glanced at some reports. I made a few phone calls. I tried to watch TV, but I was exhausted. I leaned back in an easy chair and closed my eyes. Soon, my attempt at a catnap was interrupted by muffled sounds emanating from the adjacent bedroom. The thin hotel walls broadcast everything.

All we needed now was for the Senator to have a Nelson Rockefeller–type heart attack. I felt like throwing the TV through the window.

Why am I putting up with this? I asked myself. *This is absurd.* Suddenly I stood up, ready to pound my fist on the bedroom door to get them to quiet down. Then I realized it wouldn't do any good anyway.

I stepped out of the room, into the hotel hallway. My eyes met those of two Secret Service agents at the far end of the hall. They, too, had heard the noises, and had moved discreetly away. We didn't say a word.

I slipped back into the suite. A few minutes later, when Cindy and the Senator emerged from the bedroom, I muttered, "Well, you certainly made sure that I heard everything."

They both laughed.

"Oh, Ricky," the Senator said, "I need *some* stress relief!"

"Stress" and "persistence" were, indeed, operative words for us. Often I would tuck the Senator into bed about one in the morning and head for the hotel bar to unwind and get feedback, usually from speechwriters Parker and Shrum.

As the critical Illinois primary approached, the situation appeared dismal. Our private polls showed the Senator way behind. By coincidence, the day before the election was St. Patrick's Day, and the Senator determined to make a final gesture for support from his ethnic constituency. He decided that he and his family would march in Chicago's St. Patrick's Day Parade.

When we informed the Secret Service of our plans, some of the agents appeared to be near hysteria. Throughout the campaign, the Senator had never risked such exposure. They strenuously argued against it, their faces getting redder by the minute, but the Senator's mind was made up.

On the day of the parade, Chicago greeted us with snow and freezing rain. But the Senator appeared to be in a jovial mood as he emerged from his limousine and, like a drill sergeant, mustered his forces: Joan, Kara (armed with a supply of campaign buttons), Teddy, and Patrick, as well as Eunice and Maria Shriver. He handed each of them an Irish walking stick and directed them to fall into step behind Mayor Byrne. "Remember to stay together," he commanded. "We want to stay smiling now. Show them those smiles."

As many as 150 agents—the Secret Service, augmented by local and state forces—lined the route. An ominous-looking SWAT team in khaki army jackets stood near heavy cases full of weapons. Police helicopters circled overhead.

At least he was wearing his Kevlar bulletproof vest.

Amid a snow shower, the family set off on its march down State Street. Joan's arm clutched at her husband's shoulder. They had walked only a short distance before we heard the *rat-a-tat* of what sounded like gunfire.

The Senator's knees buckled as he instinctively sought the ground. Already nervous Secret Service agents swooped around him and Joan, forming a protective cocoon. It was several minutes before we realized that some happy Irish reveler had set off a string of firecrackers. The culprit turned out to be a young man who had dyed his beard green in honor of the day.

Soon after that, agents spotted a long lens peering out of an open window, and they hurriedly guided the Senator to the other side of the street.

Mobs of people turned out for the parade, and some were in a feisty mood. As Mayor Byrne, wearing a mink coat and a festive green hat, marched past one surly group of onlookers, she was greeted with boos. The Senator slackened his pace so as to distance himself from her. But as he approached the group, the jeers continued. Joan's face showed terror.

The Senator gamely tried to work the crowd. He drew looks of horror from the Secret Service agents as he barged through police barricades to offer a handshake and a "Hi, how are you?" to the spectators. At one point, finding a friendly reception, he turned and called out, "Joansie, Joansie, over here."

"Go get him, brother," a black man yelled. "Get that Carter."

The Senator grasped the man's hand and implored, "Help me."

Not everyone was so genial. Someone yelled, "You stink!" Another voice shouted, "Carter's gonna kill you, bum."

The Senator beamed when he encountered a group of nuns. "Sisters!" he shouted. "Good to see you."

One of the nuns responded, "Go get him, Teddy."

The Senator laughed and said, "I'm trying." He turned and called back into the street, "Kara. Kara. Where's Kara? Get a button for the nuns." He explained to the group, "Kara's got the buttons."

The procession moved on. As he neared Goldblatt Brothers department store, the Senator noticed a woman behind the police barricade, sitting in a wheelchair. He stopped, leaned across the barricade, and touched her hand.

"Please win," she said, probably aware of his dedication to the handicapped.

Security men tried to push the Senator along, but he resisted. "Wait a minute," he complained. He wanted to present something to this loyal fan. "Get me a button. Get me a banner or something." He noticed a woman nearby holding a supply of green-and-gold Kennedy banners. "Can I have one?" he asked, then placed it on the lap of the wheelchair-bound woman, thanked her, and finally moved along.

When it was all over and I was ushering the family back into the limousine, one of the Secret Service agents muttered, "Thank you, God."

Unhappily, the results that came in late that night indicated that despite the Senator's presence at the parade, the public was indifferent. Carter won 165 of the Illinois delegates, while the Senator gained a meager 14.

Afterward, when we asked potential contributors for money, they would respond, "Why aren't you getting out of the race?"

It was an increasingly difficult question for the Senator to respond to, but he held tough. He kept saying, "There's this thing inside of me; I've got to get the message across." More firmly than ever, he believed that it was important to try to make a difference, no matter how the votes tallied. The more his advisers lost heart, the more he seemed to rally his own spirits.

Dissension plagued us. We had wonderful personnel to run the campaign, but no one was ever designated as *the* boss. At various times Steve Smith, Paul Kirk, and Phil Bakes pretended to that throne, and predictable jealousies gnawed at efficiency.

The clashes among his campaign brain trust forced the Senator to call more and more of the shots himself, even though he might be three thousand miles away on an airplane when a critical decision had to be made. At one point I said, "This is crazy. We're up in an airplane trying to say who is going to be assigned to different states." The chaos was very counterproductive.

Still, money was the most diabolical pressure. On several occasions the Senator mused, "Hey, Ricky, is there any chance we can go back and do another fund-raiser in Puerto Rico?"

And there were other problems. We could not shake the specter of Chappaquiddick. On March 20 the Senator presented a speech on foreign policy at Columbia University. His delivery was smooth, his message concise, and his criticism of Carter effective. Afterward, as we drove down 114th Street, we heard some music blaring out of the window of a house on fraternity row. Someone had chosen the selection with care. The title "Bridge over Troubled Water" mocked the Senator as he rode past.

The following day, *The Boston Globe* ran a piece that told of an elderly Jewish man, sitting in the sun at Grand Army Plaza on 59th Street. He was asked which Democrat he preferred in Tuesday's New York primary. "Carter," he responded. "I forgive Carter. He made a mistake and he said so." Asked about Kennedy, the man shook his head, saying, "I'm sorry, but there are some things you don't forgive."

On an evening flight to Buffalo, the Senator slugged

down several stiff drinks. At the airport gate we were met
by a member of the advance staff whom I had never seen
before. I had spoken with her by phone, however, and I
knew that she was a veteran of the '72 McGovern campaign and the '76 Carter campaign. The Senator greeted
her with unusual warmth and quickly threw a sidelong
glance at me. Immediately I sensed trouble. She was
extremely attractive. Worse, she was blond.

She accompanied us in our limo to a scheduled speech,
and I watched and listened warily as the Senator labored
to be charming. Prior to his speech, he drew me aside for
a moment and told me, "Well, Ricky, she's pretty entic-
ing, wouldn't you say?"

I didn't say a word.

After the speech, we piled back into the limo and
headed to our hotel. Several times during the ride, the
Senator's eyes caught mine, communicating an unsubtle
message. It was about 10:00 P.M. by the time we had
checked in. As we stood in the lobby, the Senator suggested that the woman come up to the suite with us, to
discuss the next day's schedule. We had a 5:00 A.M. start.

"No," I interjected sharply. "You wait down here," I
said to the woman. "I'll come back down—"

"No, no," the Senator countermanded genially. He
turned to the woman, all charm and smile and said,
"Come up to the suite."

I backed off. Secret Service agents and reporters were
all over the place.

Agents quickly completed their check of our suite,
then locked us inside and took up their posts in the
hallway.

The Senator ushered the woman to a comfortable sofa
in the parlor of our suite, took off his suit jacket, loosened his tie, settled heavily into a chair, and said with a
casual air, "Well, let's talk about tomorrow." Suddenly

he glanced at me and suggested, "Rick, why don't you go off to the other room and make your phone calls?"

I disappeared dutifully. But I sat for only a few minutes in my own wing of the suite before hurrying back into the parlor and declaring, "Senator, it's time for bed!"

His face flushed with anger. "Rick, I—"

"Your tub is ready," I lied. "Get back into the bedroom." I turned to the woman and said brusquely, "You'll have to leave." I ushered her out the door with little ceremony.

"What did you do that for?" the Senator raged after she was gone, livid that I'd interrupted him before his act could begin.

"Because I told you—the staff is off limits. Now, just get in there and get in the tub."

He stared at me, eyes burning, and then grew calmer. After a moment he burst into laughter. Then he said in that familiar petulant tone, "You never let me have any fun."

One night on the campaign trail in mid-March, Sheila, my own long-suffering girlfriend, finally reached her breaking point.

"I can't take it anymore," Sheila said to me over the phone. "You can't make time for me. The only person who is important to you is Ted Kennedy, and I've had it. I just can't live like this, Rick. Do you hear me?"

I had no defense.

We left New York the morning of primary day, March 25, and took the Eastern shuttle to Washington. Along the way, the Senator chatted with columnist Jimmy Breslin. He spent the rest of the day in McLean, trying to relax. His spirits were buoyed when Steve Smith called at about three in the afternoon with word that early exit polls looked good. By 7:00 P.M. we were on the shuttle again, heading back to New York. The Senator, Paul

Kirk, and I sat three abreast in the front row of the plane. The rear of the aircraft was filled with newsmen.

The routine approach was boringly familiar. We circled slowly, gradually descending closer to Long Island. The flaps were down, the gear locked. The plane hovered in that seemingly slow-moving glide toward the runway. Out the window to the left, I could see that we were already below the top of the nearby apartment buildings. We skimmed over water and cleared the jutting edge of the concrete runway. I waited for the pilot to cut the power sharply, allowing us to settle to the ground.

But suddenly the engines roared. The aircraft jumped in response and veered to one side, gaining altitude rapidly. The Senator glanced at me and exclaimed, "Oh, my God!"

Within moments the pilot's voice came over the intercom, calm and cool, apologizing for the missed approach. "We'll circle and try again," he said.

A Secret Service agent checked with the flight deck and reported that a second aircraft had been using the same approach path.

"Aren't you supposed to check these things out?" I snapped.

"Yeah," the agent admitted. He assured us that the control tower had been informed that the Eastern shuttle was bringing in a presidential candidate. He speculated that at this very moment an air traffic controller was catching hell.

Once we made it safely to the ground, we sped off in a motorcade. We picked up Joan at a Manhattan hotel and went to campaign headquarters to claim our victory. The Senator had a celebratory cigar at the ready. He won the Jewish vote by a 4–1 margin and captured 164 of the state's delegates, compared to 118 for Carter.

Three days later Mark Shields, of *The Washington Post,* declared that the Senator had evolved into "a confident, forceful candidate," who projected the image that he truly believed in the importance of his message. In *The Wall Street Journal,* Norman Miller praised the Senator's "gutsy performance" and scorned those who questioned "Ted Kennedy's character." Even crusty columnist George Will offered a left-handed compliment. Although the Senator "is almost perfectly wrong" on the issues, Will said, "he is cheerful, passionate, a believing professional."

22 By midspring our campaign was in somewhat better financial shape. In two months' time, we had reduced the debt from $1 million to about $545,000, partly because we had developed a novel fundraising strategy. We had persuaded about a dozen artists—including Andy Warhol, Robert Rauschenberg, Robert Morris, Richard Serra, and Jamie Wyeth—to donate original lithographs to the campaign, which we could sell to replenish our coffers. Now, new contributions were flowing in at a rate of about $250,000 each week.

Pointing toward the all-important "Super Tuesday" primaries on June 3, we enlisted the aid of David Sawyer, a New York political consultant who had worked in more than fifty other election campaigns. Sawyer produced slick new TV spots that highlighted the Senator's record in Congress on issues such as the economy, inflation, foreign policy, and energy.

We needed all the coverage we could get, and part of our strategy was to encourage Joan to speak out more, even though we knew from past experience this could have a downside. She granted a lengthy interview to *Women's Wear Daily* and, sure enough, the publication overemphasized portions of her comments that caused considerable controversy. Comparing herself with the present First Lady, Joan declared herself to be "a very sophisticated lady," whereas Mrs. Carter "doesn't have a master's." She wondered "how many First Ladies there are with graduate degrees." Joan contended that her husband would make a better president than Mr. Carter because he would surround himself with better advisers. "I've got nothing against Georgia," she demurred, "but I'd prefer to have Ted in the White House listening to the best brains in our country on matters like foreign affairs."

When the Senator read this, all he could do was roll his eyes and make himself a drink.

For my part, I survived on adrenaline, and we were so busy that I didn't even think about the toll this was exacting. In one particularly grueling week, we traveled from coast to coast eleven times.

Our biggest problem in California was voter apathy. Although polls indicated that we could narrowly beat Carter with a good voter turnout, Californians were more interested in local concerns than the national race. We had no choice but to stump California at an exhaustive pace.

We were doing so, driving through vast rolling hills, when the Senator said suddenly, "Uh, you know, Ricky, Joan Baez has a ranch somewhere around here."

I nodded, but kept going through my notes.

He, however, wanted to talk. "Ah, did you see that recent magazine piece on Baez, you know, saying she had had a lesbian affair?"

"Heard about it," I muttered.

"Well, she's not a lesbian. She's definitely bisexual," he reported, as if this were some new, wonderful species he was delighted to know about. The window was up, separating us from the Secret Service driver.

"How do you know for sure?" I asked, guessing the answer.

"Well, uh, you remember, she's been out to McLean, when she's in town . . . and she usually has a girlfriend with her. But she doesn't just get into women. . . . Boy"— he grinned—"she's a real number, Joan is."

The Senator was loosening up on the whole gay rights issue, anyway, realizing that everyone assumed—as we'd said—that he supported the idea from the start. This was the first presidential campaign in which gay rights was a featured issue, and the Senator had met with gay leaders at various campaign stops. He didn't vigorously declare an advocacy for gay rights, opting to stress that he was in favor of equal rights for everyone.

Now, to increase the campaign cash flow, he had decided to become the first presidential candidate to attend a gay rights fund-raiser with the national press corps along. The event was held at the Beverly Hills home of a gay rights activist.

"Ummmm," the Senator whispered as we entered. "Can you believe how good-looking everybody is? The men are really knockouts."

The event was a garden party and the Senator was to be the featured speaker. It went very well.

Afterward, our motorcade headed back toward downtown Los Angeles, to an evening fund-raising event staged by prominent Taiwanese citizens.

"What the hell are we going there for?" the Senator asked. "What are they gonna get for me? How many Taiwanese do you think there are in L.A.—a hundred thousand at most?"

I said, "Well, they tell me that those hundred thousand people can raise four hundred thousand dollars for your campaign."

"Oh, really? Well, why didn't you say so?" Then he scrunched down in his seat and joked in pidgin English about all the money that the Taiwanese were going to give him. It wasn't done in a mean-spirited way; he just loved to mimic people.

We were both roaring with laughter when the Senator realized that we were driving through an area of West Hollywood populated by head shops, stores that sold drug paraphernalia.

"You know, those shops, uh, they . . . sell poppers. Let's stop and get some," he said, peering out through the window.

"What do you mean?" I asked, raising an eyebrow.

"Well, I don't have any. I forgot," he explained with mild irritation. "I'm all out of everything. So let's stop somewhere along here and you run in and buy some."

He may have been semi-serious at first, but he quickly realized the impossibility of his request. "We have a whole—there must be thirty cars in this motorcade," I pointed out. "You've got a caravan of Secret Service cars and tons of press vehicles, and we're gonna stop at some head shop and I'm going to run in? You think the national press corps is not gonna cover that?"

"No," he said in a petulant tone, deciding to tease me a bit. "I want poppers, Ricky. I want poppers. I really want them. I'm all out. And listen—we could go out later, you know, to a disco where everybody uses them."

I shook my head, feeling an approaching headache and wondering where I'd put my ever-ready supply of aspirin. "You've got to be crazy. We're gonna make a popper run and then hit a disco with a bunch of popper-crazed kids?"

"Oh, come on," he chided, sitting back in his seat. "Tell the driver to stop."

My eyes must have been the size of golf balls.

Seeing my expression, the Senator started laughing. He pointed to a large head shop and said, "I betcha they have poppers in there."

"Are you nuts?" I asked, laughing along with him, realizing he was getting a great kick out of all this.

"Either you stop the car now or we're gonna come back later," he decreed ominously. He pounded his fists against his thighs and repeated in singsong fashion, "I want poppers! I want poppers!"

"I am not doing it," I declared. "If we stop, *you* are going to get out and buy the poppers."

He glanced out the rear window of the car and glumly took in the sight of the caravan full of Secret Service agents, aides, and reporters. He turned back and said, "You know, Ricky, you never let me do anything."

On June 3, as voters headed for the polls in the Super Tuesday states, the Senator was up at dawn, with Joan, Kara, Teddy, and Patrick at his side, greeting workers at a Lockheed aerospace plant. "I'm an old plant-gater," he quipped. As the balloting proceeded, we flew back to Washington.

The Super Tuesday results were among the most bittersweet of the campaign. On this day, we won the battle and lost the war. We captured California, New Jersey, Rhode Island, New Mexico, and South Dakota. Carter's greatest success was in West Virginia, but he had also won Ohio and Montana. The President now had 1,982 votes compared to about 1,125 for the Senator. At 9:15 P.M. Carter appeared on live national television to crow over his "wondrous victory." He declared triumphantly, "It's over now."

But the Senator declared that it was not: "Tonight is the first night of the rest of the campaign. Today Democrats from coast to coast were unwilling to concede the nomination to Jimmy Carter. And neither am I."

Hearing this, Ronald Reagan must have realized that he was the biggest winner of the day. Upon learning of the Senator's intention to carry on with his campaign, he told the press that the Kennedy forces "could make some mischief" at the Democratic Convention.

Everyone within our campaign organization was exhausted, but the Senator appeared fresh and ready to go on Wednesday morning. We flew to Boston to attend Caroline Kennedy's graduation from Radcliffe, then headed back to Washington for strategy sessions regarding the next act of the extended drama.

On Thursday, the Senator met with the President in the Oval Office. During the forty-five-minute session, Kennedy surprised his adversary by repeating calmly in private what he had said publicly Tuesday night. Despite Carter's numerical lock on the nomination, the Senator had no intention of dropping from the race. Instead, he renewed his call for a televised debate. Once again the President declined.

For the next two months we were reduced to figuring out strategies to win certain critical rules fights at the convention.

To make matters worse, we were bankrupt. We cut the paid staff by 45 percent and closed off much of the office space. What was left of the campaign would be managed from one corner of the building.

Our staff tried to unwind during the preconvention lull. Almost all of the campaign workers—those few we could afford to keep on the payroll—took extended vacations. Joan journeyed to a spa. But the Senator stayed in Washington and I remained at his side.

I was enjoying a rare day off when Cindy joined me at poolside to seek some relief from the legendary Washington humidity. With the campaign over, she was back in Washington, looking for a new job. I detected tension. She shifted uncomfortably in her lawn chair. A frown crossed her face. "What's the matter?" I asked.

"I don't know," she said. "I think I've got a problem." She explained that she had developed a suspicious discharge. She was concerned that she had picked up some type of infection.

It was a weekend, so doctors' offices were closed. I suggested that she go to the Georgetown Hospital emergency room immediately, and she agreed.

Later that afternoon she returned and announced, "They think they know what it is, but the results won't be official until Monday. They gave me a precautionary shot of penicillin."

My immediate concern was for the Senator. Once again—damage control. We decided to wait until Monday, after the hospital test results were completed, before we mentioned anything to him.

Around ten o'clock on Monday, Cindy phoned the office to tell me that the test results confirmed the preliminary diagnosis. She added, "Margo has it, too. She's gone in for the shot."

Margo was a Hill staffer. Who gave what to whom was unimportant. The day's priority now was to load the Senator with penicillin as a precaution. At the moment he was on the Senate floor, but I needed to deal with the problem immediately. I walked into a small private office adjacent to the Senator's, closed the door, picked up the telephone, and dialed Stu Shapiro at the Health Subcommittee.

"Stu? It's Rick," I said. "Are you alone?" He was, so I got to the point quickly. "We have a problem. We need penicillin."

"Ooohh-kay," he drawled.

"Do you have any in the kit?" I asked.

"Yeah."

"The Senator will be back at noon. Be here."

When the Senator returned for lunch, I followed him into his office and shut the door behind me. Sitting at his desk, he glanced up over the rim of his glasses, waiting.

"We have a problem," I began. "Nothing to worry about. We'll take care of it."

"What's the problem?" he asked, ready to dig into his lunch.

"It's Cindy and Margo. They both have the clap and you have to get a shot."

He stared at me as if to say: After all that we have been through during the previous months, after flying back and forth across the country umpteen times, after kissing babies and old ladies, eating bad food and staying in lousy hotels, after fighting for our political life, after grappling with the President of the United States, we now have to worry about *the clap*? He shook his head and muttered, "You gotta be kidding."

"I'm not kidding. Both Cindy and Margo have it. Stu's got the penicillin. He'll be here shortly."

The Senator squirmed in his chair, shaking his head. "Awww, Ricky—a shot? I have to take a shot? Are you sure? Are you sure I have to take a shot? C'mon."

I shrugged and walked into the reception area to wait for Shapiro. When he arrived, every eye in the office focused a quizzical stare on his large black medical bag. I instructed my assistant, Connie, "We're not to be disturbed."

Shapiro and I entered the Senator's office. As the doctor searched through his bag, I moved to each of the three doors, locking them.

The Senator watched wide-eyed as Shapiro extracted a huge syringe from his bag. The needle was about four inches long.

"Drop your pants," Shapiro ordered.

"Ohhh, no," the Senator vowed, "you're not going to put that thing in me."

"Come on," Shapiro said, "get up and take your pants down."

The Senator stood, reluctantly dropped his trousers

and pulled his boxer shorts to his knees, still protesting: "You are *not* going to put that thing in me!"

Shapiro took a step forward and the Senator backed away. He waddled about the room with his pants half-down, trying to keep the desk between himself and the business end of the syringe. Neither Shapiro nor I could restrain our chuckles, and soon the Senator was laughing with us.

I could picture the scene in the outer office. I knew that everyone had stopped work to stare at the door, wondering what was going on. "Will you keep it down?" I pleaded. "Be quiet!"

Finally Shapiro bagged his quarry. The needle hit its mark and the Senator squealed. Shapiro withdrew, a look of triumph on his face. All of us collapsed into chairs, trying to stifle our laughter.

Shapiro managed to calm himself enough to explain that he had administered a substantial dose of penicillin. "I think this should do the trick," he said. "But if you have any difficulty, let me know."

As I escorted the doctor back through the adjoining office, several women asked in unison, "What was going on in there?"

"None of your business," I snapped. I pushed Shapiro out the door and returned to my desk, cementing a stern expression on my face so as to discourage further inquiry.

But a potential problem like the clap wasn't about to deter the Senator. During the down-time between the last primary and the forthcoming convention, there was too much free time on both of our hands.

There were days and nights in the hot tub, taking ever-increasing hits of coke and tossing back more booze than was needed to cover the pain of defeat. One weekend ran into the next in a blurry haze.

One day Steve Smith came to the Senator's house for

a midafternoon staff meeting, but the session was delayed because the Senator and a woman were locked away in the master bedroom at the back of the house.

"I want to see the Senator, Rick," Smith said to me.

"You better not, Steve," I replied.

He grabbed me by the lapels of my suit jacket and pulled me off into a bathroom so that we could speak privately. His face looked drained. "What the hell is going on?" he snapped. "We're supposed to be having a meeting and the Senator has somebody in the back room! How the fuck can you let him do this?"

I answered in a tired voice, "Steve, I can't control the man. It's an impossibility."

"We have staff here, for godsakes—" Smith said, leaving unspoken the rest of the sentence—how could the Senator flaunt his behavior so? Instead, he just mumbled, "I'm so fucking sick of this."

"Steve, I'm not his baby-sitter. I can't do anything," I said.

"You two are just alike," he hissed and left me standing there in the bathroom, and I thought, *What a jerk.* Then I shut the door, took a hit from a bullet, and went and pulled the Senator out of the back bedroom for the meeting.

After that incident, Smith spent most of his time in New York, away from Washington, away from the campaign, away from the candidate himself.

Soon after that, Kitty Brewer came to town to spend a weekend in McLean. Cindy, recovered from her infection, was back in the picture, too.

That Saturday afternoon as I sat by my pool, Kitty and Cindy suddenly appeared. The Senator was committed to attending some function with Ethel's children, which he was sure was bound to be a nightmare, so the two women decided to spend their Saturday night with me.

"Last night was *wild*!" Kitty said breathlessly. By now they were used to the Senator's inclinations, but on this Friday night he had phoned some additional women and invited them over for an impromptu party. "Boy, was it . . . Rick, we did tons of coke," Cindy said. "And 'ludes. Poor Ted, he didn't know whether he was coming or going by the end of the night."

The women went back to McLean on Sunday, but on Sunday evening I drove Kitty from McLean to the airport. She was agitated and complained bitterly that the Senator had refused to give her more cocaine, pointedly telling her she had had enough. "He's so selfish, Rick. Couldn't he have spared a little blow after all I've done for him?"

The next day the Senator asked me, "Did you go into my desk for any reason?"

"No," I answered. "I never go into that desk unless you ask me to."

He looked puzzled.

Suddenly I feared what might have happened. I told him about my conversation with Kitty on the way to the airport. "Kitty must have done it," he concluded.

He was furious. *Nobody* ever went into that desk unless he wanted them to. When she came back the following weekend, he had put a new lock on his desk.

He was very protective of his stash, just as I was protective of mine.

There were nights that summer when it seemed we were twins, competing to see who could beat the other, whether it was at sex or drugs or alcohol. And yet we managed to function fairly well during the days. Later, in their book *The Kennedys*, Peter Collier and David Horowitz observed, "In the last weeks [prior to the convention] Teddy was haggard and pale."

People thought it was sheer exhaustion. If they had only known what to look for, they would have seen telltale signs. Not that it would have mattered. Neither one of us knew, or even cared at that point, how destructive our lives had become, though at times I tried half-heartedly to rationalize it. This was just an aftereffect of the campaign, I told myself. But I knew that wasn't really true. Our destructive behavior had started long before this race. And when I looked around it seemed that nearly everyone involved in the campaign was showing signs of stress.

And then, unexpectedly, we received an emotional boost from the President's brother. In the midst of the Republican National Convention in Detroit, the news broke that the controversial, beer-loving Billy Carter had signed a consent agreement with the Justice Department acknowledging that he had received gifts and loans totaling $220,000 from the quasi-outlaw government of Libya to act as its agent. (Billy had previously responded to the criticism of Jewish groups questioning his Arab ties by suggesting that they "kiss my ass.") Perhaps the most damaging disclosure was that Billy had registered as an agent for a foreign government only *after* the Justice Department began looking into the matter.

Attorney General Benjamin Civiletti first denied that he had ever discussed Billy Carter's Libyan ties with the President, then admitted to a "brief, informal" conversation. The issue was clouded when the President's National Security Advisor, Zbigniew Brzezinski, declared that the White House had sought to use Billy to influence Libya's dictator, Muammar el-Qaddafi, to intervene with Iran in an attempt to free the hostages.

None of this played well across America, and the Senate Judiciary Committee appointed a special subcommittee to investigate.

President Carter held a nationally televised news conference on August 4 to address "Billygate." He proclaimed: "Integrity has been and will continue to be a

cornerstone of my administration." He acknowledged
that his brother was "a colorful personality," but that the
President would henceforth forbid anyone in the Executive Branch from dealing with members of his family
under any circumstances that might "create either the
reality or the appearance" of improper influence.

Unfortunately, the speech seemed to satisfy the majority of Carter delegates.

And so there was nothing we could do but wait.

One day one of our staff workers returned from a
vacation that happened to coincide with the Republican
National Convention in Detroit.

"It was just crazy," she confided in me, acknowledging
that she had been in the enemy camp. "I spent most of
the week in a hotel room with ————."

My ears burned as she mentioned the name of one of
the nation's most prominent Republicans.

"Did he know where you worked?" I asked incredu-
lously.

"Yeah. I told him."

"What did he say?"

"He just laughed."

How, I wondered, had we gotten to this point? More
important, how had *I* gotten to this point? There just
didn't seem to be any perspective anymore.

The issue took on deeper significance for me when my
father called our family together in Connecticut for a
meeting. My seven brothers and sisters had all been very
close during our childhood years, and, even as adults,
everyone—except me—got together for frequent weekend functions. At this gathering I found myself surprisingly unsettled by the images of my siblings, each of them
married and focused on their families. Sure, I realized,
each of my brothers and sisters had his or her own problems, but each had someone to share them with, and they
all seemed to be close. I had been so consumed by my

own career and life, rarely making time for them, that I was now the outsider.

Dad announced that for the first time in the history of his company he was going to bring other family members into the business. He turned to my oldest brother and my youngest brother and offered them key positions. His eyes quickly passed by me, and with momentary pain I wondered, *Why didn't he pick me?* And then I realized my own professional life was so intermingled with the Senator's that Dad hadn't even considered it a possibility.

Later I maneuvered my father into a private meeting and said quietly, "I'm thinking of leaving Kennedy's office."

A spark of approval flashed across Dad's face. Still, he did not offer me a job. He waited to hear what was next.

I noted that there might be a congressional vacancy in the district where Dad had a plant, which would make it easy for me to establish a legal residence. I asked, "If I ran for Congress, would you support me in the effort?"

Dad looked at me, love filling his heart—but pragmatism overruled it. His response was tepid. He wondered if it was the right move for me. He wanted to make sure that I really wished to pursue a public career for the rest of my life. He was an intensely private person, justifiably proud of the business he had built. For years now he had followed my career with, to be sure, a certain sense of pride, but he had seen me in the nightly news, and this went against the grain of his personal style.

With a sigh, he asked about money. I told him that the cost of a congressional campaign could run as high as $500,000, and I would need his assistance in raising it.

He expressed his concern that the spotlight from a campaign would bring an unwanted invasion of family privacy. He did not slam the door on my plans, but he was far less enthusiastic than I had hoped.

Later, as he drove me to the airport for my flight back

to Washington, I asked tentatively, "What are you doing in the future, as far as the business is concerned?"

"I'd love to have all my kids in the business," Dad said. "But I'm going to let every kid make that decision."

I asked myself again, *Why didn't he pick me?*

But I knew the answer: It was my own fault.

23 We arrived in New York the Friday prior to the opening of the Democratic National Convention and rented out the entire sixteenth floor of the Waldorf-Astoria. Kara, Teddy, and Patrick were housed in rooms along the hallway, as were various staffers. Joan occupied a small suite and the Senator was in a larger, adjacent suite situated at the very end of the hall. Joan had originally been scheduled to stay at Rose Kennedy's three-bedroom apartment on Central Park South; she said she'd wanted the solitude and peace, away from all the craziness. Then she complained that she felt out of the mainstream action, and our feeling was that it was better for appearances to have her at the Waldorf anyway. So she came. A stairwell led directly down to my suite, one floor below, where we could hold strategy sessions out of public view. Its other benefit was that it provided an accessible retreat for the Senator.

Steve Smith resurfaced for the formalities of the convention; he was still frustrated by the Senator's behavior but ready to rally with the family.

We knew that the Senator had only the slimmest of chances to wrest control of the convention from the President, but we knew, also, that we would have our shining moment. In return for the Senator's agreement to drop some of his minor rules changes, the Carter camp agreed to allow the Senator to address the convention on Tuesday night during the debate on an economic plank of the platform. The speech was scheduled for prime time.

Arthur Schlesinger, Jr., came to see us that week, armed with a draft of a speech. We all read it, and none of us liked it, but we held our counsel until we learned the Senator's reaction. He hated it, too. The correct concepts were there, but Schlesinger expressed them in his own words, and did not seem to grasp the Senator's style of speaking. Everyone much preferred the draft that Parker and Shrum were working on. They were preparing two slightly different versions of the speech—just in case we were able to pull off a miracle on the convention floor.

Schlesinger's enthusiasm for his own draft presented us with a problem in diplomacy. He was an intimate of the Kennedy family, and it was going to be difficult to tell him that the Senator had decided to scrap his speech. Kennedy met with Schlesinger a few times, halfheartedly reviewed the draft and pointed out portions that needed work, but could not bring himself to drop the ax. Schlesinger, wrongly encouraged, ensconced himself in his room and dutifully worked on the revisions.

The Senator finally persuaded Smith to break the news to Schlesinger. Just that suddenly, Schlesinger was gone.

Meanwhile, on Thursday, August 7, Frank Mankiewicz, a longtime press consultant to the Kennedys, penned a memo to the Senator entitled "When to Hold 'em and When to Fold 'em (apologies to Kenny Rogers)." Mankiewicz strongly suggested that if the Senator lost the rules fight—which would allow for an "open convention," letting the delegates vote as they wished, instead of the candidates they were charged with voting for—he should free his delegates from their own first-ballot commitments, ask that his name not be put in nomination, and leave New York immediately. He characterized this as the "dignified" way to bow out, a tactic that would make it clear that the campaign had been a serious one, that the Senator had been "fighting for the 'soul' of the party."

We filed that advice and turned our attention to the battle. At a noontime rally on Friday, the Senator insisted vehemently that he was the only Democrat who could defeat Reagan in November.

We tried desperately to persuade Carter's thirty-four Massachusetts delegates to lead the fight to open the convention, but very few were receptive. Our other hopes lay chiefly in the large, powerful delegations of Illinois, Pennsylvania, Michigan, and California. We counted as many as thirty-five possible rebels in the Illinois delegation alone. We heard that Carter delegates from Minnesota were wavering, but Carter people won them back by promising platform time to right-to-life supporters within the group.

We also learned that Vice President Walter F. Mondale was on the phone constantly, stroking Carter delegates, trying to keep them in line.

Sunday's preconvention television coverage reflected the media's assessment of the probable outcome: The Senator appeared for a half-hour on the low-rated "Face the Nation" show, where he pledged that, regardless of Carter's actions, he would free his own delegates from their first-ballot commitment. The chief question in the interviewers' minds seemed to be whether or not the Senator would support Carter's nomination. He replied enigmatically that he would never endorse a nominee "just because he has a 'D' after his name." He said that the key to his support would be whether or not the convention incorporated his key economic proposals into the platform. When asked about the challenge from the Republican nominee, Ronald Reagan, the Senator noted that the former California governor was addressing the number-one issue, economics, and was articulating his positions well. He added the warning, "I think the Democrats risk losing the election."

In contrast, President and Mrs. Carter received a full hour on "60 Minutes." Carter told Dan Rather that there was "no doubt" in his mind that he would receive the convention's nomination. When Rather asked whether the President would release his delegates from their first-ballot commitment, thus demonstrating his confidence in them, Carter replied that the chances of that were "none at all."

Paul Kirk met with Richard Moe, Mondale's chief of staff, in an effort to reach compromise on some of our platform proposals, so as to present a less disruptive posture to the viewing public. Moe yielded on four platform planks, all Kennedy programs, and, in some cases, directly contradicted Carter's current stands. Moe also surrendered on the issue of "platform accountability," agreeing to the rule that, prior to the balloting for the nomination, any candidate must publicly accept the Democratic platform or publicly list his objectives.

Moe told the press that his action was "strictly a gesture of conciliation." While conceding that the new platform planks were "not our preferred positions," he insisted that he and Kirk had "found language we could live with."

But according to Kirk, Moe admitted to him that the Carter camp thought it would lose the fight on these planks anyway.

The Senator commented, "This is getting to be the kind of platform I could run on."

Carter campaign manager Robert Strauss pooh-poohed the upcoming rules fight. He told a group of reporters that, after Carter won the nomination Wednesday night, the key question would be whether the Senator would endorse the ticket in a show of party unity. For his part, Strauss said, there was "just so much peacemaking" he was willing to undertake.

Meanwhile, Kirk was insisting to the press that we were within one hundred votes of our goal to free the delegates, dump the President, and nominate the Senator. He predicted, "I think we may be on the threshold of one of the major political stories of recent political history."

The Senator added, "I see the numbers being there."

During the day on Monday, August 11, House Speaker and Convention Chairman Tip O'Neill entered the hall at Madison Square Garden and worked his way around technicians preparing for the opening ceremonies.

O'Neill was aware of the Democratic party's penchant for disarray as he strode to the microphone for a sound check. He drew a smattering of laughter when he bellowed, "Now is the time for all good men to come to the aid of their party."

At the opening session, Millie O'Neill, Tip's wife, led the delegates in the Pledge of Allegiance.

On the issue of convention rules, we now had only two minority reports for the delegates' consideration, one of which was to free the faithful delegates. New York governor Hugh Carey, ready to lead the fight for us, asked rhetorically, "Would you say that Roger Staubach couldn't throw a touchdown pass in the last two minutes?"

The definitive end to the campaign came with the roll-call vote on Rule F(3)(c), which we had been pushing to overturn. Carter's forces kept the bulk of their support intact. The delegates voted to uphold the rule locking themselves into their first-ballot votes, and the President's renomination was assured.

As we watched the voting, I felt my mouth turning dry.

It was the beginning of the end. What we had feared for so long during the down-time before the convention was now turning into a depressing, cold reality. I tried to steel myself against the overwhelming sense of despair. After all, I had to be strong for the Senator. Other staffers were more open with their emotions, and reacted to the news with tears.

The Senator, seeing the rejection of his candidacy by the convention, gave me a grim smile. Pain filled his eyes. But he was determined, I could tell, to maintain a brave front. He was, after all, a Kennedy.

We returned to the Waldorf-Astoria, where the Senator phoned President Carter at Camp David and offered his congratulations, but he remained vague on two key questions: whether he would campaign for the President and whether he would appear on the podium with him after Carter's acceptance speech on Thursday night.

Following the phone call, the Senator held a press conference in the ornate function room at the Waldorf— away from the convention hall to prevent any demonstrations by his supporters. He drew cheers when he said, "We didn't come to this great city of New York not to fight." But then he declared, "I'm a realist and I know what this result means. My name will not be placed in nomination."

"No!" someone shouted.

The Senator reassured his supporters that he would continue to fight "for a truly Democratic platform," and reminded them that he would speak to the convention on the following night "about the economic concerns that have been the heart of my campaign."

When he left the room, a chant arose: "Eighty-four, eighty-four, eighty-four!"

Reporters cornered the Senator in the hotel lobby, and one posed the question of the moment: Would the Senator now endorse Carter's candidacy? He responded,

"When an umpire up at Yankee Stadium sees a pitch cross the plate, he calls whether it's a strike or a ball. . . . We'll make the judgments as we hear them and see them."

Back at Madison Square Garden, Carter's chief of staff, Hamilton Jordan, heard the news and said that he had "every hope" that the Senator would campaign for the President. "I'm assuming that Senator Kennedy wants to help us in unifying this party," he said. Jordan reached Paul Kirk by phone and offered to hold talks through the night in order to resolve the platform differences between the Senator and the President, so as to present a unified front to the nation. Kirk responded that we would not compromise; if Carter was unwilling to cave in on all of the Senator's platform proposals, there was no need to talk. In turn, both Robert Strauss and Richard Moe took the phone, trying to convince Kirk at least to agree to a meeting.

Kirk said no.

"We've got 'em where we want 'em," Rick Stearns joked to a reporter. He called the rules vote "just a ruse to make the Carter people overconfident."

But, in truth, it was over, and we now concentrated our attention on the Senator's speech for Tuesday night. The Senator's back was bothering him, and he, like all of us, was exhausted. His spirits, however, were surprisingly good. I told a reporter, "He was better than any of us last night, and he was better than any of us this morning."

We devoted most of our day to fine-tuning his address to the convention. The Senator took time to lunch with his sister Pat Lawford at her East Side apartment, but returned to rehearse in a side room at Madison Square Garden, equipped with a lectern and a TelePrompTer to simulate the podium environment. The Senator decided that only Parker and Shrum could man the machine, for they were the ones who best understood the proper cadence. Thus, the two men who had labored over the words were destined to listen to them as they crouched into a cramped cubbyhole, out of public view.

"Oh, my God . . ." the Senator worried aloud during the rehearsal. "What if the TelePrompTer stops working and here I am in front of all these people?" He grabbed me and pointed to a cubicle of space directly beneath him. "Rick, can you fit under here?"

"What good will that do?"

"You can keep track of the manuscript, and in case this TelePrompTer breaks down, you can sort of point up to where I am."

"Right," I said. "What am I gonna do, stick my head up, with all the TV cameras around, and say, 'You're supposed to be on page eight'?"

On Tuesday evening, as the fight over the platform loomed, the Senator and I sat alone in a room off the main floor, reviewing the speech one more time. I advised, "Whatever you do, at the end, warm up. You know, hug and kiss everybody."

He knew that I was talking principally about Joan, who waited in a nearby room, along with Kara, Teddy, and Patrick. Even in defeat, his supporters would want to see them all together, the illusion of the happy family presented for at least one last time. It was, I thought, probably a farewell for the Senator. It seemed impossible that we would ever be able to pull off another campaign like this one with Joan and the kids rallying around. Things were changing in all of their lives.

At the appointed time we linked up with Joan and the children. In an attempt at jocularity, the Senator said to Patrick, "I hope I don't flub it."

Accompanied by a phalanx of Secret Service agents, we strode down a long, narrow hallway. The agents and I stopped at the entranceway to the convention platform and the Senator and his family stepped onstage, and into the glaring lights of Madison Square Garden.

The packed convention hall erupted.

Delegates set their personal allegiances aside and paid tribute to the renowned Senator from Massachusetts. As one, the crowd was on its feet, clapping and screaming. The band blared and a sea of KENNEDY signs swayed to the rhythm. For a time the chant "We want Ted! We want Ted! We want Ted!" took over the hall.

From my post at the doorway, I could see Parker and Shrum, huddled beneath the TelePrompTer, looking very nervous.

I had heard the speech numerous times in rehearsal, but as he presented it now, speaking for thirty-two minutes to the delegates, the nation, and the world, he brought tears to my eyes. The text was lyrical in its beauty, and the Senator presented it with power and emotion, performing far better than he had at any other time during the long campaign. Parker and Shrum were flawless on the TelePrompTer. As the words tumbled forth, I knew that everyone—no matter their political bent—would remember this as a special moment.

He took on Reagan, saying that the Republican nominee "is no friend of labor . . . that nominee is no friend of this city and our great urban centers . . . that nominee is no friend of the senior citizens of our nation." He directly attacked Reagan's call for severe reductions in government spending:

> It is surely correct that we cannot solve problems by throwing money at them. But it is also correct that we dare not throw out our national problems on a scrapheap of indifference. The poor may be out of political fashion, but they are not without human needs. The middle class may be angry, but they have not lost the dream that all Americans can advance together.

In all, he characterized Reagan's philosophies as "a voyage into the past."

He touched upon other key themes, such as the importance of passing the Equal Rights Amendment and the critical need for a national health insurance program. He reminded the delegates of the party's commitment to economic justice, calling it the "cause that brought me into the campaign and that sustained me for nine months across a hundred thousand miles."

He was perhaps most forceful when he spoke of the need for jobs. Calling this "a moral issue," he threw down the gauntlet to the Carter forces, declaring that "we will not compromise" on the controversial minority platform plank proposal we had been seeking for a $12 billion federal jobs program. He urged the delegates to "pledge that there will be jobs for all who are out of work."

Then he turned to more personal concerns. "There were hard hours on our journey," the Senator said, as some delegates openly wept. He continued:

> Often we sailed against the wind, but always we kept our rudder true. There were so many of you who stayed the course and shared our hope. You gave your help, but even more, you gave your hearts. Because of you, this has been a happy campaign. . . . When I think back on all the miles and all the months, and all the memories, I think of you.

He quoted from A. E. Housman's "A Shropshire Lad": "What golden friends I had."

The network cameras caught poignant scenes in the audience. Here was a black woman wearing a "Kennedy" hat, tears pouring down her cheeks; there was a young couple, both holding "Kennedy" posters, hugging one another as they wept.

On cue, Joan, looking radiant, relieved that it was

finally over, and Kara, Teddy, and Patrick walked out onto the platform and joined the Senator in full view of the national audience. The nation was mesmerized as the Senator concluded:

> Someday, long after this convention, long after the signs come down and the crowds stop cheering and the bands stop playing, may it be said of our campaign that we kept the faith. May it be said of our party in 1980 that we found our faith again. May it be said of us, both in dark passages and in bright days, in the words of Tennyson that my brothers quoted and loved and that have special meaning for me now: " . . . To strive, to seek, to find and not to yield."
>
> For me, a few hours ago, this campaign came to an end. For all those whose cares have been our concern, the work goes on, the cause endures, the hope still lives and the dream shall never die.

The convention hall again erupted in a combination of planned and spontaneous celebration. Remembering my advice, the Senator headed straight for Joan and embraced her warmly. He brought her and the children forward, to the front of the platform, and the family waved to the delirious, emotionally charged crowd.

For an instant Camelot was revisited.

Tip O'Neill's gavel was overwhelmed by the standing ovation. The demonstration continued for thirty minutes as various Democratic dignitaries made their way to the podium to shake the Senator's hand.

In the NBC booth, David Brinkley asked rhetorically, "Wasn't that the best speech you ever heard from Edward Kennedy?" ABC's Ted Koppel called it "perhaps . . . the best speech in his long and distinguished career." CBS's Bill Moyers spoke wistfully of the "Kennedy magic." Even the President's press secretary, Jody Powell, called it "a barn-burner."

After a time, Joan and the children were shunted off to

one side. The Secret Service agent next to me met my gaze, and we moved onto the platform to take up unobtrusive positions near the family.

Still the celebration continued, and the Carter forces sought to regroup. Referring to the $12 billion federal jobs proposal, Richard Moe now conceded, "I think we are going to get whomped." At this moment it was obvious that the Senator, even though he had lost the rules vote the previous night and had withdrawn from the race, had carried *this* evening. Even prior to the Senator's speech, the Carter camp figured to lose the jobs platform plank vote by a 300-delegate margin, and *now* it seemed likely that the euphoric delegates would rubber-stamp all four of the Senator's minority platform planks and deal the President a crushing defeat. So, to cut their losses and promote some sense of unity, Carter advisers spread the word that they wanted to talk.

After some initial argument between the Carter and Kennedy teams right there onstage, Tip O'Neill insisted on bringing an end to the televised dissension. If compromise was not in the wind, then he wanted to get on with the roll calls and bring an end to the business.

The President's campaign counsel, Tim Smith, made a frantic call to Hamilton Jordan in the Carter trailer and came back with a quick compromise: If we would capitulate on our call for wage-and-price controls, Carter would agree to the adoption of our other three planks, including the critical jobs program. It could all be done by a voice vote. We agreed, and O'Neill was happy.

From time to time during the extended celebration, my eye caught the Senator's. His unspoken message was, *When I give you the signal, let's get the hell out of here.*

When he finally left the platform, the applause died quickly and Tip O'Neill moved to reassert control. Wielding the heavy gavel, he called for a voice vote on the four contested platform planks. "Yeas" and "nays" tumbled forth in uncountable confusion, but O'Neill claimed to have a discerning ear. He announced that three of the Kennedy planks had been adopted. Only the call for wage-and-price controls was defeated.

In the NBC booth, commentator John Chancellor noted, "Four hours' work in two minutes."

Thus, Carter would be the nominee, but he would have to run on our platform.

Back at the Waldorf, we threw an end-of-the-campaign bash that night in the Senator's suite. Liquor flowed freely and was consumed by campaign workers and members of the press alike, but my own revelry was interrupted by a conversation with Paul Kirk. He reported that Hamilton Jordan had called him to communicate President Carter's congratulations on the great speech. Jordan and Kirk had danced around the next topic: Would the Senator now publicly endorse Carter's candidacy? Kirk informed Jordan that Kennedy had not yet made a decision.

As the party progressed, the members of the advance staff chose their moment and assaulted me en masse, pouring their beers over my head. They presented me with a card saying that no matter how hard I had pushed them, they had always known I loved them.

The Senator gulped heavily at glasses of scotch; he was somewhat annoyed. We had advised that it was better if he remained in Joan's presence this night—reporters were present—so Cindy had not joined the party; she was already en route to the Cape, where the Senator would meet her in a few days.

"It's sad that he lost," Melody Miller admitted to a reporter, "but thank God he's alive."

After several hours, the Senator gave me the signal to clear things out. I circulated, and let it be known that the party was drawing to a close. Gradually the room emptied out. Joan went off to her own suite. The Senator said that he was exhausted and was going to bed. He asked me to wake him in the morning.

He disappeared into his bedroom, alone, and only one other campaign worker remained with me. She was a woman I knew well, supremely loyal to the Senator, but one who had always been careful to maintain a strictly professional relationship with him.

She saw that I was drained and suggested, "Rick, why don't you just go and I'll finish cleaning up. I'll close the door and lock up."

"Okay, fine," I agreed. I headed down the back stairwell to my own suite and sank into bed.

Some hours later, in the midst of a troubled night, I was awakened by a familiar rhythmic cadence above my head. It took me a few moments to clear my thoughts before I identified the sounds of pounding bedsprings in the room above. In an instant I realized what was happening, and I was furious. The Senator had willfully violated one of our strictest rules: He had invaded the inner circle of the campaign.

The next morning, when I entered the Senator's room to awaken him, I found the woman staff worker there, in bed with him. She stared at me horrified—dumbfounded and embarrassed. Quickly she gathered herself together and ran off.

The Senator, rubbing the sleep from his eyes, treated me to a sheepish grin.

This was a slap of reality that I did not wish to deal with. I returned to my room to cool off.

When I rejoined the Senator for breakfast, he said pointedly, "Don't take this out on her."

"I have no intention of taking it out on her," I replied, "but I think it never should have happened."

"I was wrong," he said, pouring coffee.

I pushed back my chair, still furious, and began pacing

the room. "I can't believe you did it!" I raged. "I just can't believe it."

He had, at last, gone too far. Not for the first time, but with far greater force than ever before, the thought came to me: *I want out.*

24

"I hope I will have his support, but that's a decision for him to make," the President responded, when asked whether the Senator would endorse him.

Someone observed that what had been whipped now had to be kissed.

It was a tricky question, with issues that ran deeper than the obvious. Should the Senator issue an immediate endorsement for President Carter? Should he appear on-stage with the President on Thursday night? Tip O'Neill let it be known that he expected the Senator to do the right thing, which was to close ranks with the nominee. In fact, both CBS and NBC picked up an exchange at the convention podium that was not intended for broadcast. Democratic party chairman John White said, "It's my understanding that Kennedy . . . will not come unless the President invites him himself."

O'Neill responded, "Hey, listen, he's going to be here."

At another moment, when O'Neill knew that reporters were listening, he revealed that he planned to speak to the Senator, to urge him to appear with Carter. O'Neill said: "I'll tell him, hey, you did pretty good for a guy who was knocked down a lot in the first three rounds. . . . You stayed on your feet. . . . Now, don't piss in your own bucket."

But the cons seemed to outweigh the pros. Someone suggested that the Senator borrow a response from Senator David B. Hill, after he had lost the 1896 nomination to William Jennings Bryan. When a reporter asked, "Senator, are you still a Democrat?" Hill replied, "Yes—very still."

Carter's people kept up the pressure. Vice President Mondale phoned the Senator and attempted to arrange a personal meeting, but was rebuffed. Dick Drayne denied an account that the Senator had agreed to meet with the President. "They never quit, do they? I wonder if they keep on conniving in their sleep."

The issue came down to money. Publicly, the Senator decreed that he would announce his support for Carter only if the President agreed to support the $12 billion jobs platform plank. Privately, Steve Smith and Paul Kirk raised another issue with Hamilton Jordan. "We gotta have help," Smith said. He spelled out the details of our huge campaign debt. Our contributions had not even reached Phil Bakes's most pessimistic projections.

Smith and Kirk made it clear. If the Carter camp would agree to help reduce the campaign debt—significantly—then the Senator would offer his visible support.

On Wednesday morning David Brinkley and John Chancellor of NBC News arranged to interview the Senator in the Waldorf's Louis XIV Room. Joan readied herself for the occasion, assuming that she was to be included. When she walked in, she looked surprised to see only one chair set up in front of the camera.

"Aren't I in this interview?" She addressed the question to Dick Drayne, who was at my side.

"Um, no," Dick replied. "It was supposed to be just the Senator."

"Oh, well," Joan said crisply. "Then there's no reason for me to be here."

Later, I learned that Joan was miffed. Given that this would probably be the last time in a long time that she and the Senator would be together, I could understand her wanting to be supportive even in defeat. But it was the network's decision to have the Senator alone, not ours.

Instead, the Senator lunched with Joan at The Box Tree, an exclusive East Side restaurant. He thought it would be a chance to thank Joan for her work on our behalf. Unfortunately, the press, which followed the Senator everywhere, barged into the restaurant and they couldn't really talk. It just wasn't a good day for her.

After lunch the Senator sent his wife off in a car to the airport to fly back to Washington. Then he canceled an afternoon tennis match so that he could be available for negotiations with Carter concerning the jobs plank.

That afternoon, Tip O'Neill spent much of his time on the telephone in the dressing room of the New York Rangers hockey team, located beneath the convention podium, trying to hammer out a position that would be acceptable to both sides.

Finally, Hamilton Jordan came to the Waldorf to deliver a copy of the President's "platform accountability" statements. We studied it carefully. Carter accepted the jobs program in principle, but still balked at its price tag.

At 4:15 P.M. the Senator took a call from the President. We characterized this event to the press as a "private conversation" and we released no details. In fact, the President and the Senator covered several important subjects. The President repeated for the Senator what he had already made clear in his "platform accountability" statement: He accepted the concept of a jobs program, but would not commit to spending $12 billion on it. In turn, the Senator told the President he would support the President's campaign, but would not commit to—or rule out—a public appearance with him on Thursday.

The two men spoke obliquely about the burden of the campaign debt. "I know Paul and Jordan have talked about certain issues," the Senator told the President. "And I have to be assured on those issues before I can come out and support you."

"We'll make sure we work that out," the President said.

That evening I was with the Senator in his suite, along with Sargent Shriver, Carey Parker, Bob Shrum, Dick Drayne, and the Senator's longtime friend, Washington lawyer John Douglas. The Senator spoke several times with Paul Kirk, who was stationed at the convention; they were finalizing the words of a statement. I attended to scheduling details. We all worked with drinks in our hands, and with our ears tuned resignedly to the television convention coverage. We watched as Florida governor Bob Graham placed Carter's name in nomination and as the interminable seconding speeches droned on. We were at first pleased when a Carter statement was read to the delegates, accepting in principle our controversial jobs proposal, but we were irritated when the statement added the caveat that "the amounts needed to achieve our goals will necessarily depend upon economic conditions."

Most of us had been drinking, but became subdued when the roll call vote began. The Senator's name was not even placed in nomination, but he captured considerable blocs of votes. Carter's delegates, of course, remained not only loyal but committed to following the rules. There was no drama. Upon the final vote, the Senator issued the following statement:

> I congratulate President Carter on his renomination.
>
> I endorse the platform of the Democratic Party. I will support and work for the reelection of President Carter. It is imperative that we defeat Ronald Reagan in 1980. I urge all Democrats to join in that effort.

As the delegates burst into applause, O'Neill shouted, "So, united we stand!"

By Thursday evening the auditorium was jammed with 20,000 people, the vast majority of them Carter supporters, who cheered wildly at all the appropriate presidential pauses. Carter was well into his speech, and in the Senator's suite at the Waldorf, we paid scant attention. The Senator, with a drink in his hand, paced the room aimlessly, occasionally stopping to huddle with one or another clique of advisers.

However, we all turned our eyes to the television screen when we heard a loud, rapid *pop-pop-pop*. A member of the Communist Workers Party, who had managed to smuggle in a string of firecrackers, had set them off. When the Senator realized the innocent source of the noise, he grinned. He watched the now-distracted President stumble comically over his next line, referring to the Democrats as "the party of a great man who should have been President, who would have been one of the greatest Presidents in history, Hubert Horatio *Hornblower*—"* This blunder ranked with the best of the Senator's misstatements, and we roared with laughter.

The President had to shout to make his voice carry through hot, overcrowded Madison Square Garden, and before long his face was covered with perspiration. Enthusiasm was difficult to maintain.

Suddenly the President stared straight into the televi-

---

*Horatio Hornblower was a fictional British sailor created by the late C. S. Forester.

sion camera and drawled, "I'd like to say a personal word to Senator Kennedy." All conversation in the room ceased. The Senator stood framed in a doorway. One hand grasped his drink. He listened as the President said:

> Ted, you're a tough competitor and a superb campaigner—I can attest to that. Your speech before this convention was a magnificent statement of what the Democratic party is and what it means to the people of our country, and why a Democratic victory is so important this year. I reach out tonight to you and I reach out to all those that supported you in your valiant and passionate campaign.
>
> Ted, your party needs you—and I need you—your idealism and dedication working for us. There is no doubt that even greater service lies ahead of you—and we are grateful to have your own strong partnership now in the larger cause to which your own life has been dedicated. I thank you for your support; we'll make great partners this fall in whipping the Republicans.

Slowly the activity in our suite resumed. No one said anything about the President's personalized remarks.

I was numb from the combination of liquor and exhaustion. I thought, *I just want to be out of here. I just want this to be over.*

After speaking for nearly an hour, Carter limped to the end of his speech. The wild demonstration that was supposed to accompany this finale was to be cued by thousands of balloons falling from two plastic bins hanging from the ceiling. Carter waited in embarrassment as the balloons remained in place, his famous toothy smile strained. Television cameras caught a number of workers climbing into the rigging in order to liberate them. A few floated free, and the crowd of Carter supporters attempted to respond with their programmed passion.

Democrat dignitaries made their way to the podium, each appearance timed and calculated to escalate the applause. Meanwhile, the President glanced about, clearly searching for the Senator.

At this moment, we were still at the Waldorf, still drinking. Our agreement with the Carter people was that we'd leave for the convention hall the instant his speech was over.

"Oh, Ricky, do we really have to do this?" the Senator asked.

"Yes, we do," I insisted, trying not to think about how humiliating this was going to be for both of us. "Come on. I've already got everybody else in the car."

His eyes were bloodshot, and he didn't say a word. I straightened his tie. "We're going to be late," I warned.

"I don't care," he growled.

"You know, if you screw up, they're not going to help pay off our debt."

That motivated him. Reluctantly he allowed me to lead him from the Waldorf suite toward the elevator.

By the time we finally arrived at Madison Square Garden, pleading the excuse of a traffic jam, the Carter celebration was waning. We headed straight for the holding room, where the Senator grabbed for a drink as members of Carter's advance staff hustled us out the door and down the corridor.

"Ricky, I don't want to do this," the Senator complained, loud enough for all to hear.

But he was grinning now. Somewhere deep inside, he had tapped into his extraordinary reservoir of energy. I knew that he was teasing me. I growled at him, "You gotta do it. C'mon. Let's get this over with."

I pushed him onto the stage. He stepped forward with a resigned expression. His appearance elicited the loudest roar of the evening—more than the President's speech—igniting, in some corners of the convention floor, a systematic chant of "We want Ted! We want Ted!"

The Senator halfheartedly shook the President's hand and patted him almost condescendingly on the back. Meanwhile the crowd was continuing to roar. He glanced at Rosalynn but neither acknowledged the other's presence. Then he moved to one side of the podium and raised a clenched fist. He knew better than anyone how well this would play on television. Commentator Theodore White described this as a "seigneurial wave . . . like a grand lord tossing a tip to the coachman."

The Senator left the platform before photographers had a chance to snap a shot of him and the President joining in the traditional hands-held-high victory salute.

"Let's get outta here," he said to me.

A large Secret Service detail, red lights flashing, moving briskly through traffic, drove us to La Guardia, where a Learjet—lent by union supporters—waited to take the Senator to Washington. I had to remain behind, to clean up the convention details.

The campaign was officially over now, and so was the Secret Service protection; this was as far as the agents were going.

As the Senator walked up the steps of the plane alone, I thought he had never seemed so vulnerable.

25 Cindy was determined to break away to a life of her own. She rented a home not far away from mine.

I saw her frequently. At times she was strong in her resolve to strike out on her own. At other times I suspected she was hiding the fact that she had just been with the Senator.

One evening, when I arrived to take her out to dinner, she invited me in for a drink first. She chatted idly for a few minutes before she said bluntly, "You know, I'm pregnant."

"Are you sure?" I asked.

"Yes. I don't know what to do. No, I *do* know what to do."

I had heard these same words from her before. I asked, "What ever happened the other time?"

"I went out to California."

"I remember you were scared."

"Yeah," she admitted. "I'm going to do the same thing this time."

I was curious, and I asked, "Did he know before?"

"No. I didn't say anything to him."

"Is he aware this time?"

"Yeah," Cindy said. "He's aware of this one. He said he would do whatever I wanted to do."

We talked about that. Cindy was not excited about the prospect of becoming a mother under these circumstances. She did not know what she wanted to do with her life. There were still times when she fantasized that the Senator would make a wonderful husband. But then she felt he would never really change.

She left; when she returned, I asked her how it went.

"Fine," she said through tight lips.

Back at the office little seemed to have changed. One day I walked by my desk and saw that Gertrude's familiar box of chocolate chip cookies had arrived. I picked it up along with some files and carried them into the Senator's office.

He beamed, ripped open the box, popped a cookie into his mouth, and reached for another.

As I worked my way through our agenda, I noticed that Gertrude's cookies were disappearing at a record pace.

"You're not going to eat that whole box, are you?" I asked.

"I'm going to do what I want to do," he said between mouthfuls.

Since there was still the campaign debt to pay off, the Senator reluctantly agreed to tape three television spots promoting the Carter/Mondale ticket. But at one point during the taping, the producer had to urge the Senator to show "a little more enthusiasm." In return for the Senator's help, the White House openly urged Democrats to help erase the $1.7 million Kennedy campaign debt.

The President also extracted a promise that the Senator would make campaign appearances on his behalf.

A contingent of Secret Service personnel, smaller than before, was assigned to accompany us on the campaign trail. On the handful of occasions when the Senator and the President made joint appearances, the Senator invariably drew the more enthusiastic response. The press reported that the Senator found this embarrassing, but privately he was likely to grin and say, "Ricky, did you hear that? Did you hear the crowds?"

Shortly after that, we flew to Texas on a jet paid for by the Carter campaign, but found little enthusiasm for Carter's candidacy. A *Wall Street Journal* reporter observed that campaigning for Carter appeared to be, for the Senator, "a little like swallowing castor oil." That same reporter noted that the Senator was gaining weight, particularly in the gut.

The most poignant moment of the trip occurred in San Antonio, on October 22, at the John F. Kennedy High School. President Kennedy had visited this building site the day before his assassination, and had promised to return for its dedication. The Senator, in his speech, reminisced. "The thousand days are like an evening gone, but they are not forgotten." His voice quavered when he said, "In remembering Jack, we remember the best in our country and ourselves."

Behind him was a banner proclaiming: ONE MAN CAN MAKE A DIFFERENCE, AND EVERY MAN SHOULD TRY.

From Texas, we headed for Puerto Rico. Somehow we found one precious afternoon there for the Senator to spend with Patrick and his cousin Dougie Kennedy. We all went deep-sea fishing, with Secret Service agents along in the boat. Others stationed themselves on the rocks offshore, and a single agent patrolled in a second boat nearby.

Rolling seas made all of us feel a bit queasy. After a time, Patrick and Dougie were so sick that they wanted to jump into the water just to get away from the motion of the boat. The Senator agreed to this, to the consternation of an agent who expressed his worries about sharks.

The Senator laughed and helped the boys jump overboard. He shot a glance in my direction and without another word both of us jumped into the water. We romped with the boys as the agents trained their rifles at anything resembling a shark fin.

On October 26 the Senator was scheduled to present a speech at Hiram Bithron Stadium, an outdoor soccer field. Originally we expected a crowd of about 25,000 people, but the morning of the speech, Secret Service agents warned us that enthusiastic Puerto Ricans were arriving from all over, jamming the access roads, screaming for a chance to view the Senator. The Secret Service now estimated that at least 250,000 people would attend, the largest crowd ever to assemble at this location.

Agents scouted the area with an armored van. Sharpshooters stationed themselves along the roof of the grandstand that ran across one end of the soccer field. They made no secret of their apprehension.

Our caravan was forced to approach the stadium via a maze of back roads in order to circumvent stalled traffic. We entered the grandstand through a private back entrance.

As we waited for the Senator to go on, I produced a bulletproof vest, but the Senator balked at wearing it. The day was boiling hot. "You're not going out there unless you put this on," I dictated. He did as he was told, but throughout the long walk up the stadium access ramps he complained about the agonizing pain in his back.

The Senator reached the podium and greeted our host, Rafael Hernández-Colón, the Democratic candidate for governor of Puerto Rico. I found my own vantage point and looked out at the crowd. In front of me, as far as I could see, was an ocean of people, fanning out well past the confines of the soccer field into the parking lots and grasslands beyond. They cheered wildly at the first sight of the Senator, screaming "Kennedy! Kennedy! Kennedy!" After a time the chant subsided, but when the Senator was introduced, it began all over again. "Kennedy! Kennedy! Kennedy!" the shrill voices screamed in an ever-growing crescendo.

"He's got to hurry up," a Secret Service agent advised me. "The crowd is turning into a mob." On the fringes we could see fences collapsing as people struggled for a vantage point. What concerned the agents most was that, with the fences down, some of the crowd was able to sweep around the back of the grandstand, encircling us.

Finally the Senator began to speak, shouting over the crowd until the audience grew quiet enough to listen. His words, in favor of social justice and equality, took on greater power and authority as he responded to the thrill of the moment. His listeners reacted with wild enthusiasm.

Afterward, Secret Service agents had to push and shove to clear a path for us back to the caravan of vehicles. Even when we were inside our car, we were not safe. Excited faces pressed onto the window. Our driver forged ahead, carefully, but with earnest intent. As the crowd thinned and we were able to pick up speed, a few cars pursued us. I turned to see a Secret Service car run one of them off the road.

On the plane trip back to Washington, the Senator busied himself by penning thank-you notes to his key campaign workers. Meanwhile, I found myself reflecting upon the scene in the soccer stadium. It had been so awesome, so overwhelming at the time, that I really didn't have a moment to think about it. Now, in the quiet of the evening, I thought, *If someone had blown up that place, I'd be gone, too. . . .*

Back in Washington I discovered that while we were away, a pale blue envelope had arrived in the mail, postmarked October 23, 1980. It was addressed to "Ms. Angelique Voutselas, Office of Senator Ted Kennedy," and marked PERSONAL. This had to be from someone who was unaware that I had replaced Angelique more than three years earlier; the return address included only the letter writer's initials: L.C. Following the usual procedure, I opened it and read its contents.

It was from Lana Campbell, the countess who claimed to have had a long-standing affair with the Senator; her claims had been widely reported in the press, and she had become a part of the Chappaquiddick lore. The Senator had claimed that the night of the tragedy was the first time he had ever been on Chappaquiddick, but Campbell had told the *New York Post* that there had been previous occasions, beginning in 1966, when she and the Senator had initiated their relationship. She said that three weeks after the accident, she had met the Senator secretly in McLean, where he told her that because of the spotlight of publicity they had to end their affair.

Now she wrote of her profound love and went on to agonize over a recent encounter she had had with Lem Billings, who had told her that the Senator would "never never" forgive her for speaking so candidly to reporters. She pointed out that other politicians had survived admitted infidelities, and added that people were not as puritanical as the Senator and his advisers seemed to think. She said that after seeing the Senator repeatedly looking "wounded and trapped" at the mention of Chappaquiddick, she had decided to "rescue" him and had told the *New York Post* that the Senator had been drinking heavily during the late sixties and suffering blackouts as a result. She hoped her revelations would explain Chappaquiddick, she said.

I replaced the five-page letter in its envelope, placed it inside the Senator's briefcase, and thought, *I hope she doesn't do us any more favors.*

Days passed into weeks, and the depression we both

felt prior to the convention magnified as the Senator performed his bare-bones duty to Carter. From Cindy, I knew that the Senator was drinking heavily and that his use of cocaine was escalating. Since the Secret Service protection had returned with his campaign efforts for the President, the Senator was forced to use my bedroom for many of his romantic interludes. Once I found two neat lines of coke on my glass desk with a note, penned in the Senator's nearly illegible hand, offering me a "present."

I found another note in my mailbox, also handwritten on the Senator's personal stationery.

Dear Rickie—

We have traveled many miles together in the Senate and the 1980 campaign. I am grateful to you for all your help in so many ways—with the family—running the Senate office and being by my side when we challenged the Party and the country in 1980—

My thanks for your concern your decency your loyalty and your friendship.

As ever—Ted

As the campaign progressed, the Republicans attacked the incumbent President without mercy. In the process they systematically dismantled the ideals we held so close to our hearts. The Senator had reason to be so glum.

But not until we saw the scope of Carter's defeat in November did we realize what an incredible battering the party had taken. Now it appeared that the Republicans would control the White House for at least the next eight years.

"It's going to be different," the Senator admitted honestly when cornered by a reporter after arriving at Boston's Logan Airport. During the interview, a bill fell from his pocket. Bending his sore back to retrieve it, he said, "Five bucks. We need that to pay off the debt."

Perhaps worst of all from our standpoint was the fact that the Republicans not only won the White House but took control of the Senate. Thus, when the 97th Congress convened in January 1981, the Democratic chairmen of fifteen major Senate committees would be forced out in favor of Republicans, and the chairmanships and Democratic staffs of approximately one hundred lesser committees and subcommittees would also be lost. The Senator would relinquish the chair of the Judiciary Committee to seventy-eight-year-old conservative Senator Strom Thurmond—who quickly announced that he would seek legislation to reinstate the death penalty, limit abortions, rescind busing, and dilute fair housing laws.

Everything the Senator had spent the past ten years working for was slipping through our hands. The Senator would also surrender control of two influential subcommittees dealing with health and energy matters. They were cutting him off at the knees.

As a member of the minority, the Senator would be placed in the role of one merely reacting to the chairman's lead. Somehow the Senator had to set himself to the task of rebuilding a legislative agenda and, at the same time, attempt to regain his image as a viable candidate for the future if, indeed, that was the course he chose to take.

Now that the Senator no longer had to be in proximity to the Judiciary Committee offices, he wanted to move out of Eastland's old suite in the Dirksen Building, back to the Russell Building. I had to survey the makeup of the Senate to determine what space might be available.

The painful problem, however, was not where we would locate, but who would come with us. Over the years I had seen the office and committee staff grow from about twenty-five into the hundreds. Due to the campaign, we had added additional employees, bringing the total to more than three hundred. There was no longer any need for campaign workers, and we were losing control of more than fifty staff positions on the Judiciary Committee. Dozens of longtime staffers who had taken deep pay cuts to join the campaign committee expected to return to Senate positions that no longer existed.

The Senator could not bear to break the bad news; he made a few attempts to tell key employees, but had trouble making himself clear. One man spent a few minutes in the Senator's office listening to Kennedy hem and haw and make vague suggestions that he should move on to a new position. The unfortunate man came out and said to me, "I think I've just been let go. Is that true, Rick?"

After a few more attempts, the Senator said morosely, "You take care of it, Rick."

I had to approach one of my very close friends and announce, "You don't have a job." I had to cut men and women who had been my close associates for a decade. Occasionally I ended up crying. Often I felt a curious but acute sensation of *personal* guilt. *I'm getting irrational,* I told myself. And I was certainly getting depressed.

But it was a depressing time for everyone, especially for the Senator. He gained a considerable amount of weight, and in his sadder moments he spoke about quitting the Senate and buying a company. He bandied about the idea of trying to become the Secretary General of the United Nations. The current Secretary General, Kurt Waldheim, was nearing the end of his second five-year term, and the Senator spoke with some advisers about the possibility of gaining that post and turning it into a more meaningful office.

In the past he had used cocaine almost exclusively on weekends. One morning he arrived in the office with watery eyes and sore nostrils, looking completely out of sorts.

"You have junk coming out of your nose." I sighed, realizing he was pretty much at the end of the line.

He didn't protest as I took him by the shoulders and steered him into his private bathroom. "Aw, Ricky," he said as I straightened his tie and made him as presentable as I could before I sent him onto the floor of the United States Senate.

On another occasion Larry Horowitz emerged from the Senator's office and commented, "He was fine yesterday. Why does he have such a bad cold? His nose is dripping."

"I don't know. . . . I don't know," I said, tired of thinking of excuses. .

As soon as Larry left, I walked in and said, "Hey, it's obvious even to Larry that you have a problem."

Yet another time, a staffer emerged from the Senator's office and warned me bluntly, "There's coke coming out of his nose."

I sagged and went into his office. He was attending to business with apparent efficiency, unaware that a dusting of white powder clung to the edges of one nostril.

This is absolutely crazy, I thought. Again the conviction came to me: *I have to get out of here.*

To add insult to injury, the National Conservative Political Action Committee announced that it was placing the Senator's name on its hit list of legislators it would seek to defeat in 1982. An anti-abortion group made him its number-one target. And the 1981 edition of the Social Register decided to drop Senator and Mrs. Kennedy from its list.

That evening I called Cindy and asked her to come over. "We've got to talk," I said. We spoke at length about what we might do to persuade him to moderate his behavior—missing the irony that both of us were using coke with increasing frequency and that our behavior needed modification, too.

And yet I was, for the moment, determined to keep up appearances. As the holidays approached, I decided to give my second annual Christmas bash. Cindy agreed to be the hostess. I invited the Senator and staffers from our campaign office and our Hill office as well as friends and a heavy contingent from Washington's working press corps, including Mary McGrory, Tom Oliphant, and Susan Spencer.

"Should I invite Mudd?" I asked the Senator.

He screwed his face in pain. We both knew that Mudd was battling Dan Rather for the chance to replace Walter Cronkite as the anchorman for the CBS "Evening News." He was an important man in Washington, and soon might be even more important. We decided that my Christmas party might provide the proper opportunity for the Senator to mend his fences, so we issued an invitation to Mudd and his wife and son.

"No scenes or anything like that," I counseled, and the Senator promised to be on good behavior.

In the meantime another issue arose. On Thursday, December 18, the day before the party, the Senator's private line rang. I picked up to hear the Senator's son declare, "Rick—I have a problem. . . ."

Teddy was supposed to be en route from Wesleyan University, coming home for the holidays. He was planning to arrive in time for my party. "What's up?" I asked.

"I got busted," he said. He explained that he was stopped by a state trooper in Upper Pittsgrove Township, New Jersey, charged with driving his Jeep sixty-four miles per hour in a fifty-mile zone. Peering into the car, the trooper had noticed a small, partially opened wooden box containing a suspicious substance.

My ears were on alert, worried that he would say the word cocaine.

"Just a little pot," Teddy said.

Well, that was sort of a relief. Nevertheless, we had to

swing into action. The Senator instructed me to call John Douglas, who put a New Jersey law firm onto the case. Soon, Teddy was sprung from the custody of the state troopers and was back on his way home, but the incident did little to improve the holiday spirits.

Early the following evening, after only a few of the guests had arrived, Mary McGrory ran up to me. "Oh dear!" exclaimed the tough-but-proper reporter. "I've ripped my dress."

I located my housekeeper and said, "We need your help."

The three of us adjourned to my bedroom. Mary stepped into my bathroom and took off her dress. She reappeared, clad in a bath towel, handed her torn dress to my housekeeper, and sat on the edge of my bed. I sat next to her and chatted.

A few minutes later Roger Mudd poked his head into the room, took one look, laughed, and said, "What a story this is going to make!"

We all laughed. Then Mudd said, quite seriously, "Thanks for inviting me."

We decided to rejoin the party. I was on the staircase, with Mudd behind me, when I noticed that the Senator had arrived, along with Patrick. The Senator was busy greeting people, so he did not see us coming.

Mudd reached the bottom of the stairs, caught the Senator's eye, and held out a friendly hand.

The Senator refused to shake it. Without a word, he moved off into another room.

I mumbled my own apologies, but Mudd left the party immediately.

I hunted up the Senator, found him downing a drink, and demanded, "Why did you do that?"

"Because the guy skunked me."

"But I asked permission—"

"Yeah, well, I just decided I didn't want to deal with him."

But there were other things he *did* want to deal with.

In Aspen for the holidays, the Senator met two women in their early twenties, and the occasion developed into a rambunctious night. One of the women bragged about it afterward.

Soon we received a letter from a Kennedy supporter who had heard the story from this woman and wanted to know how a United States senator could behave in such a manner. She threatened to take the story to the press.

The Senator read the letter and laughed.

"Did you have a good time?" I asked grimly.

He laughed again, but he said, "We may have a problem here. You better call her. Take care of it."

I phoned the irate letter writer and did my best to appease her. I managed to handle the situation, but it added to my growing conviction that things seemed to be getting out of hand. Shortly afterward I noticed the Senator paying particular attention to Betty McKay, one of our staffers. This upset me, not just because she was staff but because the Senator *knew* that she was the longtime girlfriend of one of our recently laid-off campaign workers, a man I still counted as a good friend. She told her boyfriend, and he told me, that the Senator was plaguing her with phone calls. "You gotta say something to him," the man pleaded.

"I just hope there's nothing going on between you and Betty," I said to the Senator, who shrugged it off.

One Sunday evening the boyfriend called in alarm. "Rick, something's going on. She's really upset. She won't talk to me." I drove over to visit Betty and found her distraught. I said simply, "I *know* you slept with him. What happened?"

She said that she had finally relented to the Senator's constant phone calls and agreed to visit him at McLean.

They drank. They snorted coke. They went to bed. "What should I do now?" she cried. "Should I leave the office?"

"Calm down," I advised, though by now I was deeply agitated myself. I thought about the dozens of other times I'd said those words to women upset with the Senator. "We need to talk. Want to go out for a drink?"

We went to Morgan's, a fairly new restaurant and dance club, and proceeded to drown our sorrows. After a while she began to feel better, but I didn't. Things were eating away at me.

Near two in the morning, when I took Betty home, she suddenly realized that she had forgotten to bring her keys. "I've got a spare hidden near the back door," she said. I drove into an alley around the side of her town house. Then I boosted her over a high fence.

I was standing in the alley, peering over the fence to make sure that Betty located her key, when I noticed a red flashing light. *Uh-oh,* I thought. A D.C. police officer approached and asked gruffly, "What are you doing?"

I was pretty drunk and painfully aware I had a vial of coke in my pocket. Somehow I had to talk my way out of this. I stammered, "Uh—my girlfriend forgot her key. And I was just helping her—"

"Show me your driver's license," the officer commanded.

As I fumbled for my wallet, a moment of inspiration struck. I pulled out my Senate card, which clearly identified me as the administrative assistant to Senator Edward M. Kennedy. I handed the laminated document to the officer, gave him a moment to study it, and then apologized, "Oh, I'm sorry. I gave you the wrong card."

The officer asked quietly, "Will you be okay to drive home?"

"Yeah," I assured him.

"Be careful," he advised.

On Monday, when I next saw the Senator, I said, "I thought we had an agreement. The staff is supposed to be off limits—and Betty has been dating my good friend for four years."

The Senator grinned, then, realizing I was distinctly not grinning back, he shrugged.

"I should've known." I turned on my heels and stormed out of the office.

Everything seemed to be coming apart, beginning to run out of control. In my coke-filled, stressed-out state I could feel a building sense of anxiety and frustration, and now added to that was a welling anger. The whole melange was made more blurry by my confusion about what to do. On the one hand I tried to get on with business as usual, and on the other I found myself repeatedly thinking, *I've got to get out.*

But how? Always with me was a further preoccupation that was to be a dire influence over the next few weeks: The fact was that though I wanted to leave the Senator, I also wanted to remain his friend, an accepted member of his circle. The Senator had a history of branding as a traitor and actively shunning an aide who had walked out on him. Illness, divorce, personal crisis—these might be acceptable excuses, but nothing much else was. I was haunted by the Senator's enduring animosity toward Jim King, his former advance man who left to join the National Transportation Safety Board. He sent me a note expressing regret at being unable to attend my Christmas party. The Senator saw it and scribbled the word "Ugh" on the note. When I asked him why, he said, "Because I wouldn't want Jimmy King coming to the party."

Angry though I was at him, I confess that something within me cringed at the idea of his rejecting me that way.

On the morning of January 19, the Senator said, "Rick, can you come in?"

I grabbed my notebook, went into the office, and closed the door behind me.

The Senator looked tired and sad. He said softly, "Joan and I are getting a divorce."

I was shaken, not just by the news, but by the realization that he and Joan and Dr. Hawthorne had been discussing it and I knew nothing about it. I had never been shut out of so fundamental an issue in the Senator's affairs before.

"Call in Carey and Bob," the Senator said. "We need to get a statement together."

Two days later, while most of official Washington was recovering from the Inaugural festivities of the day before, and the press focused on the long-awaited release of the American hostages (which the Iranians timed to coincide with President Reagan's ascension to power), the Senator formally announced that he and Joan would seek a divorce after twenty-two years of marriage. The carefully worded statement declared,

> With regret, yet with respect and consideration for each other, we have agreed to terminate our marriage. We have reached this decision together, with the understanding of our children and after pastoral counseling. Appropriate legal proceedings will be commenced in due course, and we intend to resolve as friends all matters relating to the dissolution of our marriage.

Father James English, the pastor of Holy Trinity Church in Georgetown, disclosed that he had discussed the situation with both Joan and Ted. "They're very fine and mature people," he commented, "and when they came to the decision . . . I said it was the best thing." He added, "They understand the Church won't recognize this."

The *New York Post* ran a tabloid-style piece about the divorce announcement that included a partial "Who's Who" of some of the Senator's "playmates." Included were ski champ Suzie Chaffee, Countess Lana Campbell, American socialites Helga Wagner and Amanda Burden, former British debutante-model Louise Steel, and Princess Angela Wepper of West Germany. The *Post* quoted Suzie Chaffee: "I think it's very sad. . . . She is a wonderful lady." Discussing the Senator, she said, "In the years I've come in contact with him . . . I found he has wit, compassion, and a hell of a lot of energy."

Together with Paul Kirk, the Senator and I pored over printouts of the family's expenses over the past five years in order to determine the proper alimony settlement. Once Paul said, "Hell, there's a lot of cash expenses here." But he did not push the issue.

Patrick Kennedy, now fourteen, moved to Boston to be close to his mother. Twenty-year-old Kara was at Trinity College in Massachusetts, and nineteen-year-old Teddy was safely back in Wesleyan, after paying thirty dollars in fines and court costs. Despite Teddy's recent arrest and other minor problems, I considered all three to be wonderful kids, with a great deal of promise. I knew that the Senator would miss them.

The McLean house was an empty shell.

26

In the early morning hours of Friday, February 6, 1981, I was home in my bedroom, dressed in a bathrobe, when I heard what sounded like knocking at the door.

I went downstairs. When I stepped into the kitchen, I found a black man on the patio, trying to get in the kitchen. He looked like a vagrant. Panicked, I screamed, "Who the fuck are you?"

He turned, startled, and took a step toward me.

I fled upstairs, locking the bedroom door behind me. Several minutes passed as I struggled to catch my breath and force my pounding heart to relax. I listened carefully, but heard nothing.

After some time I ventured out and carefully checked the entire house. I was relieved to find that the intruder, probably as frightened as I was, had fled.

I called the police to report an attempted break-in. Nothing was taken, I said, and the man was gone.

The police dispatcher recorded the details and blandly informed me that an officer would stop by to write up a report, sometime in the next two or three days. Whether or not I would have reacted the same way if I were in a normal state of mind I don't know, but in my strained mood the police nonchalance infuriated me. Two or three *days*?

At work on Friday, as I recounted the story to my colleagues, one of them asked, "Well, do you have a gun? You should be careful. It's a big house."

I phoned a Secret Service agent whom I had befriended, told him the story of the attempted break-in, and admitted, "It shook me up. I'm a little alarmed."

The agent agreed to lend me his spare revolver. When we met later that day, he took some time to show me how to use the gun, but then he had second thoughts. After all, I had no permit, but he allowed me to keep the gun anyway. I placed it in a bedside table, just in case.

A difficult weekend began. I was depressed and spent a great deal of time in the house, listening to music, doing lines of coke, and tossing back scotch. How had I let my life sink to this?

And I brooded about the nonresponsiveness of the police. *What the hell do you have to do to get some attention from those guys?*

Over Friday night, Saturday, and Saturday night, the gales of thought and emotion built, and though I couldn't realize it, they were about to organize like a tornado into a moving column of irrational behavior. I emphasize "irrational" because later, after the events of this night and the three weeks following, friends have asked me, "Why did you *do* it?" and they suggest possible answers to me, always phrased in rational terms: "Was it a survivor-instinct device for *ensuring* that you left the Senator?" or "Was it a cry for help?" and so forth. I can only shake my head in uncertainty, because my behavior over those days was so inconsistent that no attempt at a clear-minded, logical explanation holds up. The man who, asked to account for some egregiously foolish act, says "I was drunk," is not justifying himself, but he may be giving as valid an explanation as he can come up with.

The man who in a fit of frustration breaks something, smashes, say, some object that he treasured when he was sound, both explains and fails to explain when he says, "I just snapped, I guess."

In any case, in the growing swirl of cocaine, alcohol, fatigue, stress, new depression, and high jitteriness that Saturday night there began to stir a wild germ—to call it the germ of an "idea" is probably to dignify it too much; "impulse" is closer—and this germ would quickly infect many parts of me.

It seemed to start narrowly enough with a determination to get some attention from the police, whose blasé attitude had fermented in my teeming mind to the point where it seemed an intolerable outrage.

Obviously they hadn't responded to my intruder because the details were too mild. Well, I could fix that!

And so, in my hectic haze, I concocted a *fake* break-in, complete with all the trappings—a smashed window, alarms going off, a call to 911, and by the time the police arrived, which they did in a hurry this time, the pièce de résistance—a kitchen knife stuck into my bedroom door. I felt triumphant. At last the police took me seriously. And, of course, at last I had gone totally out of control.

On Sunday Betty called me, exasperated. "I thought you said you'd talked to the Senator, Rick!"

"I did," I replied.

"Well, it didn't do any good. He just called again, wanting me to come over."

"I don't believe it!" I said, furious with him. "I *did* say something to him, told him the staff was off limits. Period."

"Well, he didn't listen. He said he wanted to see me."

"What did you say?"

"I told him to get lost."

God! I seethed. *It wasn't just the cops, the Senator too was incapable of paying attention!*

By Monday night I was crashing again, plunging back into gloom and anxiety. More cocaine and scotch. I felt a strong but fuzzy sense that I was careening off course, but at the same time I was seized by the need to *do* something. I had to change my life, I couldn't go on like this, I would go to pieces—thus I jabbered at myself.

What I needed was to take a drive, I decided, get out of this house, clear the head. Then my newborn worm of paranoia whispered: *Take the gun; you never know. Right! Good idea!* My drugged-out, stressed-out mind listened to the worm's wisdom and I tossed the gun in the glove compartment.

I started driving.

I can't recall with surety everything that stampeded through my head that night. I don't remember where I went at first. I do recall I began to cry, and prayed aloud in the car: *God, please help me.*

Finally I found myself near CIA headquarters, across the river in Virginia. I was in an isolated section, heavily wooded. I pulled off the road and parked. I would take a walk in the cold night air. I would take the gun with me. A wild new scheme was hatching.

I needed to get away from the Senator, but I didn't know how. I couldn't quit, he would write me off forever, and I just couldn't accept that. But my life was going to hell. And now I even had a housebreaker threatening me.

At some moment during these agonized thrashings, several of these elements must have come together because the last pieces of the wild scheme clicked into place. Or did they? I can't pretend that now, eleven years later, I recall with utter clarity all the thinking of that befuddled night. How much of what I did was a calculated plan to expand the scenario that my life was being threatened ("And so, Senator, I know you'll understand that, much as I hate to leave you, I must withdraw from the scene") and how much was simply rage's appetite to express itself by breaking something, I'll never know.

This is what I did. I found myself back at my car. I raised the gun I had been carrying, aimed it at the rear window on the driver's side—and I fired.

I felt the kickback, heard the explosion, saw the window shatter. And yet, for milliseconds I didn't take it as real—just as while we're sleeping we adapt into our dream a voice or telephone ring until, abruptly, we wake up and realize it actually *is* ringing.

And that's what happened to me. Suddenly I was wide awake, back in reality, looking at a broken window and God only knew what else broken with it.

Looking back, I now can see that was my moment when I could have said, *should* have said, "There it is, hard evidence that I've lost it, I'm out of control. I'll show it to the Senator and say you know I'd never leave you voluntarily but you must see I'm stressed out, exhausted, whatever, I'm no good for you this way, I need to go away, take a rest, et cetera."

But I didn't do that.

No. A decision like that would have taken a clear and reasonable mind, and though the gunshot had woken me up, it did not wake me to a well-rested, drug-and-alcohol-free mind. Or to a mind instantly freed of the automatic responses of the past ten years. *We got a crisis here!* What's the first thing to think about when you've got a crisis? *Damage control.*

Not the truth. Damage control. You shot your own car window out! What's the best kind of damage control on a wacky fact like that? Total suppression. Don't tell anyone. Just take it in first thing in the morning and get it fixed. Make it go away. *But how could I do something like this? Shoot my own car?* Forget that now. Think about that later. Right now, damage control. All notion of an I'm-being-threatened scheme was blown away—temporarily.

I got back home, parked the car in the driveway. Within a matter of minutes a couple of my friends dropped by for a late-night visit. Talk about bad timing. The car was in plain view.

"What happened to the window?"

I looked at the window and I looked at them, and in that instant Rick Burke the damage-control expert became a damage-multiplication expert.

"Oh, uh, I was in the driveway, getting into my car and somebody . . . took a shot."

"Oh, God!" one of my friends said.

The other said, "We've got to call the police."

That was the last thing I wanted, but I couldn't come up with a reason to refuse. So we called them, and it was as though I'd seen myself ignite a powder trail and now the sparks were racing away from me toward what surely was a keg somewhere in the distance.

The police raced over—five squad cars in all—examined the damage, and recorded a statement from me. I told them that I was getting into my car when someone—I did not know who—fired a shot.

All of this was perfectly in line with my original death-threat scheme, but still I did not sleep that night, and by morning my bedsheets were wet with perspiration. Oh, God . . . I'd filed another false police report. I tried to tell myself that everything would blow over, but when I drove into the private garage underneath the Senate Office Building, the guard glanced at the shattered window and said, "Oh . . . I heard about what happened."

The office was abuzz with it, and I had to repeat my story to numerous concerned coworkers. The Senator was working at home that day and I clung to the hope that he would not learn what had happened. Just how he was supposed to agree to—indeed maybe even *suggest*—

my resigning rather than risk my life without his ever learning I'd been threatened, don't ask me. I've already confessed that logic was not the commanding factor in these last days with the Senator.

But of course he did hear about it. Some time during the afternoon he called, trying to conceal his puzzlement that I had not told him the news myself. "What happened?"

A brief spurting impulse to tell him I'd shot the car myself came and went. I couldn't do that now, I figured. Because now it entailed *two* admissions: I shot the car *and* I lied to the police about it. The police report was now official—and false. This would give him fits. No. I took a deep breath and repeated the lie I had told the police. I did it with a curious, jangling combination of dread and hope—dread that he wouldn't believe me and this wouldn't work, hope that I was convincing him and this would blow over; dread that he *would* believe me, hope that he would see through me, stop me from this out-of-control binge.

But he accepted my story.

His only concern was that someone might be trying to intimidate me. "This could be a very big problem, Rick . . . ah, you know, what if somebody's trying to extort money or, worse, information? Information about . . . about me? I think we better inform the FBI."

In fact, as soon as the Senator hung up, he phoned Walter Sheridan, the ex–FBI agent who had worked as a security consultant for Robert Kennedy and, later, for the Senate Judiciary Committee. He was a pro. His first act was to inform the FBI.

When I heard this my alarm cranked up still more. Now the FBI was involved?

That evening two FBI agents interviewed me at home. Their demeanor was polite and professional, but in my scrambling anxiety it never occurred to me to do anything but stick to my story.

Over the ensuing days one thing led to another, but what it *didn't* lead to was my cleaning up my act by getting off coke and booze. I continued to "mastermind" my whole scheme in a bewildered mixed-media haze of intoxication.

But this time I was deeply recommitted to the somebody's-threatening-me plan. I began to invent and report threatening phone calls.

Bill McMannus, a friend who was an officer on the D.C. police force and a former linebacker for the Philadelphia Eagles, had offered to come by my home for a while. He would monitor all my incoming calls.

One night I scrawled a note threatening both me and President Reagan's son Ronald and left it leaning against my mailbox. Then I took off for the evening and did not return until I was sure that McMannus had already been there. He left me a message telling me about the note and saying he was taking it to drop off at the FBI lab. My reaction to this news, as with each new step of my ruse, was an inconsistent combination of exhilaration and alarm.

The threat to the President's family now brought the Secret Service into the case.

As it happened, I had to travel to Boston, and I stopped off in Connecticut to visit my parents. When I repeated the story to them, my father advised, "Get protection if you have to."

"I'm handling it," I insisted.

I "handled it" by fabricating new threatening calls and notes, and the snowball of lies grew bigger with each day. I hired operatives from the Vance Agency, owned and operated by Bill Vance, the ex–Secret Service agent who had married Susan Ford. I wrote a wildly fictional summary of events for Walter Sheridan.

Mom wrote to me: "I pray & pray this nightmare will end."

Reporters pounced on the theme, calling me for details.

Then one day, the two agents came back to my house and asked if there was a place we could talk privately. I said, "Sure. Come in." When we went inside they said, "There are several points in your story that just don't add up. Is there anything you want to change, or do you want to retract? If you do, we'll just drop the whole thing."

They cited some of the inconsistencies they'd found, they offered to give me some time to think it over, and they went into another room. A short time later I told them I stood by my story.

Finally, some nights later I took a long drive. For two hours I maneuvered in and around Washington. An unaccustomed sobriety had a chance to take hold. I knew my lies were collapsing under their own clumsy weight. The FBI was closing in. It was only a matter of time before I would be confronted with what I had done. By the time I got home, it was obvious there was no alternative: I had to tell the investigators the truth. I couldn't bear the thought of facing the Senator yet, but I knew I had to 'fess up to the "cops."

I pulled into my driveway to find two Secret Service agents awaiting me. I asked them to come in.

"Where were you, what's going on?" one of the agents asked.

"Why?" I replied.

"The more we dig, the more questions we have," he said.

The decision that night to confess began with an awareness that the investigators were closing in.

But there was also a substantial element of sheer exhaustion, of the need to get out from under the crushing strain of trying to maintain the whole preposterous scam.

And at last there was even an element of appetite—successfully suppressed for too long—to do the right thing.

Still, all those reasons did not make it an easy thing to do. Thus it was that for a few minutes I was unable to speak. Finally it came to me how it should be done and I said simply, "Take me to Paul Kirk."

The agents agreed to do so first thing in the morning.

After another all but sleepless night, I met with Kirk at his law office. "Paul," I confessed, "this shooting and the threats? They didn't happen."

With those words a flood of emotions arose, but by far the dominant one was a surge of relief.

Kirk listened without comment as I poured out the story of my life with the Senator. Then he dialed the number of a psychiatrist at George Washington University Hospital and took me over for an examination.

After the doctor pronounced that I did not pose a physical threat to myself or anyone else, I called the Senator and requested an immediate appointment. Kirk made another phone call just before I left, but didn't say to whom, and I didn't ask.

The Senator and I met in his library in McLean.

"It didn't happen," I admitted. I detailed for him the truth behind the events of the past few weeks and concluded, "I'm just completely burned out. I need to take a leave of absence to find out where I'm going, what I'm doing."

"You know, uh, Ricky, I was concerned about you," he said softly. "If you need any help with anything, I'm here."

We covered a few essential details. My assistant, Connie, could handle the brunt of the work, at least for a time. Paul Kirk would be on call to help. I agreed to stay in touch with both of them.

As I rose to leave, I asked, "Did you know what I was coming here for?"

"Yes," he admitted. "Paul told Walt Sheridan right after you talked to him. But I wanted to hear it from you."

My sister Peg and my brother Len flew down from Connecticut to offer their support. I spoke with them for hours at a time. I told them how painful it had been to fire so many of my friends over the past few months. I hinted at the stresses caused by the Senator's womanizing, but I shied away from the topic of drugs.

When Peg said, "I'll always be proud of you," tears filled my eyes.

What about the future? I wondered. I remembered the Secret Service agent who had remarked that I looked, sounded, and even *thought* like the Senator. What else could I do but work for the Senator? My social station, my job, my very identity were linked to him. I found it difficult to picture myself in any other job. Was this why longtime staffers such as Angelique and Eddy and Paul found it so hard to leave? On February 25 the staff threw a party for me to note my twenty-eighth birthday, although very few knew at that point that I was leaving. The Senator came, accompanied by Cindy.

He chose his moment and drew me off into a bathroom, where we could speak privately. He embraced me and I realized that, for the first time in a decade (except when dealing with his children), I saw the shimmer of tears in his eyes.

What was this man to me? I wondered. What was I to him? During the past few frantic years, I had served as his employee, friend, brother, son, image consultant, confidant, and—though inadequately—his conscience. We celebrated our successes together. We mourned defeat with a common sorrow. We drank together. We shared drugs. We were romantic rivals.

He handed me a print of Jamie Wyeth's portrait of JFK, signed by the artist. The Senator had also signed it, adding the personal note: "To Rick, who keeps the rudder true."

He said, "Rick, you've done more for me than anybody."

On March 19 the Senator issued a statement: "I have accepted Rick Burke's resignation with regret and with deep gratitude for his extraordinary service as my administrative assistant. I value his friendship; he has my total support during this difficult period."

Judge Reggie B. Walton of the Superior Court of the District of Columbia accepted my plea of guilty to the charge of carrying a pistol without a license. Charges of filing false reports to law enforcement agencies were dropped. The judge sentenced me to one year in jail, but then suspended the sentence and placed me on three years of supervised probation on the condition that I pay a one-thousand-dollar fine and participate in a program of psychiatric therapy. After considering early psychiatric reports, which indicated that my behavior was "triggered by the exceptional circumstances" of my employment and that I was cooperating in therapy, the judge further reduced the sentence to one year of unsupervised probation.

Whenever you leave a position in a public way, it brings a focus and spotlight on others in your life as well. This was especially true for my family, and I felt enormous guilt about involving them in the matter. My mother was very understanding, but very confused.

Dad advised, "Move away from Washington."

"My counseling is here," I protested. What's more, all my friends were Washington based. I owned a house in Georgetown. My therapy was going very well. I was seeing a psychiatrist a couple of times a week and we were beginning to make important inroads. Professionally, I even had a few business feelers out.

"You can find a good therapist in another city," Dad insisted.

Eventually I accepted the wisdom of his counsel. By then I was gaining the upper hand in my fight against cocaine, having decided life was difficult enough without that complication, and my alcohol intake was minimal, limited to occasional dinner wine. I didn't join any program for either the coke or alcohol abuse, but worked with the therapist, determined that I would overcome these demons with his help on my own. I flew to Connecticut, unsure of my plans, and held a long discussion with Dad. It was the first time we spoke in depth about my years in Washington.

I studied him closely. I remembered him as a rather distant figure from my childhood. He loved us, but he was not a "hands-on" type of dad. Now, perhaps, he was growing a bit more mellow. His business was successful. For the first time in his adult life, he allowed himself leisure. I thought that I saw in his face a twinge of regret that he had not spent more time with his children when they were younger. If he could, he seemed determined to atone for that now. He wanted to help.

He reminded me of the night in 1979, shortly before the presidential campaign, when he and Mom had come to Washington and I had taken them to dinner at The Foundry. I remembered, and I squirmed in my chair as I recalled thinking that they were taking up my "valuable" time that night.

"Remember when you excused yourself to make a phone call?" he asked.

I nodded.

He related that, while I was gone, Mom remarked about all the people in the restaurant who seemed to know me. She asked, "Isn't it wonderful that Ricky has so many friends?"

Dad had replied, "If you believe that any of these people are his friends, you're fooling yourself. These aren't friends. These are people who want something."

He let that story sink in for a few moments, then he said, "I was always afraid that you'd get caught up in the false glamour of life." He added bluntly: "I'm sure there are things that you and Kennedy did together. From what your sister has told us, I have to believe that there's a whole lot of drugs and sex involved in this."

I admitted, "Yes, there was. I did things I would never have conceived of doing."

"You don't need to go into it," he said quickly. "But I figured something was going on." He was quiet for many moments, then asked softly, "What do you want to do with your life?"

I saw no choice but to start over. I agreed now that it was essential for me to get out of Washington, so I planned to sell my house and move to New York, or perhaps back to Connecticut, and try to find my niche in the business world. "Of course," I said, "it's going to take me about a year just to get over this."

My father predicted: "You'll be lucky if five or six years down the line, you are not still dealing with this thing."

EPILOGUE

My father was right. In some real sense, I'm still "dealing with this thing" more than ten years later.

In the decade since I left the Senator's staff, my life has had some surprises, some high points, and some lows.

During the first six months after my resignation, I regularly visited a therapist. With his help, I fought my dependency on cocaine, and by the time of my father's death in 1983 I had all but rid myself of the drug habit. By the mid-eighties I was free of it entirely and I've stayed that way.

In 1984, from my continuing friends on the Senator's staff and his social world I heard that the Senator was considering a presidential bid.

"You can't let him run," implored a close friend, a woman who knew almost as much about the Senator as I did. "It would be crazy to let this man run for President." This was no easy thing to hear and face up to, but I knew she was right. The Senator, albeit without intending to, could still bring tension into my life—and into other lives. Visions danced before me of a President addressing crisis decisions while impaired by the excesses I knew Ted Kennedy was prone to. Yes, I'd have to do something if he decided to run.

To my great relief, he did not run. I turned back to my own life, which still called for a lot of rebuilding. Because I admired many of his legislative initiatives and harbored a lingering yearning for revival of that old Kennedy flame, I hoped that the Senator had the capacity to remedy his personal failings even though he was in his fifties. But as the years passed I periodically heard reports about his conduct that made me shake my head.

In 1985 among other activities I joined the Board of Trustees of the Martha Graham Dance Company. In 1987 I was elected its president, and my primary assignment to myself was to work to eliminate a $1.5 million budget deficit. The National Endowment for the Arts turned down our grant application, so we decided to see if Congress itself would help us address the debt. To plead our case, Martha Graham, Mikhail Baryshnikov, and I went to Washington. We were sitting in the office of Senate majority leader Robert Byrd, talking with several influential legislators, when Ted Kennedy walked in.

"Rick!" he exclaimed, clearly surprised.

We shook hands and our eyes met briefly for the first time in six years. His demeanor was polite, but at this public moment I could read discomfort and worry in his face. Through my mind ran something that a friend and former colleague had once told me. "The Senator is terrified of you. He's afraid that you're going to tell what you know." I had also heard he'd been given this counsel by one of his advisers just after I'd resigned: "You've got to distance yourself from Rick—he knows too much." But I was in Washington to talk about Martha Graham's activities, not the Senator's or mine, so the meeting proceeded in a formal way until we all parted—with no further personal exchange.

That same year, 1987, I invested in a faltering company and agreed to become its chairman because I thought I saw how to turn it around. And it did become profitable—until the recession. Creditors called in their loans, many of which I had personally guaranteed for the business. The result was personal bankruptcy for me in 1991.

Nineteen ninety-one was a bad year for Ted Kennedy, too. The events in Palm Beach involving his nephew William Kennedy Smith and a charge of rape became a public relations nightmare. The image of the Senator himself prompting his son Patrick and nephew Willie to go bar-hopping late at night, and the carousing ending in an arrest—it all brought a grimace to the faces of millions.

In June, confronted with friends who were concerned about his drinking, he rejected the notion. "I don't have a problem," he announced publicly.

In the summer of 1991, after weeks of televised coverage of Willie Smith and the Senator both in and out of court, a writer friend who knew some of my history prompted his agent to call me. I took the call.

Early in October I met for the first time with a publisher, signed a contract, and by the end of October the writing had begun.

The background for the negotiations and the commencement of work on the book was again the picture of Senator Kennedy on television, and never did he look less comfortable or effective in front of a camera. The occasion was the Clarence Thomas hearings. The Senator, obviously forced into silence during the discussion of Anita Hill's sexual harassment charges, was a classic portrait of a man whose private conduct was forfeiting his public usefulness.

In October he delivered at Harvard what quickly became known as his "mea culpa" speech. "I recognize my own shortcomings—the faults in the conduct of my private life," he told his home-state audience. "I realize that

I alone am responsible for them, and I am the one who must confront them."

That was it, the entire mea culpa, and for many it was not enough. "It was a tantalizing tidbit," wrote Michael Putzel in *The Boston Globe,* "but there was little hint of what he thinks those faults are or of how he is working to confront them."

"He seemed to mention it merely in passing," wrote Curtis Wilkie, also of the *Globe,* "as if he were talking about the fact that he didn't brush after every meal, or failed to clean up his room."

None of this served to discourage me from pressing on with the book.

Inevitably, within a matter of months the Senator knew of the project and the calls began.

Old acquaintances were suddenly interested in my activities, my welfare, many of them people I hadn't heard from since leaving Washington ten years before.

These "friends" were politely inquisitive: How was I doing? What was I working on? Simultaneously, others in the Senator's entourage worked on contacts with high officials of the publishing house.

Some of the conversations grew heated. There were veiled threats. There were equally vague intimations that, should I drop the book project, my success in business could be assured.

Finally, one day in a private club I was approached by Paul Kirk, former Chairman of the Democratic National Committee, and the man to whom I had gone to confess eleven years earlier.

He was now a successful Washington attorney and retained a close relationship with the Senator. He asked bluntly if I was writing a book. I had no intention of answering that question, but contractually I wasn't allowed to answer anyway, just as the publisher could not acknowledge that it was being written prior to publication. When I refused to respond he told me that he *knew* that I was, and he warned me that the Senator's friends would utilize every resource, every legal option, every influential connection, to thwart the book.

He argued that the timing was horrible. The Senator's image was at a low ebb, as low as it had been since the Chappaquiddick tragedy.

I reminded him: The timing is never right. There is always an excuse, be it an upcoming election, bad polls, or another personal controversy.

The exasperated Kirk flared, "I know *some* of the things you know about the Senator, and I know there's much more. Why are you doing this? Can't you just forget about what you saw?"

"No," I said.

"Fine. You're going to go down in history along with Lee Harvey Oswald and Sirhan Sirhan."

Furious at this form of attack, I rose from the table, more determined than ever to continue.

But the Senator's people were not giving up. During the writing and final drafting of this book, they phoned relentlessly. I did not engage in conversations with them beyond mere formalities, but finally they got to the bottom line: They were sorry they hadn't been of more help with my businesses during the late eighties and early nineties. They had heard about the bankruptcy. If I were to drop the book, one of the Senator's friends conveyed that he would be willing to gather a group of investors to buy a company that would in turn buy out mine, or they would come up with several million dollars in working capital via various lines of credit.

The amount they were discussing was many times greater than I would receive as a book advance. They were right to think the advance money was important to me, but they were wrong to think it was *the most important thing*. I told them no deal.

I've written this book for several reasons; one of them has been the sharp sense that I have a story to tell, not just about the Senator, but about myself. My immediate intended audience for this personal story is those who have been close to me over the years, but I'm also convinced there is a larger audience out there to whom my story can be valuable, both as a cautionary tale, and as an aid to understanding how someone *they* are close to may have gone drastically awry at some time in his or her life.

I have watched from a distance as members of the Senator's family challenged adversity and moved on with their lives. Joe Kennedy is a well-regarded and competent congressman; Bobby, Jr., has overcome his problems, raising a family and helping in the battle to preserve the environment; Chris Lawford, likewise, is leading a productive family life and making a successful career in California. Watching the Kennedy children face their problems and move forward confirms my belief that people are capable of conquering their internal demons—when they want to.

I'm ashamed of some of the things I've done that I've described in this book. But for many reasons it has seemed important to me throughout its writing to be as honest as possible, not bent on making myself look fine, innocent, blameless back then. Nobody ever held me down and forced cocaine up my nose, nobody coerced me to lie to the FBI, or, more painful to remember, to my friends and my family.

There were people that I used back then, people that I deceived, people that I hurt. I owe them this apology. I owe it to a broader readership to say that my own excesses, including my own substance abuse, made me unfit back then to hold an office with critical decision power. I must own up to this.

But I am not the only one who should own up.

I've been told to be prepared for attempts to see there *is* no owning up, and indeed even before publication of this book those attempts were under way, the damage-control team at work.

The first aim of such teams is to see that such a book as this is never published, or failing that, to see that when it is published no one believes it.

In particular I have been warned that the classic control method—either to suppress the news or then to discredit it—is to attack the messenger. He's a liar, he's crazy, he's only doing it for the money.

As I write these final words of the book that campaign has already started. If you are reading these words it means that the initial aim of the campaign has failed; it could not prevent the book and what it says from ever being seen by you.

The original would-be publisher in fact did withdraw. Whatever her reason was, it *wasn't*, she said, because she believed the history I've recounted here is false.

For St. Martin's Press the first and last question was: Is what's in the book true?

The publisher read my admission of lying in 1981. He knew I'd spent six months visiting a therapist. In hours of talks together he came to know lots more about my personal life and business in the years since 1981. He took calls attempting to influence him and discredit me. He sent me to spend even more hours with the company's lawyers.

He read the book.

And in the end he decided, yes, he believed the book. In whatever approaches were made to him, he did not encounter a line of successful indictment of the book's essential truth.

He tells me to expect the book to be microscopically examined by its opponents with an eye to finding something—a date, an hour, an exact location—that's inaccurate. The detail will then be waved around as sufficient grounds for dismissal: How can you trust a book like this? I have scoured my memory, referred to my daybooks, and checked whatever references I could to verify such matters. I *think* I have each detail right, but I *know* this: Every event described here did take place. Did we all plan these things, did we do these things, did we say these things? Yes, we did.

The publisher was aware of legal moves against me that might prevent St. Martin's from paying me any money at all, and he asked me: If that happens, if you can't receive any money from the book, do you still want to go ahead? My answer was yes.

John F. Kennedy once said, "From those to whom much is given, much is required. And when at some future date the high court of history sits in judgment on each one of us—recording whether in our brief span of service we fulfilled our responsibilities to the state—our success or failure, in whatever office we hold, will be measured by the answers to four questions: Were we truly men of courage? Were we truly men of judgment? Were we truly men of integrity? Were we truly men of dedication?"

I agree with this—except for the suggestion that the judgment should always wait for some future court of history. Voters rightly feel they should make that judgment every election day. Indeed it's not wrong to say that they are entitled to make it every day of an office-holder's tenure.

In doing so, it's madness to demand perfection. It's always a case of taking some bad with some good. But to exercise this judgment, to weigh the bad and the good, the opportunities and the threats, the evidence is required, the truth is needed.

Everything described in this book did happen. This book can't pretend to be the whole truth, but it is part of the truth, and it certainly is nothing but the truth.

Index

BESTSELLING BOOKS FROM ST. MARTIN'S PAPERBACKS— TO READ AND READ AGAIN!

BESTSELLING BOOKS

FROM

ST. MARTIN'S PAPERBACKS

FLASHBACKS: On Returning to Vietnam
Morley Safer
_____ 92482-8 $5.95 U.S./$6.95 Can.

THE SILENCE OF THE LAMBS
Thomas Harris
_____ 92458-5 $5.99 U.S./$6.99 Can.

BORN RICH
Georgia Raye
_____ 92239-6 $4.95 U.S./$5.95 Can.

WEST END
Laura Van Wormer
_____ 92262-0 $5.95 U.S./$6.95 Can.

THE WESTIES
T. J. English
_____ 92429-1 $5.95 U.S./$6.95 Can.

HOW TO WIN AT NINTENDO GAMES #2
Jeff Rovin
_____ 92016-4 $3.95 U.S./$4.95 Can.